EMERGE
CRACKING THE COCOON OF MEDIA SOCIALIZATION

LISA K. DUNNE, PH.D. (ABD)
WITH JOEL JOHNSON

EMERGE
Cracking the Cocoon of Media Socialization

Copyright © 2010 by Lisa Dunne, with Joel Johnson
All rights reserved.

Published by 4GENPRESS
www.4GENPRESS.com

ISBN: 978-0-9824967-5-6

All rights reserved. No part of this book may be reproduced or transmitted in any form or by any means, electronic or mechanical, including photocopying and recording, or by an information storage and retrieval system, without permission in writing from the author.

Printed in the United States of America
Cover design by modedesign.us,
photography by www.antoinettephotography.com

Contact the authors:
Lisa Dunne
contact@4GENpress.com

Joel Johnson
joel.johnson@teenmania.org

Visit www.4GENPRESS.com for living lessons from *EMERGE*, recorded by readers for readers.

SOCIAL SCIENCE / PSYCHOLOGY / RELIGION

Dedication

Dedicated to Clara Mae Biby:
great-grandmother, teacher, and naturalist.
1913 - 2009

> "Sunlight is the great disinfectant."
> — *C.S. Lewis*

Contents

PART I:
KNOWLEDGE IS POWER: THE SOCIO-BIOLOGICAL FOUNDATIONS OF SOCIALIZATION

Chapter 1: Testing the Tainted Water — 11
Chapter 2: Applications of Social Psychology — 19
Chapter 3: The Anatomy of Association — 29

PART II:
NO MAN IS AN ISLAND: MASS MEDIA'S COLLECTIVE INFLUENCE ON WORLDVIEW AND BEHAVIOR

Chapter 4: Subtle Socialization — 45
Chapter 5: Cinematic Contagion — 61
Chapter 6: Historic Concerns — 77

PART III:
ALL THAT GLITTERS IS NOT GOLD: EVALUTING LIFE THROUGH THE LENS OF THE PAST FOR THE SAKE OF THE FUTURE

Chapter 7: Tragic Timeline — 87
Chapter 8: Media-Centrality and Multigenerational Socialization — 103
Chapter 9: State of Affairs — 115
Chapter 10: Hey, Mom, What's for Dinner? — 147

PART IV:
NOT EVERYTHING THAT COUNTS CAN BE COUNTED: ASSESSING THE EFFECTS OF THE SOCIALIZATION MACHINE

Chapter 11: Land of the Lost Literacy   185
Chapter 12: F2FMIA   209

PART V:
ANTIDOTES TO THE PANDEMIC: INTERVENTION STRATEGIES FOR COMBATTING THE SOCIAL, FAMILIAL, AND CULTURAL INFLUENCE OF MASS MEDIA CENTRALITY

Chapter 13: Hope for a Breakthrough   229
Chapter 14: Staying Afloat in the Midst of a Media Deluge   241

PART VI:
CRACKING THE COCOON: THE BUTTERFLY EFFECT

Chapter 15: Strategies of Healing   249
Chapter 16: The Butterfly Effect   257

About the Authors   266
References   268

Foreword

There are two challenges inherent in a book of this nature. First, a subject of this magnitude tends to introduce more questions than answers, which means that the goal of the text must be tragically truncated; instead of solving world problems, I am relegated merely to drawing attention to them. Space limits the textual sprawl of further ramblings. Second, because the topic of study in this book is one of sweeping, revolutionary changes taking place at an ever-escalating pace, some studies and stats herein will be outdated even before the paper hits the pavement. However, it is my hope that the spirit of the idea can be communicated clearly and somewhat succinctly, and that, while the numbers may wax or wane at press time, the essence of the message will remain steady, meaningful, and inherently transformative.

I am grateful to a number of individuals who have helped inspire the writings in this book. First, I appreciate the astute professors from my Master's degree program at Regent University, who opened my eyes to the historical path of media and its ever-encroaching presence in modern life. Additionally, I am grateful to the professors in my Ph.D. program at Fielding Graduate University for broadening my worldview in the areas of social psychology and scientific research. I appreciate, as well, the openness of discussions amongst colleagues and students at William Jessup University, where scholars of all ages have been courageous enough to discuss real issues facing real people. I am also grateful to the hundreds of high school and college students across the country who have allowed me to peer into their lives and hearts at critical periods of development over the years, from Florida to California. Your willingness to serve as guinea pigs, sounding boards, and national role models does not go unappreciated. A debt of gratitude is also owed to pastors George Brantley, Francis Anfuso, and Frank Colacurcio, whose collective words of insight and inspiration continue to fuel the fire for transformative knowledge that shapes both individuals and cultures.

Finally, thank you to my family: to my dear husband of 19 years, Adrian, and our precious children, Ethan and Cymone, who gave up so much of their wife/mommy time to allow me the luxury of staring blankly at the computer keyboard into the wee hours of the morning. May this book prove instrumental in forging a new future for you and for the generation you will help usher in.

Lastly, I owe an enormous debt of gratitude to my dear grandmother, Clara Mae Biby, who graced the planet for nearly 96 years, touching thousands of lives through her work as a teacher and through her passion as a naturalist. I still remember the first nature poems we wrote together 35 years ago. Without her impartation of a serious and calculated focus on the importance of literacy and the inherent lessons of nature, I could never have survived the media deluge to crack the cocoon for myself.

Lisa

EMERGE!

CHAPTER ONE

Testing the Tainted Water: Creatures of Context and Cohort

This book begins with a presupposition. The subtitle of the work implies that you, the reader, share in the belief that the modern Western paradigm is encased in a cultural cocoon that is fortified by a subtle socialization birthed of mass media messages. If you agree with that construct, even somewhat, read on. If you disagree with that concept, whether mildly or vehemently, may we first challenge you to read the studies and statistics put forth in this book, analyzing the scientific, biological, and sociological data thoroughly, and weighing the evidence carefully? The hallmark of a free society lies within its citizens' willingness to speak to one another respectfully and charitably—yet openly—with regard to our observations and opinions. It is to this free exchange of ideas that we, the authors, appeal.

In 1946, an experimental drug was introduced into the United States' consciousness. Its ubiquitous nature makes it as imperceptibly prevalent as water, while its potency makes it as insidiously powerful as strychnine. The drug's popularity rose from 0 percent in 1946 to a staggering 98 percent in 2009, with its early models spawning later offspring that boasted larger taps, instant connectivity, and the potential for a continuous high. Today, its wares are promulgated from every corner of the house: the living room, the bedroom, the office, the kitchen, even the bathroom. In fact, the modern American home contains more dispensers of the drug than it does indoor toilets. Over the last 60 years, the maddening concoctions spewing forth from its spigots appear to have impacted the emotional health of millions upon millions of people, spreading malaise throughout the civilized world and reaching into the far corners of the earth, leaving two generations pleading in silent helplessness for relief. Its populace, millions strong and nurtured on the mind-numbing narcotic for over 60 successive years, is characterized by a host of predictable emotions—anger, depression, anxiety, restlessness, self-loathing.

These are the effects of a media-central society.

But there is something you can do to escape the grasp of this postmodern pandemic sweeping the planet: Don't drink the water.

Or, at the very least, test the tainted water for potential aftereffects. This we shall do in the pages to come.

This is a book about paradigms, worldviews, lenses, interpretations. Our paradigms are difficult to scrutinize with great accuracy, for an intricate process is required for any of us to interpret with even relative precision the culture we live in: We are part of the system we attempt to analyze. And, as sociologists note, a fish is oblivious to the water it swims in. However, if we are able to step out of our solitary seas and take a momentary leap into the global perspective of socialization, we may be surprised at the messages that have shaped our existing paradigms—and how these messages may have kept us from the true pursuit of life and liberty.

This book is, in essence, a written quest for answers—answers that help make sense of the impact of socio-environmental influences on human behavior, connections between humans and the environment in which they live. As a doctoral student in human development, I have sought connections between biology and sociology, nature and nurture. As an educator for 15 years, and as a university professor, I seek connections between the intellect, mass communication, human development, and social change. As a parent, I seek methods and mindsets that will help create a better future for the next generation and the generations to come. In addition to the copious educational research that supports the findings in this book, our long-time family friend Joel Johnson brings an experiential focus to *EMERGE*, as he travels throughout the United

States speaking to upwards of 200,000 young people a year, hearing their challenges, seeing their struggles, and witnessing their resolute determination to break free of the choking grasp of media centrality.

As I write, I am traveling to the funeral of a much-loved relative. Anyone who has attended a funeral of someone beloved knows the process: there is denial, anger, bargaining, depression, and, finally, acceptance. When someone we love dies, the focus of relationships becomes clearer. It is as if a great lens is turned right before our eyes, and the most important aspects of life suddenly come into focus. We begin resurrecting all our forgotten-in-the-busyness-of-the-moment relationships, reminding others that we care about them. We talk to people more. We laugh more. We share more. We give more of ourselves to the true priorities of the moment, redefining what holds the focus of our attention and our affection.

In the same way, at the time of this writing, the Unites States is facing a funeral of sorts. The streets reek of death—death of the housing boom, death of the technology boom, death of the retail boom. But beneath the decay is a lone sprout of growth, a renewed hope, a focus on something far more important than materialism. To reach it, we must take an important step. We must push with all our might against the hardened shell of our cocoons until we emerge.

To avoid confusion, I will explain here that my use of the word *emerge* in this text is not connected to the modern church movement by a similar name. Instead, I have chosen the word *emerge* as the title of this work because of its powerful metaphorical connotation as well as its remarkable scientific explanation. As most students of science know, a caterpillar undergoes a radical process of metamorphosis while it lies in an outwardly dormant state within its cocoon. At the end of its two-week stay in the protective shelter, the caterpillar emerges as a winged creature, an object of beauty, a symbol of freedom—a butterfly.

For many years, scientists believed the butterfly's cocoon to be an external work of art spun by the creature itself, a shield of sorts that keeps the caterpillar safe from predators during a vulnerable period of transformation. However, with the advent of slow-motion photography in the 1950s, scientists discovered that the butterfly's cocoon was not an external mechanism at all; it was an internal agent. The butterfly convulses and wriggles and twists itself until its outer shell is turned inside out, becoming a cocoon. Remarkably, the transformative power of the butterfly has lain within the creature during its entire lifespan as a caterpillar, a dormant presence awaiting the exact moment in time where the caterpillar is destined for transformation. In the same w ay, we too possess an inner strength for transformation, a hope of renewal, a liberating paradigm that will guide us through the days ahead if we will only push through this current darkness and emerge.

The last year of American history has provided numerous opportunities for breaking free of the cocoon encasing our current mindsets. When we change our paradigm about a circumstance, our response sets in motion a chain of events that can, and often does, bear positively on the circumstance itself. When we realize the latent power coursing through our atrophied wings, we will summon the strength to push through the cocoon. I use the word *cocoon* here largely because of the striking image painted by a mid-20th century writer, Cassini (1946), who observed that culture had become so *cocooned* in the world of mass communication that individuals were no longer able to analyze or comprehend the events of life without the interpreter we had come to rely on: mass media. Our paradigm, as Cassini and many other writers have noted, was and is being shaped by the "interposition" of media. In the current economic system, there has been a stretching and twisting of paradigms, and, within that, an opportunity for emergence.

In the 1890s essay by Guy de Maupassant entitled "The Necklace," a young woman driven by materialism and greed unwittingly gives ten years of her life for an evening of frolicking at a glamorous party. Her desire for consumption blinds her to the true beauty of life, and she ends up a bedraggled, poverty-stricken, harsh old woman, unrecognizable to those who knew her only one decade prior. She learned to live without luxury. She learned to work hard. She learned to live simply, but the learning cost her greatly. The haunting theme of the story is its poignant parallelism to modern life. At the end of a decade of ultimately meaningless labor, of working to the point of exhaustion, of the denial of dreams and hope, the main character of the story learns that all she had worked for those ten years was completely worthless—a piece of fake gold whose false glitter destroyed her life.

Earlier this year, I ran into someone I had known vaguely three years prior; at that time, he was a high-powered real-estate executive. I often spotted him driving through our neighborhood in his $50,000 car, rushing here and there, holding loud, impetuous phone conversations that fell upon the ears of anyone within a two-mile radius. This brash picture is a markedly different one from the one I encountered when I saw him this last time, a meek, dressed-down real-estate agent who pulled up in a small, beaten-up Corolla, and stepped out in jeans and old sneakers. His demeanor was soft. His brashness had turned to humbled politeness. By the standards of materialism, he had lost the game. But by the standards of humanity, it seemed that he had discovered something of greater value: Character. Character is forged in the fire. It isn't always, or even often, measurable in external qualities. As Einstein once said, "Not everything that counts can be counted, and not everything that can be counted counts."

It is from this vantage point that the current writing looks out, gazing over the fallen powers of the political elite, a once-powerful country that now hang in the balance of utter dependence, extraordinary debt, and loathsome depression. Like the real-estate agent, the same heads of corporations who boasted of their "conspicuous consumption" just a few months ago are today driving beat-up Corollas and sulking humbly at the governmental door hoping for a handout. The change is palpable. For some, the change is terrifying. But as I reflect on the message of "The Necklace," I can envision a straighter path, a new generation. The United States is poised to learn some of the greatest lessons of all time, lessons that can be painful at the moment, but ones that will ultimately bring positive transformation and prosocial change.

Testing the Waters

Any book intended to help foster self and community awareness should begin with an offering of some type of self-examination. A reader must be encouraged to look inward before looking outward. In the case of socialization, we can begin to assess the dramatic changes in the outer realm by looking at the subtle changes that have taken place in the inner realm. These are illustrated both metaphorically and literally in a recent news headline that came blazing across my computer screen. The story was an exposé on hidden dangers lurking beneath our streets, microbial agents coursing through our underground waterways and into our kitchens. The authors of the study had discovered that generations of careless disposal had led to pending disaster: The water Americans use every day for cooking and drinking is laced with 56 potential toxins of the pharmacological nature. There was a ring of intrigue, a spark of danger to the topic, but beyond the curiosity birthed of such a mysterious manifestation, there was also a sense of betrayal. How could a developed nation with such educational and technological potential at its fingertips be guilty of such dramatic oversight?

Permit me to answer by way of analogy.

Imagine a bustling village tucked away in a remote tropical location. As a scientific researcher, you stumble excitedly upon this lively community, but as you watch the residents from a distance, you make a striking observation. Though they labor busily, carrying about their tasks with strong arms and legs, they share an obvious physical defect: The entire village is completely blind.

Intrigued by the widespread nature of the visual deficiency, you assemble a team of assistant researchers to ascertain the nature of the physical malady. Once the village has been scoured and the people studied, your researchers discover the secret of the blindness. A shared water source is poisoning the entire community. You bring your findings to the village leaders, excitedly informing them that their blindness is a temporary ailment that can be reversed over time with a simple change of water source. You and your team even offer to construct a new well fed by a pure source of water.

But the villagers hesitate. They like their water. It's cool. It's convenient. The poison imbues it with a unique flavor they have become accustomed to. Many have even grown to crave its odd taste. The villagers are uncertain as to whether they should trade their poisoned water for an unknown, potentially unpleasant concoction. After all, they've grown comfortable with their blindness; it no longer seems to be that much of an inconvenience. Would the newfound changes really be worth the work required to change the culture of comfort?

You and your researchers are shocked at these apathetic responses. You felt certain that the promise of clear eyesight would embolden the villagers to abandon their polluted source in place of a nourishing one. After all, the only requirement for the restoration of sight would be a simple change of intake. But the villagers reject your offer. They want to keep their water source, regardless of the consequences. You feel angry and alarmed, and you can't help but ask one question: What will future generations say when they learn that their country's leaders chose convenience over truth?

In the same way, we are facing a cultural blindness today. It is imperative that we begin an open dialogue about the challenges facing Western culture, a society steeped in the waters of media-centrality. What you read in the forthcoming pages may shock you, anger you, even frighten you. Certainly, there are segments of the book we would label PG-13 or worse. We do not shy from lucid truth in matters of social change. This book is ultimately a pragmatic approach that points to the inherent power of the human spirit to triumph over challenges, whether individual or collective in nature. The next two chapters will present the reader with the opportunity to peer into some of the most fascinating aspects of human development and their relation to media-centrality: our sociological and biological foundations.

EMERGE!

CHAPTER TWO

Applications of Social Psychology: The Socially-Constructed Self

As an educator, I have spoken regularly on media centralization and socialization, on the water source that courses through, around, among, and between us all, affecting us in various patterns—some predictable, some surprising. At times, naysayers appear in my audience. These students often argue that because their own development was not impacted by, for example, the incessant viewing of cartoon violence or the rabid consumption of MTV, that everyone else is equally immune.

It's a fair argument in a sense. It is certainly true that there is a relative uniqueness in response based on certain factors, including cohort, context, and culture, as discussed later in this chapter. However, through the course of study for this text, I have come to see that the impact of biology and sociology play a vital role on our ultimate outcome as human beings, both in the individual and in the corporate sense. Later in this book, we will explore from a macro view a certain generational positioning that is of critical concern. Before assessing these macro concepts, though, there is some groundwork that must be established. We must understand the human brain in a developmental context, and we must understand the potential power of influence outside sources can bear on the human brain. Thus, to begin a relatively comprehensive text on media-centrality and the collective impact of media on personality development, it is necessary to impart a broad understanding of the various ways that individuals are influenced to develop their sense of self and an understanding of their place and purpose (or lack thereof) in the world.

The modern Westerner is predominantly a psycho-social being, amassing behavior patterns through a mysterious amalgamation of social and psychological conditioning. To understand the self in a vacuum, devoid of social context, is both superficial and artificial. The individual (and the individual's potential for influence) must be understood within the context of the social world in which that individual dwells. Thus, in order to effectively introduce the gentle reader to the concept of socialization, it is necessary to spend a few moments immersing ourselves in the history and findings of the field of social and developmental psychology.

Vivian Burr, a well-known author in the field of social constructionism, says that the individual is a "fundamentally social phenomenon" (p. 3). Burr says that the social realm has more than just a casual or even an occasional influence on the person; instead, the influence of one's social system is a vital clue to the identity of the individual herself: "We can't understand what it means to be a person without an understanding of the way in which a person is socially embedded" (p. 34). Thus, an individual cannot be fully understood in isolation; it is only through the analysis of his or her social surroundings that the individual may be studied accurately.

This is an important consideration for the second portion of this writing, and we shall return to it in detail there. Part of the development of a human being is the creation of the group norms of the society in which the person lives. As shown by early social psychologists such as Sherif and Le Bon, the construction of a group norm "works not at the level of the individual but at the level of the collectivity," a place where the whole is seemingly unrecognizable to the parts themselves (p. 36). One's social system can influence a wide range of beliefs, which lead to a wide range of actions. One of the foundational characteristics of this fundamentally social self is the power of influence. "There is considerable concern here that rational, moral, and free-thinking individuals may be unduly influenced by their peer group if they find that their own personal views are unpopular or just uncommon" (p. 35). In fact, much of the early research in social psychology was founded on a startling revelation that stemmed from World War II—that any seemingly "normal" individual could commit social atrocities if he or she were persuaded by social norms or peer pressure to do so.

Social conformity may be defined as our inner desire to look to others for clarification and direction: "When we are unsure of the accuracy or legitimacy of our own view, we naturally and sensibly look to others for information" (Burr, p. 35). This concept of naturally looking to others for guidance seems to indicate an inherent tendency toward socio-biological hierarchies, that is, we naturally desire to look up to someone and emulate their behavior. We see this tendency in developmental psychology studies from the earliest stages of life and will talk more about the qualifications for this emulation in later chapters

As a side note on this topic, despite our seeming need for hierarchical systems as an inherent pattern of healthy growth and development, during the current generation, the playing field is being leveled at every possible opportunity. In both home and workplace, there is a drive toward stripping away all things hierarchical in favor of all things egalitarian. The team has co-captains, the parent is a buddy, the company has co-presidents, and every child on the team gets a trophy, lest someone's feelings be hurt if he must face the harsh reality that a better player than he exists in the world. It is presently unclear how this latitude leveling may play out for our species. Arguably, it does create humorous situations for television producers to exploit on sitcoms, but it may also be undermining an innate and beneficial desire for guidance. Such rugged egoism is not new for the Western world, but it does occur at a unique timeframe in the Western world. As we shall see in Chapter 7, this movement may in fact be a component of persuasive positioning that has created the opportunity for such profound influence.

The norms of a culture play a vital role in governing protective behavior: "Individuals carry around with them the unwritten assumptions of their society" (Burr, p. 91). Our frame of reference, then, both reflects and illuminates the culture we belong or ascribe to. From an individual stance, Mead referred to this as "the generalized other," the view of ourselves from the eyes of others, which offers us a "composite self-concept." In other words, society's "rules" live in us—the expectations, norms, and values of the culture in which we live. We carry within us a set of values that we have absorbed from our social worlds, from what George Herbert Mead called the "generalized other." When we look to the "generalized other," we recognize whether we are living within those guidelines—and whether we measure up to those now-internalized expectations.

These are important considerations as we begin to evaluate the influential role of one-way, centralized communication in the form of television, movies, music, internet, newspapers, and other modern mass communication channels. For media have, in many ways, become the ever-present peer, the "generalized other," dictating rules and norms of right and wrong—from dress to hairstyles to teeth to belief to behavior. Through any expression of a view or any taking of a stance, says Burr, we are expressing that generalized other. Now, it should be understood that the expectation of the generalized other can be a benefit, keeping us, for example, from breaking legal and social norms that might cause embarrassment, awkwardness, or legal ramifications. However, in the same way, a persuasive perception of the generalized other can create an unhealthy expectation or value system that becomes embedded in our neural structure, and while we may not be aware of it until we "breach the culture," we are nonetheless governed by its potentially injurious expectations. As Mead and Burr both point out, there is no self but the social self: "The self is thoroughly social in origin" (Burr, p. 93).

A similar concept of the self was put forth by Charles Horton Cooley (1902) in a notion he called the "looking-glass self." Our understanding of who we are, Cooley said, is derived from the existence of others. When assessing ourselves by looking "in the glass," said Cooley, "we always imagine, and in imagining, share the judgements (sic) of the other mind." In Cooley's view, says

Burr, the self is simply an amalgamation of the views of ourselves as reflected in and apprised through the views of others (p. 93).

Like Cooley, Mead studied the ongoing relationship between mind, consciousness, and society, discovering that we are largely influenced and at times even governed by the social systems we find ourselves within. Would it not be a great disservice to both individual and culture alike if we failed to assess and address these notions carefully? The modern author Ashworth (2000) notes that our ability to analyze the concepts externally permits us to escape from the "tyranny of other-determinism" (Burr, p. 93), but this is a decidedly modern lens, as modernists tend to view ourselves much like those of the Enlightenment, as omniscient and omnipotent sojourners. Perhaps, though, we are far more likely to be slaves to emotionalism and determinism than we would readily like to admit.

As mentioned previously, early social psychology was concerned with the potentially negative ramifications of the subtle peer influence exacted on the social self. In the famous Stanford Prison Study, Philip Zimbardo (1975) found that individuals could enact disturbing behaviors if they felt relatively anonymous and if they believed the behavior was "expected" of him. That is, if an individual believed his identity to be protected and a person of influence placed upon him a clear "standard" of behavioral expectation, the individual would willingly violate his conscience in order to fulfill the expectations of the other. In considering Zimbardo's findings, one cannot help but think of the violent interplay that has emerged of late in the virtual realm with its inherent anonymity and propensity for aggression. Perhaps if we told children (and adults) their ISPs were being recorded and observed, they would be more mindful of their online actions. Certainly, it seems that such anti-anonymity methodology has achieved a measure of success in this regard: the "most watched city" in the world, London, has enacted a lower crime rate just by videotaping would-be criminals—and thus stripping them of potential anonymity.

As Zimbardo says, "Individual behavior is largely under the control of social forces and environmental contingencies rather than personality traits, character, will power, or other empirically invalidated constructs." However, it is easy to underestimate the power of these forces because they are subtle and often unnoticed. Burr counters this concept by saying he was simply analyzing within the "frame of reference" of his day, hence his "power to the forces that be" mindset. But if Zimbardo is looking through a glass darkly, the same must be said of us. Like Zimbardo, the blind spots that we remain oblivious to in the early 21st century may be aptly (and appropriately) mocked by future researchers denouncing our inherent bias to our own lens. Whatever the cultural or generational avoidance, it does seem clear that our behavior is largely governed by factors we are not aware of, and we often tend to delude ourselves into thinking that we have control over our responses when in fact, to a large degree, we do not (Burr p. 58).

These characteristics are visible in both the individual and the corporate realms. "Institutional settings develop a life of their own independent of the wishes and intentions and purposes of those who run them" (Zimbardo 1971). Like MIT's robotic cockroach, entire organizations can find themselves loping along determinedly but obliviously as they hurtle toward destruction. There is, to quote Pearce (2007) a logical force that compels individuals and organizations to spiral forward, even when all the road signs warn of unstable surfaces ahead. As the snowball grows, social forces that may have been created by individuals may one day swell far beyond the paradigmatic possibilities of the initial creators.

It is important, then, that we make ourselves aware of both the individual and the social process, and we might do well to begin with an analysis of some recent social trends that are reaching epidemics levels. One such change can be analyzed in light of anthropologist Ralph Linton's (1945) status theory, which Burr believed to be most compelling and promising as a key concept in Mead's symbolic interactionism (the concept that people act in certain ways toward certain symbols based on the meaning those symbols hold—meanings that are founded on social influences). Status theory is a component of role theory, the tendency for human behavior to form a predictable pattern within a certain social context: a role being played out. Linton's theory says that the rapid changes taking place in modern society are a result of intergenerational disintegration; he believed that the system of status and roles inherited from previous generations is "breaking down," and we will thus be increasingly uncertain of our status or role. Many would agree that this description mirrors the present-day crisis of aimless drifters awash in the "Me Generation." In several segments of this book, we will examine some potential contributors to this social transformation.

As humans, our upbringing is reflected in both our biological heritage and our external socialization. No longer do scientists duel over nurture versus nature debates, for modern developmental research demonstrates that both influences play an important role in our development. There is a powerful interface between biology and sociology: In fact, it might be said that sociology and biology work in tandem. For example, if a person grows up in an angry household, there may be biological underpinnings of anger or over-reactive tendencies, but there are also sociological ones; that is, the trait of explosive expression is taught as much as it is caught. A person growing up in an overweight household may have a genetic predisposition toward a larger physique, but there were also household practices, such as sedentary lifestyles and high calorie diets, that support this body type as well. As one developmentalist puts it, "fat runs in families, but so do frying pans" (Berger 2007). In other words, both nature and nurture are at work in our patterns of development.

Another example may be found in food consumption. We eat for biological reasons (to sustain life), for sociological reasons (our friends are going out to eat and we don't want to sit at the restaurant drinking lemon water), and for emotional reasons (sadness, boredom, frustration). Crunchy foods are linked to stress relief, while soft foods are tied to comfort-seeking. These examples persist at the cellular level as well. For example, the consumption of certain foods such as olive oil triggers the production of oleoylethanolamide (OEA), a fatty substance that travels to the nerve endings to tell your body that you are full. That's biological. However, we are capable of overriding that biological base through our Pavlovian connection with food: TV-watching triggers a desire to eat. Driving in the car triggers a desire to eat. Going to a ballgame triggers a desire to eat. These desires are not based on physiological need—biology. They are based on socio-emotional training. Instead of being driven by biology, in this case, the sociological indicators outweigh the biological ones.

On many levels, we know that sociology can profoundly alter biology. For example, acting on the desire to do a good deed for someone else creates positive alterations in our personal biochemistry. Studies on oxytocin, the hormone known for its role in childbirth and parent-child bonding, show an increase of dopamine levels in the brain's reward center when we perform what we consider to be a "good deed" for someone else. This act takes us out of our own microcosm and connects us to a larger sphere so that, as one author put it, "we feel within ourselves something greater than ourselves" (Maloof 2008). The sociological surroundings in which we find or place ourselves play a vital role in our overall development. From our first connection to humanity, where the biologically-wired dyad of mother and child experience shared physiological expressions of love at the cellular level, we can witness the beautiful connectivity such as that which happens when a parent smiles at his or her biological newborn: the heart begins to beat more rapidly, simultaneously, in both beings, a phenomenon known as parasympathetic acceleration of the heart (Siegel 2007). And like the physiological influences at work here, in the same way, for better or for worse, there are agents of influence in our social realms that are providing the psychological foundations for the paradigm we will hold tomorrow.

Three Cs of Impact: Culture, Context, Cohort

Within the social realm, there are numerous categories of influence that bear an impact on human development. Three of those that carry some of the greatest weight are culture, context, and cohort. The culture in which we live and were raised has bearing on our interpretation of events, and it also impacts our response to those events. People from expressive cultures, for example, may be more likely to vent verbally than to stew silently over a problem. People in small towns are normally more prone to greet one another on the streets than are people who live in large cities. When I moved to Miami from my small Illinois town of 2,100, I couldn't figure out why no one responded to my courteous "good morning" addresses to passersby. Small town behavior did not translate accurately into the big city experience. The size of the city of residence plays a role in the individual's upbringing and development, hence the saying, "You can take the girl out of the country, but you can't take the country out of the girl." A culture can be a family, a town, an ethnicity, or a larger whole that shares some value or connectivity around certain components of development. The culture one grows up in will determine, to some extent, one's interpretation of and response to life events.

Additionally, life events are interpreted through context, that is, what has happened around, before, or after these events. The context of school shootings in the United States means that raging journal entries by silent, brooding students are given more serious attention than they were just a decade ago. Just a few years ago, a traveler could take a refreshing bottle of water onto the airplane for consumption, but given the context of post-911 travel, such luxurious opportunities have ceased to exist. The context of a conversation or a book or a movie can bear profoundly on the audience's interpretation of that work. An anti-war movie situated just after the commencement of a war, for example, yields a different interpretation than it would if the movie aired when there was no threat of war. The context of the situation determines the interpretive slant of the communication effort.

Lastly, the interpretation of life events is dominated by one's cohort. A cohort is a group of people who share roughly the same age category (Berger 2007). A cohort experiences a connectedness through shared events of impact. For example, when I ask my Millennial students (18-25) what they were doing when the news of

911 reached them, they remember with vivid detail. They are connected by the event in the same way that the cohort before them might have been connected by the assassination of John F. Kennedy. Cohorts can be bound by a common language, a fascinating method of connective tissue that encompasses both individualized interpretation and the fluidity of language, which is constantly evolving to reflect its users. For example, for Boomers, Busters, or Gen Xers, the word *gig* might mean an opportunity offered to a band to play in a club. For Millenials and some Gen Xers, a *gig* is a measurement of space on a computer. The word *driver* means something different to a golfer and a techie. Once, many years past, when I asked students to take out their *notebooks*, they interpreted this to mean a small writing tablet, not a laptop computer. Similarly, many other words have different connotations for different generations: *cutting*, *a gay affair*, and any use of the word *virtual*, which, interestingly enough, just a decade ago meant *unreal*. Though this linguistic elasticity is entertaining to note, it also underscores the rapidity with which language and meaning are changing. Language is a reflection of its users, and its users are a reflection of their society. Our cohort influences our interpretation. I will always maintain a different view of cell phones and computers from that of my 11-year-old son, for I grew up in a world that lived without them, and he is growing up in a world that is dependent on them.

Thus, there are a number of considerations to bear in mind as we approach the topic of development, for it is through both biological and sociological underpinnings that we grow and become, and it is through the lens of culture, context, and cohort that we interpret the events of life. Let's look now at some of the biological aspects of human development, specifically the influences of the human brain; for a deeper understanding of how the brain interprets information will offer a great level of comprehension regarding the powers of influence, both within and without.

CHAPTER THREE

The Anatomy of Association: Neural Networks and Socialization

As we have discussed, there are multiple lenses through which we may view human development, and philosophies within each realm of possibility range from singularly myopic to broadly inclusive. One of the most fascinating methods for analysis of development is a relative newcomer to the field, an intriguing blend of science, biology, and psychology known as *neuroscience*. This methodology, introduced in the 1990s, offers great potential for analysis, interpretation, and healing through a combination of both internal and external observations. Through the use of brain imaging technology, neuroscientists are able to analyze development from a hitherto untouchable realm—the brain itself. In fact, neuroscience experts such as UCLA's Daniel Siegel use a combination of psychoanalytic, behavioral, and cognitive approaches to appropriate radical changes in thought and behavior.

Through studies of the brain's anatomy, we can glean incredible insights into the realm of the potential for sociological influence. Later in the text, we will observe some future implications of this work, for these neuroscience experts labor to show that change is possible; even deeply embedded emotional and physiological connections can be altered to promote hope and healing.

In "An Interpersonal Neurobiology of Psychotherapy," Siegel (2003) explains that neural connections respond to experiences during every span of life, which means that the human brain is continually experiencing, linking, adapting, and responding to life's challenges. In his quest to discover "the power of relationships to nurture and to heal the mind" (p. 3), Siegel encourages practitioners to ask not simply what the problem is, but how that problem can be fixed. This is a refreshing turn from the diagnosis of many popular psychologists, who seem bent on problem-analysis but remain tragically allergic to the pragmatic functions of hope and healing. Siegel believes that both individual minds and communities of minds can be defined as complex systems; that is, they have a propensity for self-organization, they have internal and external constraints that can govern their eventual trajectory, they move toward "maximal complexity," and they must ultimately balance both differentiation and integration to achieve or maintain wholeness and health (p. 4). "Systems that are able to move toward maximal complexity are healthy systems. They are the most stable, adaptive, and flexible. What a wonderfully concise definition of well-being!" (p. 4). Mental health, thus defined, is a system—"be it a person, relationship, family, school, community, or society"— that progresses toward a state of maximum complexity (p. 4). To get a better sense of the possibilities here, let's take a look at some of the amazing functions of the human brain.

Biology of the Brain

The brain is driven by both experiential and genetic factors, and is capable of neural firing patterns upwards of ten to the millionth power (Siegel, p. 4). Memory, essentially, is the manner in which these neurons fire from within distributed areas. Most strikingly, our present-day mental realities are configured by the linking together of neuronal firing patterns—in other words, a new concept links to an existing concept in whatever way the brain considers them to be categorically associated. "Learning requires that we create linkages to alter the nature of our future neuronal firing patterns" (p. 5). This means that future learning, for example learning in adulthood, will be associated with existing learning (e.g., learning that took place in childhood). This is why a young man raised with a controlling mother might later link all women into this same frame of reference: "All women are alike" might become his silent mantra. He would then be limited in his assessment of reality by what his brain is linking together in experience-based interpretation.

Because there are "inevitable ruptures" in our social lives, it is helpful to note that healing can take place as "overwhelming events and suboptimal developmental experiences...become freed from their restrictive or chaotic patterns" (p. 7). We saw in the last chapter how the social environment serves as a conductor of information and interpretation for the individual, that our worldviews and behaviors are formed in the context of relationships in society. Neuroscience helps make sense of the biological foundations for this sociological phenomenon: As Siegel points out, the brain is "genetically programmed to be social...(it is) hardwired to take in signals from the social environment to alter its own internal states" (p. 7). Did you catch that? At the neural level, our brain is cueing in to the culture around us to model, to mirror, the actions of those within our social circles.

As Albert Bandura's Social Learning Theory teaches, humans learn through social interactivity and behavior modeling. Thus, community, both familial and extra-familial, is an important component to the healing process. Ironically, this same community often perpetuates the injuries (knowingly or unknowingly); thus, individuals must learn to face, accept, and deal with interpersonal challenges, both present and past. As Bono, McCullough and Root found (2008), forgiveness is a key component to well-being. The early years of life are crucial to such development, as there is a sort of time-release development that occurs throughout the lifespan, a critical period where certain life lessons seem to form a mindset, a "working model," as Bowlby (1969) called them. These mindsets, such as Erikson's (1959) trust versus mistrust, develop in almost-automatic fashion, usually unbeknownst to the individual.

The mind is formed through "the interaction between neurophysiological processes and interpersonal relationships" (Siegel, p. 9). There is a foundation laid in early life in this regard; however, this shaping, this alteration, continues throughout life. Awareness of the patterns, specifically through interpersonal communication, "can create lasting changes in neuronal structure and function that can in turn powerfully transform the mind. In other words, the mind can alter the brain and the brain can alter the mind" (Seigel p. 9). It is this continual shaping, this pliability, that creates new growth. "It is not a matter of nature versus nurture, but rather that nature needs nurture" (Seigel p. 10). As an interesting side note in this regard, Carol Dweck (2008), former Stanford psychology professor and author of *Mindset: The New Psychology of Success*, points to the importance of early awareness of correctly-directed praise. She says that parents must model "growth mindsets" instead of "fixed mindsets" to help children believe that they can progress throughout life. Praising intelligence over perseverance, for example, gives a message of an innate trait (fixed) rather than a progressive one (growth-based). Of her work with students, athletes, and other Generation Yers, Dweck says, "Parents and educators tried to give these kids self-esteem on a silver platter, but instead seem to have created a generation of very vulnerable people."As a result, she says, many people are fearful of making a mistake and are thus held back from attempts which could lead to personal growth.

From Blank Slate to Full Plate

How does the brain develop and change? Let's take a bird's eye view of the remarkable capabilities of the human neural network. The adult brain is made up of billions of cells called neurons (over 10 billion neurons!) with axonal fibers winding two million miles in length. Each of the neurons is connected to the others at a synapse, where neurotransmitters are released. Depending on the chemicals active in that region, the result will either be activation or inhibition of neural firing. It is these "neural net profiles," these patterns of firing or not firing that create a mental process.

Though schools such as the University of Manchester, England have made news with their arguments against the blank slate philosophy, Siegel says that the brain is the least developed of all organs at birth. Its hierarchical symmetry exists prenatally (right and left hemispheres, regions, systems, circuits, neuronal groups, single neurons), but the functions of perception, memory, and the regulation of emotion must be fashioned outside of the womb. In essence, all these developmental aspects are *dependent on socialization*. And, depending on what percentage of development is biological and what percentage is sociological, it is possible that the environment in which a child (or an adult) develops may hold the key to potential relational health or dis-ease.

As noted earlier, there are a number of critical periods of development within the lifespan. The early years are one such developmental stage, and the adolescent stage is another major phase of development. This is not to say that these are the only two stages of development and that adults do not continue to develop throughout their lifetimes, only that these two stages appear to be the most pronounced of all life eras in terms of radical, rapid development. Interesting to this study, there appears to be a physiological link to the Judeo-Christian spiritual concept of "putting away the old self" or "being transformed" in the renewing of one's mind. As Siegel puts it, "In some cases, lack of use leads to impaired synaptic growth and to a dying away process-called pruning-in which connections are lost and neurons themselves may die. Such a pruning process appears to be a major event during the adolescent years, in which the huge increase in synaptic density created during the early years is then pruned to the lower densities of the adult years" (Spear, 2000).

Many parents, Siegel says, seem to feel that sensory overload is the infant pathway to later relational and intellectual success. Instead, though, it appears that "the experiential food for the mind is in the form of collaborative communication rather than sensory overload" (12). In other words, instead of the latest and greatest toy, school, or learning "tool," children need one-to-one connectivity with parents in order to feel secure and complete. When early socialization creates an unhealthy view of self or others, whether through a caretaker or a media source, this lens persists until consciously replaced. When there is an inability to "process" the events of life with a caring adult, a child will adapt in ways that are less than healthy. For example, when a child lacks an environment of closeness and responsiveness, he may develop unhealthy response patterns, such as the inability to feel a longing for closeness that might be "unbearable in sustained family environments of rejection and emotional neglect" (Siegel 2003). Later in life, these responses can continue to impair relationships and "inhibit the readiness to enter into authentic ways of being" (Siegel 2003, p. xx). The treatment process is intended to help individuals integrate the experiences into the larger self, much the way someone with body dysmorphic disorder might glance painfully into the mirror, focusing on one part of her body with disgust before treatment, but might look at herself in the mirror as an integrated whole afterward, seeing the entirety of the person, not simply the real or imagined flaw. These are important worldview considerations as we begin to look at the impact of our current socialization.

As a hopeful side note, a point of healing is recognizable when it is integrated into what neuroscientists call a "coherent" narrative. I think of how many of my students want to stab at a memory from the distance as with a stick, then immediately bury it once again. I recall one student, who, when she was required in my class to discuss a narrative account of a past experience, told the group that she had quite literally "locked those memories up in the attic." At the end of a connective and engaging semester, the student actually climbed up into her physical attic and brought out some photos to share with the group. It was a beautiful, transformative moment for her and the others in the room. She integrated some seemingly insignificant but extraordinarily painful pieces of the past into her whole self—developing a coherent narrative.

As Siegel and others have shown, emotionally healthy people seem to use their challenges as a point of reference to understand life and to help others do the same. This, too, is an example of the coherent narrative, making sense of life's challenges, finding purpose in the pain. Restorative resources can be found in a number of places, and even when they have been absent in phase one development (infant-parent attachment), they can be later forged through what Siegel calls "two person governed self-regulation": Through these therapeutic alliances, "experiences (external constraints) can help modify the synaptic connections (internal constraints) that enable the individual to achieve new levels of flexible and balanced forms of self-regulation" (p. 14). It is this locus of control, this inner ability to balance that is a vital component of growth: "Self-regulation is a key to mental health" (p. 13). As the saying goes, healthy body, healthy mind. For generations that have lacked connection as well as awareness of the potential for transformation, these lessons have been too long silent.

The realm of emotion and processing may seem trivial to scientific research, but as some authors have pointed out recently, "the relationship between emotion and health is...more important...than most of us could have imagined" (Merriam 1999, p. 191). In fact, this nebulous affective realm appears to be grounded in physiological phenomena: "Viewed through the lens of 21st-century science, anxiety, alienation and hopelessness are not just feelings. Neither are love, serenity and optimism. All are physiological states that affect our health just as clearly as obesity or physical fitness...The challenge is to map the pathways linking mental states to medical ones, and learn how to travel them at will" (Benson 1999). Perhaps even more fascinating is the link between emotions and reason—or lack thereof: "(E)motions are enmeshed in neural networks involving reason...Emotions increase the strength of memories and help to recall the context of an experience, rendering it meaningful" (Hill 2001).

In a media-central culture, where emotional manipulation through television, music, and advertisements has become so commonplace as to be virtually undetectable, a study of the link between emotional recall and academic success is indeed a valuable undertaking. As researchers are now discovering, "neurological and emotional pathways are impossible to separate: There is no such thing as a behaviour or thought, which is not impacted in some way by emotions. There are no neurotransmitters for 'objectivity'; rather even the simplest responses to information signals are linked with possibly several 'emotional neurotransmitters" (Haberlandt 1998). Because the neurotransmitters, which carry messages of emotion, are integrally linked with the information...there is not thought, memory, or knowledge which is 'objective,' or 'detached' from the personal experience of knowing (Merriam). It benefits us greatly, therefore, to look at the whole being, for attempting to compartmentalize the emotions, thoughts, and responses is an exercise in futility.

Possibilities and Potential

Regarding the possibilities of lifelong transformation, whether for better or for worse, Kegan says the word *transformation* is itself a useful clue in the search. "At the heart of the word is "form"...Transformation entails a reconstruction of basic forms of the distribution of energy or information or production" (Debold 2006). Kegan says we must consider "what *form* is transforming." He describes socialization as a time in adolescence and early adulthood where "we become more a part of society because the society actually becomes more a part of us. Thus, the self feels whole, connected, and in harmony through its identification with a set of values and beliefs that both make the self up and simultaneously preserve its intimate connections—relationships to the bigger tribe or to the culture of which one is a part" (Debold 2006).

In a pluralistic culture, Kegan notes, there are constant and competing demands for our loyalty, so we must develop an internal locus of control, a compass to guide us in the evaluation of what is valuable, real, and worthwhile. A small percentage of Westerners, he says, have reached that level of cognitive ability (21%), and some of those have moved even beyond that to a unifying concept, an awareness that we are moving through a process together, that we are all participating in a journey where each individual transformation affects the corporate whole. "(E)ach living thing in the universe has the opportunity, through the process of transformation, to move toward a more complex form. Maturity has something to do with the fit between the person and the nature of the demands of the surround" (Debold 2006). Kegan's idea of unity at the macrocosmic level provides an interesting parallel to Siegel's notion of unity at the neural level; one small shift affects the whole system.

Transformative Potential

To understand the potential for transformation, we must first look at the functions of the most amazing central processing unit known to man—the human brain. How does the brain learn? The brain is known as an "associational organ," which means that experiences are embedded in neural connections in the brain (memory), and the brain literally "matches present firing patterns with those of the past" (Siegel 2003, p. 21). In fact, at the neural level, our very expectation of what is to come influences the reality of what is to come. "The brain is an anticipation machine—linking the present with what it expects in the future based on experiences in the past" (Siegel 2003, p. 22). This realization has tremendous ramifications. What we believe about ourselves, others, and our world predisposes us to not only an interpretation of reality, but also to an adaptation of it. Additionally, Siegel says, the brain is a "social organ" that engages in development with other people, other brains—we are quite literally "putting our heads together" in order to experience growth. The development works this way: First, we have an underlying motivation, which leads to an organizing pattern, then to an operating pattern, then to an observable trait of personality (p. 24). Through these patterns, we continually reinforce what we believe to be true. Thus, we develop a paradigm: "the architecture of how we think, the scaffolds along which our thoughts run" (Pearce 2007, p. 60).

The synaptic connections are altered through "directed" experience: A child's temperament, for example is a "constitutional feature" of the child; though it is not necessarily genetic, it does have certain predispositions that will either be enhanced or overwritten by the caregivers. These attachments shape the developing mind and impact the self-regulatory circuitry. Existing attachments shape future attachments. Moreover, the potential for transformation is impossible to quantify, for "development is non-linear...small inputs can lead to large and unpredictable outcomes" (Siegel 2003).

Each hemisphere of the brain has a unique role in the processing of information; the right hemisphere's focus is autobiographical knowledge, and the left hemisphere creates and stores facts about the self. Neuroscientists have observed clear causation between socio-emotional deficiencies in the early years—from caregivers—as well as specific effects and affects later in life. For example, if there is a lack of worth, connection, assurance in early life, a pattern of anger is developed. Without connection, affection, and approval, a pattern of sadness and shame emerges. If there is a lack of assurance, certainty, security, a pattern of anxiety or fear shapes the neural world, and eventually, the individual's outer world (Siegel 2003, p. 37). In order to heal, says Siegel, there must be a move toward coherence, an attempt to integrate all of these fragmented parts into a whole and become less rigid, more adaptable. "As integration is achieved across the numerous dimensions of living, a sense of the unity of being is revealed" (Siegel 2003, p. 40). We must dissolve the connecting patterns that cause us to expect and connect information/experience in certain ways, for the anticipated outcome shapes the end result: Expectation literally creates our inner worlds. What we think, we become.

Hawkins (2004) called this physiological manifestation of incoming experiences and stimuli a "memory-prediction framework." The cortex predicts what will happen, the experience comes, and the brain links the experience with the prediction. Siegel says we live in an "optical delusion of isolation" where we feel separated but are really connected to everyone else by the shaping of our shared experiences. He encourages readers to extend this "prison" outward and recognize our connectedness, developing compassion for all things. Clearly, personal transformation and social transformation are both equally possible, but the steps must be completed in order. There must be a connection, an integration of the fragmentation, internally first, and then we can begin to integrate, to connect, externally as well.

The flurry of new developments in the field of neuroscience has led to a rush of reviews and articles that provide a striking opportunity to confuse and mislead readers. Much of that interpretation, it seems, is a result of the lens, the paradigm, through which Westerners have viewed development and disease in recent years. Let's look at a few "hot topic" issues in order to belabor the point somewhat. A parent approached me recently with the relief of "proof" that her teenage son, who had become increasingly angry, dishonest, and violent in his teen years, was not at fault for his behavior. The doctor performed a brain scan to show the parent that the young man's brain is "just different" from everyone else's. Thus, Mom was able to walk away from the doctor's office with a sense of resolve about her state of victimization: "I did nothing to cause this; there is no one to blame, and there is no cure. A lifetime of expensive medication (with no intention of psychological therapies or interventions) is the only 'hope.'"

I certainly understood the reason for her resolve; the fatalistic diagnosis of "just the way it is" has an all-too familiar ring. This was once the diagnosis for cancer as well—no hope, no answers. Now, though, a number of prominent researchers have made it clear that lifestyle changes can prevent over 50% of all cancers. Researchers sought causation in place of victimization. Not too long ago in Western culture, obesity was blamed solely on hyperthyroidism. "It's not my fault; there's something wrong with my body. Those six cheeseburgers and quart of Coke have nothing to do with it." Now that 63% of Americans, including 1/3 of all children, are struggling with overweight or obesity, researchers have been forced to look at causation there as well. In the same way, we must begin to look at some of the sweeping social changes that have taken place in our culture over the last 50 years and begin to ask questions of causation. Are we unwitting victims in the current cultural malaise of materialism, violence, and oversexualization, or is there a link to controllable causation?

Let's look at a few tough issues to break up the rocky ground here, bearing in mind both our role as a socially-constructed self and the capacity for association and socialization as a result of our neural chemistry. Let's take again as an example the connection between emotional disorders and neurochemistry, since these disorders represent some of our greatest cultural challenges today. One recent article, titled "Teen Boys' Anger Tied to Brain Development," tells readers: "Aggression in some teenage boys may be linked to overly large amygdalas in their brains." The findings post from the *Proceedings of the National Academy of Science*, and the article says that "these boys may also be unable to control their emotions." The findings, involving 137 12-year-old boys, showed that aggressive boys have large amygdales (the portion of the medial temporal lobe that is associated with arousal and fear) and small prefrontal cortexes (the portion of the brain associated with emotion regulation). While this finding is statistically accurate, it's also somewhat misleading. As we have seen in the research thus far, the brain is associational as well as social. Looking through the lens of finality creates a concrete mandate of hopeless resolution: nothing that can be done to alter the course of history. Let's just give up.

Consider, as a potential paradigm-shifter, this interesting sociological discovery: The highest rate of emotional disorders is found among children of the highest socio-economic strata (Berger 2007). In other words, wealthier kids are more likely to be emotionally imbalanced than poorer kids. Does being born into a privileged family make a child biologically-bound to emotional illness? No, that's illogical. Clearly, there is a socialization factor in effect, which means there is an element of control, an element of potential transformation in the existing system that, if applied, could alter the ultimate outcome. We aren't necessarily victims, but we have been prisoners to a problematic paradigm.

Another article, this one from *Science Daily* and entitled "Resisting Peer Pressure," quotes University of Nottingham researchers discovering that the only adolescents who can effectively resist peer pressure are those with strong neural connections. This study of 35 ten year olds showed higher levels of neural connectivity among those who self-described as more able to resist peer pressure. Again, this study can also be explained in greater depth for its causation-if the news reader were willing to look up the original findings as printed in *The Journal of Neuroscience*. From the article's sensational summary, though, the reader is left with the sense that brain development is permanent, not plastic. As we saw earlier, the brain is the most undeveloped organ at birth. It must be socialized. Teens are not born; they are made. In "Teens' Brains Explain Their Impulsiveness," the reader has more of a chance to read behind some of the political lines forming around neural research, as the article begins by offering background on one of the researchers-a man who helped draft a brief for the U.S. Supreme Court to outlaw the death penalty for those under the age of 18. Whatever one's opinion of the law, the pressure to "prove" the lack of responsibility, at least in this case at least, is seemingly clear. Fortunately, teen culture revolution messages, such as those from the teenage Harris brothers' book *Do Hard Things*, are beginning to bring some balance to all the needlessly negative nonsense of sensationalized news.

In another article bearing the ominous title "Brain Studies Show ADHD is Real Disease," NIMH researchers call ADHD a disease of the body chemistry. Though the two studies cited varied in their findings, the second one (who received the most press) had a singular focus on fixed mindsets. The first researcher, Dr. Philip Shaw of the Child Psychiatry Branch at the U.S. National Institute of Mental Health, said his findings demonstrated that children with the "ADHD gene" tended to improve as they got older. The second researcher, Dr. Jon A. Shaw, professor and director of child and adolescent psychiatry at the University of Miami Miller School of Medicine, said that his findings show ADHD to be "a heritable disease with genetically determined neurobiological underpinnings (adding) further evidence that this is a valid mental disorder, often requiring neurobiological interventions [such as] psychopharmacological treatment." The final findings of the article, again, link the reader to concreteness of mind: "Individuals with ADHD have a decreased function of the brain dopamine system...ADHD, clearly, is associated with a biochemical dysfunction."

A former student of mine comes to mind in this regard. In her later years, she had begun to struggle with ADHD and bipolar disorder. Her psychiatrist told her she must remain medicated for life and that, through no fault of her own, she is simply "incompatible" with other human beings and thus better off unmarried. So, she and her teenage son live alone on welfare in government-subsidized housing. Mia's college is paid for, her housing is paid for, her food is paid for, and both her and her son's anti-anxiety/antidepressant medications are paid for (she tells me her medications alone cost $30,000 a year)—all financed by the wonderfully supportive taxpayers in her region of residence. One semester, I overheard her advising another student who was struggling financially after a recent divorce. "Why don't you get government assistance?" Mia asked. "All you have to do is prove that you aren't competent or able to work, and you can basically live for free."

The other student stared at Mia with great annoyance: "Well, I *am* competent," she said. "It's just not easy, that's all."

The lure of ease is very tempting, especially when Americans have spent a lifetime, as Neil Postman so beautifully put it, "amusing ourselves to death." One student was willing to take responsibility, and another was content to remain a victim. But then again, why wouldn't she? She's been granted a free pass down easy street. There is no responsibility required, no change demanded. She rests lethargically under her cocoon of labels and hopelessness.

I drove past a building in downtown Sacramento recently that reads "Pain Management" in massive letters across its side. Pain management: The phrase seemed so fatalistic, that those who enter the doors will always be faced with the dreadful experience of chronic pain; the pain will just become more manageable. Pain management means we must resign ourselves to a hopeless dependency, to a lifetime of pain and distress.

Pearce (2007) asks what kind of world we are making with our communication at the interpersonal level, and we can ask the same question at the macro level here: What kind of world are we forging with such fatalistic predictions? Is this the message of hope to send to an individual or a society? It's easy to say medicine is the only alternative—it's politically correct and materially beneficial to the economy as it stimulates exorbitant levels of consumer spending. But what if the underpinnings of the "disease" are sociobiological, and what if this continued socialization forms the neurological foundation upon which all future wrongdoings are inscribed?

For the sake of paradigm-shaking, let's ask some hard questions that might cause us to squirm in our seats. Let's say hypothetically that a researcher discovers that one of the root causes of ADHD is the lack of paternal involvement at the age of two. Ahh, now the argument becomes political. These are shark-infested waters we're swimming in. No one makes money off of pushing fatherhood, and a compulsion for two-parent families stands against the I-can-do-it-myself rugged individualism of feminist theories. But what if it were the simple, statistical truth? What if healthy neurological development were dependent on early wiring systems of both biology and sociology that are either nurtured or warped in foundational familial environments? If that is the case, we would be forced out of our easy chair, and we would have to being taking seriously our own individual responsibility in the realm of both the preventative process and the healing process in our culture, both for children and for adults.

If we view the human condition as inherently hopeless, our survival depends on prisons, psychologists, and pharmaceutical companies. If we view the human condition as hopeful, however, then the power of transformation rests within each of us. For we are all in motion—and in context: "It is a mistake...to think of an organism and its environment as two entirely independent and unrelated entities; the organism does not exist as an organism apart from its environment. The environment as a whole is ...a part of the identity of the organism" (Johnson 207). The question now is to what extent has our environment shaped the individual organisms within it, and to what extent do we possess the power of altering that environment?

EMERGE!

CHAPTER FOUR

Subtle Socialization: The Intelligent Design of EE Interventions

In 1988, George Michael saturated the airwaves with his song "Father Figure," where he proclaimed his paternal devotion to all the young girls in the listening audience:

> I will be your father figure/Put your tiny hand in mine
> I will be your preacher teacher/Anything you have in mind
> I will be your father figure/I have had enough of crime
> I will be the one who loves you/Until the end of time

A generation before the song's release, the lyrics would likely have been scoffed at as anti-family, even predatorial (see verse one for greater clarity for the rationale of the latter term). But after years of rejection on the home front, teenage girls were more than willing to accept an alternate source of male authoritarianism and affection. The song's power in the era was testament to its historic impact—it was embedded in a cultural context. As Christopher Vogler explains in the *Writer's Journey*, entertainment becomes iconic when it relates to our deepest-seated needs, desires, or dreams. In fact, the best-selling writers in Hollywood use Vogler's insights to craft relatable messages that will sell their product.

This is no secret. In the same way, Michael's song became wildly popular because it resonated with the teen and young adult audiences: They were searching for a father figure. The lack of individual parental influence and connectivity had opened a chasm of fear, anxiety, and restlessness. Given the profound propensity for influence we saw in the last two chapters, biological and sociological foundations, it is important that we now look at the cultural context in which we currently find ourselves immersed, a culture of media centrality.

A few years back, I began a classroom experiment that has become both fascinating and sobering in its implications. In working on a project, I came across the site of an elementary school teacher who had created a tool for measuring socialization in her elementary school classroom (*Stay Free* 2004). I adapted her brilliant model for use in the college classroom and have had some very interesting results in utilizing it with hundreds of college students. In virtually every course I have taught over the years since I discovered her socialization experiment, I have devoted some segment of the course to the topic of media centrality, and the results have been compelling.

The lesson begins with a series of slides where students team up and attempt to identify the images accurately. The first slide is a collection of 25 common flowers and trees: magnolia, oak, birch, holly, pine, and the like. For this slide, students mainly stare at each other, gaze blankly at the slide, and then make a few daring guesses at the content. The average score per class is four answers right out of a possible 25—a 16%.

The second slide is a collection of 20 former US presidents: Lincoln, Truman, Adams, Bush, Kennedy, and the like. For this slide, the energy in the room usually picks up slightly, with students at least venturing a verbal guess here and there. Most can identify Lincoln (to my relief), and some even know who Roosevelt is (impressive!). However, the sad average score on this portion is 7 correct answers out of a possible 25—a higher (though still abysmal) score of 28%.

Then I post the final slides. As soon as these final images appear on the screen, the room begins buzzing with conversation. These slides were never taught in school; they do not contain the essence of science or history or geography. Instead, they are marketing symbols—single letter images that stand for products marketed daily in Western culture—26 letters symbolizing brand advertising (mostly, it is interesting to note, for junk food). There is a bubbly pink B that stands for Bubblelicious Bubble Gum, a fattened E for Eggo waffles, a red F that students know immediately as Frito Lay, and a C that any student can tell you stands for Campbell's, mmm, mmm good.

When these slides hit the screen, the entire class comes to life (and most students can sing the jingles or recite the slogans that accompany the products as well), for this screen contains images everyone in the room knows, virtually every student in every class—hundreds and hundreds of students in all during the time I have utilized the experiment. Compared to the meager scores of 16% or 28%, most classes score a perfect 100% on this exercise. The class always identifies virtually every single symbol (if there are any symbols not identified, by the way, they are most often the exact same ones: a domestic product and a religious one, Xtra detergent and Hebrew National). Coincidence? I don't know, but these companies might want to beef up their assault on the American airwaves, just in case.

Where did my students learn these secret truths of the brand images? Did they absorb this data through the formal educational process? No, they have been secretly socialized, trained to memorize mass media content with no conscious awareness or effort on their part. Once students see their scores, note their collective energy, and recognize their striking profile as a target market, they need no further proof; they realize they have indeed been impacted by commercialized media. The only question that remains for them is how these media messages have structured (or restructured) their consciousness. To paraphrase Samuel Morse, what hath *we* wrought?

Though it might seem trivial at first blush that we have been socialized to the tune of soup and laundry soap jingles, let us return to the concept of human behavior modeling and neural development to see what type of impact this type of socialization may have in the long term. Much of what we do on a daily basis is instinctive in nature, autonomic, reflexive. If certain behavior patterns persist as part of our habitual paradigm, if we act out of reflex instead of out of critical thinking and reflection, we are far more likely to make poor decisions, decisions that impact us not only individually, but also collectively. One of the most effective socialization strategies of our time plays on this very concept, a persuasive appeal of mass proportions known as EE.

Contemporary Persuasion: Strategic Successes of Entertainment-Education

Since the late 1980s—unbeknownst to most citizens—a number of colleges, advocacy groups, and major organizations have begun pairing up with Hollywood in order to market their particular strategic doctrines. The movement, known as entertainment-education (EE), is based loosely on Albert Bandura's Social Learning Theory, which demonstrates, in essence, that we mirror the company we keep. What is most remarkable about SLT and EE, however, is that the "company we keep" need not be in the format of fact-to-face (F2F) interaction to be influential. Through movies, sitcoms, and radio programming, EE has shaped cultures around the world, focusing on issues such as population control in Mexico and domestic violence in Africa. Additionally, in the United States, EE has also been used to market a number of socialization strategies, some seemingly inadvertent and benign, and some overtly controversial, cunning, and culturally destructive. In accordance with Ray Bradbury's prophetic 1953 observations, the television has become a member of the American family, and with this unique amalgamation of sibling status and digital domination, EE has the potential for power beyond measure.

Arvind Singhal and Everett Rogers, authors of *Entertainment-Education: A Communication Strategy for Social Change*, provide by far the most broad and accessible background for the strategy of EE, which they define as a media message that attempts to entertain as well as educate an audience, with the goal of increasing audience awareness of an issue and creating noticeable shifts in attitude and response, ultimately contributing to social change. The EE strategy was officially birthed in 1969, when Rodney Shaw began the Department of Population Problems in the Methodist Church in response to growing concerns of the then "population explosion." David Poindexter served as the director of this fledgling institute, and, since that time, Poindexter, along with his Mexico-based counterpart, Miguel Sabido, has successfully launched the EE missive around the globe.

EE serves as a catalyst for change because of its ability to persuade audience members to identify with certain characters, thus engaging them in an emulation of "positive" social behavior from what viewers perceive as a "non-preachy" role model. In creating Entertainment-Education venues, the Sabido-Poindexter team relied heavily on Albert Bandura's Social Learning Theory, the concept of learning through the modeling of others. This theory proved highly effective in developing a measurable demonstration of prosocial behaviors, a term defined as the creation of positive social behavior such as friendly interaction, aggression reduction, altruism, and stereotype reduction (Singer, p. 185). Though the process requires intensive research before, during, and after production to be highly effective, the secret of EE's success is fairly straightforward. Viewers identify with celebrities and therefore desire to model their on-screen behavior. First, the "celebrity" is given media exposure, which leads to parasocial interaction (a process in which viewers begin to feel as if they know the character personally, often talking about them as a "real" person), which leads to identification. This identification leads to changes in values. Greater identification with the character or characters produces greater audience awareness of broad social issues, often creating a movement of social change in relation to the celebrity's displayed values.

According to Martine Bouman, author of *The Turtle and the Peacock: The Entertainment-Education Strategy on Television*, people of a lower educational status spend more time watching "light" entertainment and dramatic programs compared with those with higher levels of education (59). This research begs the chicken-and-egg question: are these individuals less educated because they watch more television, or do they watch more television because they are less educated? Either way, it's a significant statistic, and it is the reason that certain diseases (which often seem more prevalent in lower income populations) have become part of the EE strategy in shows supported by the Netherlands Heart Foundation (NHF), for example (Bouman 59). As the NHF found, in as little as one hour a week, cultures could be impacted by the message of EE. But it isn't only the lower-educated masses that are impacted by EE's strategy, of course. As we saw earlier in Cressey's research, if there is a salience, a factor of relatability or personal interest, virtually anyone can be impacted, at least momentarily, by an EE message.

In both America and abroad, EE has shown itself to be tremendously effective, and participating media have proven they can disseminate EE messages and influence mass changes in human culture, achieving "widespread change" in behaviors that lead to national development (or the procurement of the producer's values, depending upon one's view).

One of Sabado's first most well-known interventions dealt with population control in Mexico. Sabido ran a serial drama, an EE strategy focusing on family planning that ran a half an hour a day for five days a week. After a one-year run of the show, Mexico's population, which was projected to double in two decades, *dropped from 3.1 to 2.7 percent* (Singhal, p. 26). Researchers and governmental officials credited the sweeping social change to the prosocial directives of the popular show. Additionally, organizations such as the United Kingdom's BBC have utilized EE strategies, with the goal of "further(ing) the national interest...through information, education, and entertainment" (Singhal, p. 244). The BBC's trust programs have taught prosocial topics in countries such as Albania, India, Nepal, Ghana, Egypt, and Niger, tackling topics like leprosy, domestic violence, child marriage, gender equality, and a host of other issues.

One of the most readily recognizable Entertainment-Education campaigns in the US was the designated driver crusade, hailed as one of the most successful media campaigns in the history of EE. The campaign, developed by a partnership between Mothers Against Drunk Driving and the Harvard School of Public Health's Center for Health Communication, had as its goal a reduction in the number of alcohol-related deaths in the US. The team knew that if they wanted to make even small changes in the behavior of the drinking population, they would have to place their persuasive appeal strategically—somewhere everyone would be sure to find it. A book? No. A classroom? No. A newspaper? No. Enter the sitcom.

During the 1988-1992 TV seasons, more than 160 prime time shows, such as "The Cosby Show," "Cheers," and "L.A. Law," included subplots, scenes, dialogue, and even entire half-hour or hour-long episodes devoted to the campaign theme. By 1990, public opinion polls indicated that 9 in 10 adults (89%), and virtually all (97%) young adults 18-24 were familiar with the designated driver concept and rated it favorably. In 1991, the term "designated driver" was included in the Random House Webster's College Dictionary (KFF). Before and after research showed that the concept had been met with widespread social awareness (Singhal, p. 18): 89% of the population reported an understanding of the theme.

The reason this particular campaign was deemed so effective was its realistic goal: it sought to make small changes in a large-scale plan over a period of years. In other words, it was strategic—and patient. Nearly twenty years later, it is difficult to find one student in any of my classes today who has never heard of (or used) a designated driver. Years after the EE campaign ended, its vocabulary and social strategy remain in place.

In the US, many of the well-known EE interventions have centered on healthcare, with their proposals appearing in the most unlikely places: Soap operas are a prime source of information for certain population groups: 69% of Black women, 56% of Hispanic, and 48% of White (KFF). Often, the EE strategy involves blurring the line between fantasy and reality. For example, in one EE campaign, Johns Hopkins, KFF, and CBS initiated an EE intervention and ended up with a new model altogether. The group introduced a disease in the storyline of the drama ER, and then after the show aired, they ran a real-life news segment featuring people who had dealt with the issue. The segment reached over 1 million viewers a week (KFF), no small audience, especially given the rate on which Westerners rely on entertainment media for medical advice. According to a CDC report in 2000, 52% of viewers say that they get—and trust—medical advice from prime time shows (KFF), and 90% report learning from television about new diseases and how to treat them. Despite its purported identity as the entertainer extraordinaire, for many people, television is much more: it's a trusted friend.

Of course, it isn't only television that applies peer pressure in a distance format. Researchers at University of North Carolina, Chapel Hill demonstrated just last year that young adults experience statistically significant levels of influence from not only television but music as well. In fact, the evidence was so strong that researchers went so far as to say that the type of programming a teen watches could be a predictor of behavior, that is, a teen who is watching sexually explicit programming is likely to be sexually active, a teen who is watching violent programming is likely to be engaging in violent behaviors. Whether broadcast through song or script, continual messages of promiscuity proved to be highly impacting on the teen's behavior. We'll talk more about the Chapel Hill study in a few chapters.

EE researchers know that behaviors demonstrated by "stars" on TV will be emulated by the general public. This, of course, was one of the reasons behind the cigarette ban on television in the 1970s. But these are examples of relatively agreed-upon positively prosocial behaviors. What about EE campaigns we don't all agree on? Are there other agents, such as political lobbyists and special interest groups, who design campaigns aimed at the general public? At first glance, EE seems like a benign influence, possibly even a positive one. Let us not, however, be oblivious for media's propensity as an agent of propaganda. Whether it's Morgan Spurlock or Michael Moore, filmmakers often have very specific opinions (agendas, as some would define them) whose goal it is to impact public opinion (and, therefore, public action). Many adults believe that these effects are limited to teens or children—a psychosociological blindness that Singer and Singer call the Third Person Syndrome. In Third Person Syndrome, participants believe that the rules and consequences apply to others, but not to the individual observer. For example, in the current obesity crisis, over 65% of the adult population in America is overweight, yet only 1/3 of adults believe that they are personally overweight. The statistics don't line up because everyone believes the statistics are describing someone else, not them.

In the same way, young children say that movies can be influential, but "only for babies" (Singer 2003). If adults and teens alike can be impacted (which high-paying advertisers certainly believe to be the case), we need to consider seriously what type of "friends" we're inviting over for dinner. Imagine a whole segment of the adult population watching a show where married women are regularly engaged in extramarital affairs. Will their behavior be changed to mirror that of the celebrities they admire? Will they become numb to the consequences of their actions and so begin to seek out elicit relationships? Or might there be smaller levels of influence over a period of time—more relational instability, less accountability, less dependence on and belief in the institution of marriage?

Film has a power that supersedes even real relationships' capacity for influence. Propaganda is powerful, subversive, not to be underestimated. When Hitler wanted to decimate the entire population of Jewish residents in Germany, he turned to film. A number of historical accounts state that Hitler hired the country's best film maker to create "educational" propaganda that would turn everyone against the Jews. It seems he knew the latent power of the image, and if he could get "his" people to believe in the image he created, he believed the world would be his. And, but for the courage of a few brave men, it nearly was.

Any type of persuasive appeal that is emitted en masse begs the question of whose values are being purported and whose pocketbook (or agenda or lifestyle or company) is being served and supported by these appeals. If we want to know what's for dinner, so to speak, we had best read the ingredients on the side of the box. For when we take an in-depth look at the media elite and run a cross-comparison on their values versus the values of the average American citizen, we see chasm of remarkable proportions. The media elite (as well as journalists) have very little in common with the average US citizen. We will return to that thought in a moment.

Why does EE work? First, we are social creatures in that we want to be like those we admire. EE uses celebrities who radiate an older-brother (or richer-friend) charm that makes others want to emulate their behavior. Another reason for EE's effectiveness is that we are psychological creatures who desire acceptance into the elite social world. To ease into social situations and understand (or circumvent) our place in the hierarchy, we find ourselves copying those we admire: "Modeling seems to be a dominant way that people get new behaviors. Whenever we are in a new situation, we almost always look around to see what others are doing" (Primer 2006).

In an era of military prowess, the saying was that might makes right. In the case of the visual culture in which we now live, it seems that sight makes right. And whether it's because of the ubiquity of media messages or a host of other factors, modern Westerners seem particularly susceptible to persuasion. What is perhaps most maddening about EE's style is the difficulty we have identifying it, naming it, fighting it. The television (like other media formats) induces relaxation, and just when we are in our most relaxed, vulnerable state, the potential power of persuasion can kick in. It is this embeddedness—this secrecy and subtlety—that make it so extraordinarily powerful.

When the British came to America to fight the Revolutionary War, they had the honor and dignity (some would say naiveté) to wear red coats so they could be distinguished from American soldiers and be made visible in the battle. Today's lifestyle marketers take no such honorable stance. Instead of wearing red coats, they wear camouflage. They blend into the culture, into the background noise of our lives. Media does not bow before us courteously, saying, "Warning: Use of this product may be harmful to your socio-emotional health." Instead, mass media messages slip rather subversively into the water source, becoming part advertiser, part entertainer, part co-creator of culture.

Many examples of socialization through mass media exist. Though some influence may indeed be unintentional, it is difficult to ignore that much of the social transformation is fostered through forms of direct propaganda. What is perhaps most fascinating—and maddening—about this system is that the financial support of the "ruling" class actually comes from those who are enslaved by the rulers. Remarkably similar is the process today to Caesar Augustus' historical army. Caesar conquered the body by force, but in order to conquer in spirit, he slipped into the corporate subconscious like an advertisement by inscribing "Caesar is Lord" on the currency. In the same way, the entirety of Hollywood is propped up on revenues from movies, products, and advertising dollars. Instead of honoring the true heroes of our culture, such as civil servants, firemen, policemen, those who work to make America and better and a safer country, the highest paid professionals are not the most astute and ethical leaders in our country. The highest-paid professionals are the most entertaining ones.

A final reason for EE's effectiveness as a campaign strategy is our human need for belonging. As Maslow showed in his hierarchy of needs, in order to reach our full potential, we must feel connected to the whole; we must have a sense of community. Community is a fascinating word today, as we can have communities based on brand names, through athletic associations, even through online groups. This latter concept relates in interesting fashion to studies on community and connectivity, including the revelation that authentic community cannot take place in an anonymous environment. This belief is echoed by "techie" author John Jewell, Internet expert, who says that without a sense of accountability in online relationships, there can be no growth, no personal or collective maturity. Kollock (1998) echoes this appeal, adding that individuals must have some framework for understanding something about who a person not only is at present, but who he has been in the past. "If identity is unknown or unstable and if there is no recollection or record of past interactions, individuals will...not be accountable for their actions." Given the sudden rise of anonymous culture around us, where we can "talk" to a hundred people in a given day who may or may not be who they say they are, the conceptual framework of true community is indeed in question.

Teacher, Preacher: The Many Modalities of Media

Looking at the human propensity for socialization and modeling behavior, as well as our inherent need for belongingness and our inborn efforts to emulate the behavior of those we admire, it is clear that EE has tremendous potential for impact. The numbers of responses to EE interventions around the globe, numbering in the millions in the US alone, demonstrate how effective a well-rehearsed EE campaign can be. The potential to influence an entire culture is truly within the hands of those leading the campaign—as long as the campaign constituents are staying connected to the source, that is, mainstream media.

Kaiser Family Foundation writes that in the United States and around the world, "Public health organizations are increasingly turning to entertainment media-from soap operas to sitcoms to reality shows-as a way to reach the public with health messages" (2004). In the US, the primary medium for EE is television (Kaiser 2004). The EE message may be generated either by a special interest team or by producers and scriptwriters who "have a particular interest or personal connection to the issue" (Kaiser 2004). In addition to the producers and scriptwriters, "Other messages result from outreach efforts of special interest groups or health agencies to deliver their message to audiences. These groups often work with Hollywood-based advocacy organizations that serve as liaisons to the entertainment community via industry forums, roundtable briefings, and technical script consultations" (Kaiser 2004).

Early EE effectiveness examples include an episode of the show "Happy Days" where the main character of influence, Fonzie, gets a library card. Following the episode, the demand for library cards across the nation increased a whopping 500 percent (Kaiser 2004). Clearly, EE has the potential for promoting prosocial behavior. Obtaining a library card and refraining from drunk driving are positive benefits of EE. However, there are also other forces at work in EE, and we may or may not always share the same values with those of the EE strategists. Kaiser Family Foundation offers voluminous research on a number of campaigns which the general public may be supportive of or opposed to.

The Media Project is one company that works with the entertainment industry to spread news of adolescent sexual "health" through numerous shows (upwards of 100 shows consult with the Project for advice). In one story, a college freshman in the show "Felicity" visits the campus health clinic to learn about birth control, where she is given a demonstration on how to use a condom, and she asks her "prospective partner" to get tested for HIV and other STDs. The Media Project has also worked with storylines on "ER," "Dawson's Creek," "Moesha," "Boston Public," "Strong Medicine," and "Judging Amy." Additionally, The Media Project works on scripts for the preteen audience (KFF).

Mediascope promotes health and social issues within the entertainment issue, specifically anti-bullying and violence prevention. Shows include "7th Heaven," "Law and Order," "Judging Amy," "24," "The Shield," "Boston Public," "The Guardian," and "All My Children" (KFF).

The Kaiser Family Foundation focuses on such diverse topics as rapid HIV testing, emergency contraception, chlamydia, insurance coverage of experimental treatments, teen sexual activity, the working uninsured, and Medicare and Medicaid. Through partnerships with BET, MTV and Univision, KFF has contributed to a number of full-length EE shows, including 19 full-length shows that appeared on MTV and reached *an audience of over 95 million viewers* (italics mine). Some KFF programs include popular musicians and other celebrities to utilize the socialization/identification factors discussed earlier, and some shows use a documentary format where the main character deals with a social issue demonstrating the desired response in order to inspire viewers to respond in similar fashion (KFF).

The UCLA School of Public Health and Department of Film and Television, in collaboration with the Immunization Branch of the California Department of Health Services, worked together to launch an entertainment education campaign regarding immunization. During the 1996-1998 broadcast seasons, stories about immunization were incorporated into scripts of over a dozen TV shows, including "ER," "High Incident," "Frasier," "7th Heaven," "Step by Step," "Sabrina the Teenage Witch," "Guiding Light," "Days of Our Lives," and "Mister Roger's Neighborhood." One show, "Fraiser," featured the lead character facing his fear of needles and getting a flu shot. The goal was to encourage viewers to follow in the footsteps of the "star."

The Last Acts Writers Project, organized by the Robert Wood Johnson Foundation, focuses its strategic EE campaign on end-of-life care, pain management, biomedical ethics, and rights of the terminally ill, having featured their messages in such shows as "ER," "NYPD Blue," "Homicide: Life on the Street," and "The Guardian," as well as the film "My Sisters' Keeper."

KNOW HIV/AIDS, a campaign launched in January 2003, incorporates HIV/AIDS messages in television shows and movies produced by Viacom-owned companies or broadcast on Viacom-owned networks such as CBS, UPN, MTV, and BET. Some of the messages are geared for the public in general, while others have targeted groups most at risk, such as youth, people of color, women, and gay men (KFF 2004). Shows featuring the KNOW HIV/AIDS message include "Becker," "The District," "Enterprise: Star Trek," "Touched by an Angel," "Girlfriends," "Half and Half," "One on One," "Soulfood," "Presidio Med," and "Queer as Folk." According to KFF, in 2003 alone, more than 58 million viewers tuned in to campaign-related entertainment programming, and more than seven million visited the campaign's website.

A few years back, I watched a personal acquaintance face some dramatic internal transformations. She had become increasingly interested in soap operas, so much so that she made every effort to watch every episode of one particular show every time it aired. She knew all of the characters' names and was actively engaged in figuring out who was going to do what with whom next. I observed her behavior over the course of a year as she became more emotionally invested in the lives of these celebrities.

After awhile, Karie found herself obsessing over the looks of a particular male actor on one of "her" shows. One night, as we were having dinner with a group of friends, she and her husband were present. During one point in the evening, she turned to the girls sitting near her and began discussing the physical attributes of this certain male star in the show. She described the physique of this actor aloud, in an admiring fashion, and compared it to that of her own husband, who was sitting next to her at the table. I watched her husband whither in his chair, his manhood seemingly sucked out in the presence of all. Shocked at her callousness, everyone sat in an awkward silence until the conversation was rescued by a waiter.

Though Karie's husband was an attractive, successful man, it was clear that he could never measure up to his wife's new Hollywood-induced ideals. Her visual addiction had colored her worldview, and she could not shake the ridiculous ideal of Tinseltown perfection. Sure enough, she soon met someone she deemed as measuring closer to the standard of impossible perfection and left her loving husband for her new Hollywood elite.

Some might say this is just an isolated case, an anomaly, anecdotal evidence at best. Perhaps it is. Surely we aren't impacted to such a dramatic degree by our intake of media, are we? What has been the global impact of the EE campaigns discussed here, and what other types of subtle media influence is expressed in the modern paradigm? In the next chapter, we'll take an in-depth look at the collective influences of mass media on worldview and behavior, from both a modern and a historical perspective.

EMERGE!

CHAPTER FIVE

Cinematic Contagion: The Social Constructionism of Mass Media

In the late 1980s, then-*Washington Post* writer Pete Hamill made an interesting observation about television in an essay he wryly titled "Crack and the Box." After covering the drug-addict beat for years, Hamill stumbled upon what he believed to be a comparative factor between drug addiction and television viewing—the "unearned high." He watched the faces of young children, surrounded by drug-addict squalor, staring vacantly at the images on a television screen in one tenement building after another. As he walked outside, he saw those same vacuous stares on the faces of the drug addicts huddled in the doorways along the streets. Through his observations of the Western world, where, as he said, "2% of the world's population consumes 65% of the world's hard drugs," Hamill posited that years of living vicariously through televised entertainment could create an insatiable drive for constant amusement rivaling an addict's craving for a drug-induced stupor. He became convinced that spending hour after hour and year after year in search of constant emotional diversion ultimately produced the empty yearning of a drug addict—and, perhaps, drug addiction itself.

At the time, Hamill's words seemed more like the incoherent ramblings of an eager journalist seeking the gratuities of sensationalism, but looking back, they have a certain ring of possibility. Is it conceivable that day after day of siphoning off vicarious emotions could lead to an adrenaline addiction? Is it plausible that the television and other forms of mass media could serve as a form of socialization? Taken together with the observations of a host of other futurists and researchers, the potential for influence seems likely. As discussed in the first portion of this study, the modern Westerner is predominantly a psycho-social being, amassing behavior patterns through a mysterious amalgamation of social and psychological conditioning. Exactly how much power does mass media have in the realm of social influence?

This next portion of the study focuses on the effects some of the most effective marketing campaigns in psycho-social development in the Western world. We will look at the history of persuasive media appeals, the power of film, the emergence of the visual culture, and a rationale for why mass media appeals may be more suggestive and salient than ever before: an idea I'll call *persuasive positioning*. Finally, we will address the overt and covert messages of media, as well as how these have affected specific people groups, and, ultimately, we'll learn what we can do to avoid being inadvertently persuaded by the powers of the image.

Influencer of the Masses

Now, let's look at a few specific examples of media influences on social behavior. One of the most interesting responses in terms of a mass behavioral shift has been the extraordinary trust and reliance on online sources that has been developed over the past decade. A majority of viewers (52%) report picking up health information *that they trust to be accurate* from prime time TV shows, and 1 in 4 (26%) say that these shows are among their top three sources for health information (KFF 2004, italics mine). Because EE strategies are based on agenda, that is, a purported system of behavior that is supported by a particular group, it is easy to see the potential for persuasion in an intended direction, especially when such a high percentage of the population has a mindset open to the possibility of trust and influence. Nine out of 10 (90%) of "regular viewers" (that is, those who watch programs "regularly") report learning about diseases and/or disease prevention from television, with almost half citing prime time (47%) or daytime entertainment shows (48%). Additionally, KFF reports that almost half (48%) of regular viewers who heard about a health issue on a prime time television show say they took one or more actions as a result of viewing that episode: 42% told someone about the storyline, an indicator of influence, as discussed earlier in the segment on parasocial interaction and influence. Additionally, 16% told someone to take action or took action themselves, 9% visited a clinic or doctor as a result of the program, and 5% called a clinic, health care facility, or hotline number for information as a result of viewing the program (KFF 17).

Additionally, KFF reports that after watching "ER," 32% of viewers sought out additional information about a health issue, with 14% contacting a doctor or other health care provider as a direct result of a topic addressed in the "ER" program. Many regular "ER" viewers show "significantly increased awareness" about health issues that were addressed on the show. For example, after a scene about emergency contraception was included in one episode of the show, KFF noted a 17% increase in the number of viewers who "were aware that a woman has options for preventing pregnancy even after unprotected sex." Among those who had heard of emergency contraception, 20% said they had learned about it on "ER" (KFF). In fact, a survey KFF completed during the 1997-2000 seasons of "ER" surveyed 3,500 regular viewers of the show yielded some interesting statistical significance: 53% of regular viewers said they "learn about important health issues" while watching "ER," 51% talk with family and friends about these issues, and 32% said that "information from the show helped them make choices about their own family's health care" (KFF 2004).

The highest rate of impact in this study was found among viewers with less education: 44% of those with no college were able to avoid the sway of the message, or at least to question it, whereas only 25% of those who had only some college education were able to withstand the sway. Data were not available for those having no college education, but given earlier research discussions on

Strasberger's work, the strata of the population that has not yet come of age for college, along with those who have not chosen a college education, seem to represent the greatest risk of influence. The statistical significance of this impact is alarming. This is not to say that a college education necessarily serves as a protection from influence; however, from a statistical standpoint, one of the benefits of a college education is that a student learns to think and reason for himself. Clearly, people are not only watching television passively; their paradigms are being actively shaped by the information taken in. The potential for information—and misinformation—in these campaigns is evident.

After an episode aired about the sexually transmitted disease human papilloma virus (HPV), the number of viewers who said they had heard of HPV nearly doubled (from 24% to 47%), and the number who could correctly define HPV tripled (from 9% to 28%). Among those who had heard of HPV, 32% said they had learned about it from "ER." And, according to the Kaiser Family Foundation's National Survey of Physicians, one in five doctors say they are consulted "very" or "somewhat" often about specific diseases or treatments their patients heard about on TV shows such as "ER" (KFF 22).

As one might expect, many daytime soap opera viewers report learning about health issues from TV as well. According to KFF, among regular viewers of daytime drama, almost half (48%) of those surveyed said they learned something about a disease or how to prevent it from watching soap operas, and 4 in 10 also reported learning about disease and prevention from prime time television shows (41%) and talk shows (38%). In terms of ethnic breakdowns, Black women (69%) were most likely to cite soap operas as a source of health information and a catalyst for personal action, followed by 56% of Hispanic and 48% of White women.

Additionally, overt strategies, such as a public service announcement being linked to a health storyline in a television show, offer viewers the opportunity for instant connectivity to a toll-free telephone hotline, where trained personnel await callers on that specific issue. These public service announcements have proven successful to special interest groups as well. For example, after an episode of "Chicago Hope" where the storyline introduced a cardiac disorder that can cause sudden death in children and young adults, a public service announcement was aired, and 1,500 people called in for information. When "The Practice" aired an episode on Tourette Syndrome, inspired by the co-executive producer's children who have TS, 500 callers connected with the hotline for more information.

The Commanding Power of the Image

Since the time of Hammil's pre-Internet observations, culture has undergone some radical changes, not only externally, but also internally. As discussed in the first portion of this study, the Western world is now lunging furiously toward a visually-centered form of communication, a concept I have referred to as *visuality*. One of the most important components of visuality is the commanding power of the image—an image that often serves to restructure our consciousness. The late Neil Postman, former Chair of the Department of Communication Arts and Sciences at New York University (and one of the most well-known media critics of the modern era) puts it simply: "We can never underestimate the psychological impact of language's massive migration from the ear to the eye" (p. 32). Though he speaks here of the movement from oral to literate culture, the transformation is even more profound when we consider the movement from the written word to the image, literacy to visuality. For the image, as we shall see, is authoritarian and omnipresent. It rules in formats both conscious and subconscious—and therefore wields the potential for tremendous power.

Prior to printing, says Postman, "all human communication occurred in a social context"(p. 27), but transforming communication strategies and technologies began to give us new ways of thinking—a new lens through which to see the world (Postman, p.

30). In the same way, the new era of visuality creates a lens through which we view the world, a way to understand the hidden hierarchy of virtual sociology-and our place in it. If the "impersonality and repeatability of the typescript assumed a certain measure of authority" (Postman, p. 32), how much more so the image? It is commanding, authoritarian, stamped indelibly on billboards and brains as a reminder of its all-consuming power. And if the book "conditioned people to think more abstractly" (p. 39), the powerful impress of visuality is conditioning people to think more concretely, less imaginatively, more media-centrally. Our vision has been dominated by a singularly-focused point of view. Finally, if the book culture destroyed "knowledge monopolies" (Postman, p. 49), the image culture has reinstated them. With only a handful of primary owners of worldwide mainstream media (including newspapers, magazines, cable, movies, and even music), it is clear that there is an elite class, one to which, as *Frontline* put it, most of us don't belong. And, as we shall see, as an insecure teenage girl seeks the approval of the domineering upperclassmen who rule her social world, so Western culture is finding itself drawn into the maddening myopia of media centrality.

When Samuel Morse sent the first distance human communication message, he asked his recipient to consider what God had wrought—a question we might understand to be an awestruck but fearful acknowledgement of the medium's potential power or purpose. He was not the only one to contemplate such staggering (or superficial) possibilities. Upon hearing of Morse's telegraph, Henry David Thoreau was rumored to have asked what two men in separate parts of the country could possibly have of value to say to one another (Postman, p. 69). We, too, find ourselves impacted by this question today. Though we are surrounded by more information than has ever been present in the history of mankind, most of what we hear and see consists of irrelevant stories and statistics; the vast majority of televised and printed news stories center on disconnected, disembodied ideas that serve to do little more than distract us from our own real lives. In this realm, as others have noted, we give up something of our individual self to gain entrance into the collective whole. As Marshall McLuhan wrote, "When man lives in an electric environment, his nature is transformed and his private identity is merged with the corporate whole. He becomes 'Mass Man'" (Postman, p. 70). As the speed of information moves far beyond the individual capacity to transport it, human communication plunged headlong into a world that can only be understood retrospectively:

> The telegraph eliminated in one stroke both time and space as dimensions of human communication and therefore disembodied information to an extent that far surpassed both the written and printed word. For electric speed was not an extension of human senses but a denial of them. It took us into a world of simultaneity and instancy that went beyond human experience. In doing so, it eliminated personal style, indeed, human personality itself, as an aspect of communication (p. 70).

If the telegraph created a world of anonymous, decontextualized information (Postman, p. 71), it was a mere infant predecessor to the sweepingly disembodied communication formats of the Internet world. Today, one can make "friends," meet a future spouse, and even interview for a job in the virtual world. But for all this communicative ability, is what we say in these formats really worthwhile? Or, has technology so transformed the very nature of communication itself that what once would have been considered meaningless and trivial conversation now masquerades as news or truth or petty public interest stories? Postman answers the question even before I get it down on paper: "The telegraph created an audience and a market not only for news but for fragmented, discontinuous, and essentially irrelevant news, which to this day is the main commodity of the news industry" (p. 71). Postman believed that television trivialized culture, bringing secrets of the psychologist's office to the public eye where, like a hideous roadway accident, the passersby can't keep from looking away. TV, he said, does not record events; it creates events (p. 83).

There have been many socio-emotional casualties associated with the rise of commercialism and media-centrality, more than space permits discussion of here. However, one relevant cultural transformation Postman speaks strongly of is the blurring of lines between the socially acceptable behavior patterns of adulthood and childhood. In *The Disappearance of Childhood*, Postman shows the rationale for the rapid decline of childhood and the subsequent rise of what he calls the "adultified child" and the "childified adult." As Postman puts it, there is an ever-increasing haziness in the lines between youth and maturity, fantasy and reality. These changes, at least in their initial phases, he links to the printing press.

In similar fashion, PBS Frontline's *Merchants of Cool* discovered a comparable blurring in the lines between adulthood and childhood, a cultural transformation the researchers linked to the frenzy of media-centrality. The modern-day portraits that emerged from the study were "mooks" and "midriffs," men who act like hormonally-driven teenage boys, and young women who act like self-absorbed, sultry princesses. In light of some of our current social struggles, there is great interest in constructs such as Postman's assertion that "The book and the world of book learning represented an almost unqualified triumph over our animal nature; the requirements of a literate society made a finely honed sense of shame necessary...demanding that body be subordinated to mind" (p. 48). This is an important consideration for the modern era, as we now see a paralleled reversal of this concept. As literacy rates have fallen in the United States, there appears to be a parallel rise of brazenness, a lack of personal responsibility (or even concern) over actions that were once considered socially reprehensible. In fact, the word *shame* has become a necessary evil in itself, decried in scores of modern self-help books, both secular and religious, as a farce, a man-made emotion of certain malevolence.

This is a far cry from the lens of earlier generations, where shame was part of the vocabulary of both adult and child (as was *discipline*, but that's another book altogether). In fact, Postman later discusses John Locke's assertions that "esteem and disgrace are, of all others...the most powerful incentives to the mind, when once it is brought to relish them" (p. 57). The failure in these areas Locke blamed unflinchingly on the child's guardians: "An ignorant, shame-less, undisciplined child represented the failure of adults, not the child" (p. 57). One can only imagine the impact of greater parental responsibility assigned to child disobedience today. If nothing else, stronger measures of parental guidance might profit society with fewer youngsters crowding the hallways of juvenile detention centers. Instead, though, many modern moms and dads seem to identify with the parents who were thrown off a United Airlines flight because they "couldn't" get their three year old to sit in her seat. Much of modern argumentation, both social and psychological, seems to erode a potentially beneficial sense of shame, replacing it with a false sense of esteem and ability, a smug complacency that is equally hollow and harmful.

I'm not the first to question the link between the frenetic structure of television's spew and the recent "discovery" of masses of children who can't sit still for a minute. Neil Postman's son, Andrew Postman, illuminates the fact that the disembodied news segments that float through on plastic smiles, with topics ranging from violent crime to tips for healthy eating to celebrity news, create "a sequencing of information so random, so disparate in scale and value, as to be incoherent, even psychotic" (Postman xi). From this, it's easy to see how children can grow up desensitized and disconnected from the stark realities of their consequences. Of his dad, Andrew Postman says, "His book urges us to claim a way to be more alert and engaged…it's time for the reins to be grabbed by those of a new generation, natives of this brave new world who understand it better" (xiii). He too, is on the prowl against the profound influence of the "absurd insubstantiality" of the media. He asks a number of thought-provoking questions in his touching tribute and forward to his father's book. With the mass of meaningless information at our constant disposal, we find ourselves, as Aldous Huxley foresaw, in a situation where "truth would be drowned in a sea of irrelevance" (Amusing xix).

Like other mechanistic inventions, Postman says the printing press took on a life of its own; a transformation he calls the

Frankenstein Syndrome: "One creates a machine for a particular and limited purpose. But once the machine is built, we discover—sometimes to our horror, usually to our discomfort, always to our surprise—that it has ideas of its own; that it is quite capable not only of changing our habits but...of changing our habits of mind" (p. 23). This is not unlike the many facets of the modern computer. One such example is spell check. Many writers and teachers concur that after years of allowing the computer to "think" for them (and for their students), the writers' own spelling abilities come into question. Instead of looking the correct spelling up in our old faithful dictionary, we allow the computer to do what our brains used to do—weigh and consider.

In the same way, speed dial and then contact lists on our telephones ultimately equaled a lessening of the dependence on human memory. As another example, consider Microsoft Word's automatic correction to the first person singular pronoun *I* when I write it in lowercase: *i* automatically becomes *I*. In the classroom, this translates into a sloppy style of students writing without capital letters. It never happened in my classroom before the domination of Word, but now the error is fairly commonplace (as are extraordinarily odd juxtapositions of words and meaning that stem from blind acceptance of spell check's mandates). These are simplistic examples of placing our brains on automatic pilot and handing the keys to the computer.

The computer gives us its own version of reality, of existence. It recognizes only a limited view of modern names and faces, casting a shadow of unreality upon historical figures by underlining their names in red. Figures of biblical history or even American history are labeled as outdated, beyond reality, by Microsoft's red pen. There are other annoying hints of habitual influence that persist in those of us who rely on the computer regularly—such as the strange inclination to press *control s* after I've been working with pen and paper lest I "lose" my handwritten data. Or, after a few years of IM interruptions and email echoes rudely elbowing their way into my workspace, I suddenly find my normally dutiful brain seeking occasional but illogical distractions, such as wondering if there are any news updates since the last time I checked (10 minutes prior). As Postman said, the machine takes on a life of its own—exacting mysterious and possibly deleterious sociological change. This has been true of machines from the printing press to the television to the Internet, as we shall see in the final section of this study.

As we analyze Postman's (and Huxley's) admonitions, that we can best understand a culture by studying its tools for conversation (8), we would do well to contemplate his conceptual analysis of media speak, where, as he said, he "found intimations on the idea that forms of media favor particular kinds of content and therefore are capable of *taking command of a culture*" (italics mine). He goes on to say, like his predecessor Ernst Cassini, that modern man is so thickly enveloped in the lens created for us by technologies that we are unable to interpret our realities except through these mediums. At first, this stinging revelation may seem a condemning reprimand—until we read the precious lines of his heartfelt plea: "Like the fish who survive a toxic river and the boatmen who sail on it, there still dwell among us those whose sense of things is largely influenced by older and clearer waters" (p. 28). Clearly, Postman's vision was hope for the future.

Sillier by the Minute: The Din of Dangerous Nonsense

One of Postman's goals was to persuade the reader that "the decline of a print-based epistemology and the accompanying rise of a television-based epistemology has had grave consequences for public life, that "the content of much of our public discourse has become dangerous nonsense" (p. 16), and we are "getting sillier by the minute" (p. 24). As I listen to the conversations of the culture, whether in written word, in speech, or in media speak, the gravity of Postman's (and Morse's and Thoreau's) observations become painfully clear: The art of conversation has been traded in for a shallow din of surface conversations, flitting from subject to subject like a news broadcast, and sprinkled with the brusque banalities of a morally-bereft comedian—indeed, content that is *sillier by the minute*.

In his sprightly yet stinging assessment of the catch phrase that has become the empty connector for two seemingly unrelated story lines in the news media ("now—this!"), Postman echoes the vacuous nature of the entertainment world: "The phrase, if that's what it may be called, adds to our grammar a new part of speech, a conjunction that does not connect anything to anything but does the opposite: separates everything from everything" (p. 99). It's easy to see how, in this world of disjointed and emotionally fragmented, seemingly psychopathic links to information, a child (or adult) could become fragmented and disconnected from the possibility of logical exposition.

This challenge is increasingly visible in the classroom, to be sure—so much so that I find myself wondering at times if intelligence and media addiction are, for the most part, mutually exclusive, in the same way that crack addiction and relational normalcy are mutually exclusive. Television jumps from such diverse, unequally yoked topics so frequently that it is impossible to do anything but react momentarily, emotionally. "We have become so accustomed to (TV's) discontinuities that we are no longer struck dumb, as any sane person would be, by a newscaster who having just reported that a nuclear war is inevitable goes on to say that he will be 'right back after this word from Burger King'" (p. 102). And the ramifications of this fragmentation, this complete disregard for seriousness or reflection, are playing out in multiple facets of our socio-emotional worlds. "One can hardly overestimate the damage that such juxtapositions do to our sense of the world as a serious place. The damage is especially massive to youthful viewers who depend so much on television for their clues as to how to respond to the world" (p. 105).

In the first two chapters of this book, the reader will recall, we discussed the human brain's propensity for socialization and how we naturally look to our social surroundings as a model for behavioral appropriateness. Thus, children reared by media bear a chilling and vacuous disconnect from reality. I use the word *chilling* because of the extraordinary implications for a generation raised without the impartations of gravity (replaced by pure levity) of empathy (replaced by mocking) or sensitivity and compassion towards all living things (replaced by desensitization and a disconnect from the reality of cause and effect behaviors).

With its focus on the irrelevant factoids that are the bread of television viewing, with its lack of complexity and nuance, with its visual stimulation substituting for thought (p. 105), television "creates the illusion of knowing something but...in fact leads one away from knowing" (p. 107). With the "now...this" mentality so firmly embedded in our culture, it is not difficult to see how students have fallen away from history, how conversations with them can jump to 15 topics in 1 minute, how speakers in my oratory class have difficulty maintaining a serious tone and repressing their television-endowed urge to draw laughter from the audience. Postman explains by saying "the public has adjusted to incoherence and been amused into indifference" (p. 111). Our collective attention span has suffered.

Today's teachers are told to lecture less than 20 minutes and preachers less than 30; the rest of the time in class should be "group work" and the rest of the time in church should be "socializing," presumably with caffeinated-laced coffee and sugar-imbued doughnuts. Given these new mandates, the attention span of the average modern American appears to have dropped to the rough equivalent of a three-year old. Thus, if a speaker plans to talk more than five minutes, he should be sure to give us some crayons and a piece of bright red construction paper to keep us entertained. Or, better yet, he should be entertaining, avoiding the fluff of substance with appropriate silliness.

As a final example from the Postman productions, the provocative book *Technopoly* provides a backdrop for the transformative culture we find ourselves in, where the tools created to serve us have instead become our masters. Technopoly, "the submission of all forms of culture to the sovereignty of technique and technology" (p. 52), found its insidious root in American culture because of a handful of simple reasons: a tendency toward restlessness, a desire to disconnect from the past, a general distrust of establishment, technological successes and promise, and a devaluation of traditionalism (p. 55). This impact is discussed by a number of authors, one of which is Richard Schickel in the book *Intimate Strangers* (2000). Schickel says that our virtual face-to-face time with media celebrities (7 hours and 2 minutes a day of TV time, he says), has created a new form of relationship based on the "illusion of intimacy" that is both entrapping and "insidiously subliminal in its workings" (4). Schickel says that while we maintain a sense of professional separation in our dealings with others in normal, face-to-face relationships, this protective distancing does not extend to celebrities.

> (The) decent wariness that protects both ourselves and the stranger from intrusion...is not operative when we are dealing with celebrities. Thanks to television and the rest of the media we know them, or think we do. To a greater or lesser degree, we have internalized them, unconsciously made them a part of our consciousness, just as if they were, in fact, friends (p. 4).

If we imagine that friend to be "present" in our lives for 7 hours a day, a soulless, empty vessel, continuously pitching products through under-the-radar marketing and secretly inducing us to buy this and believe that, the image leads us to an end result—a culture carefully conditioned under the tutelage of cynicism, materialism, and seduction. What would be the impact of such a friend's influence, this *intimate stranger* with whom we have bonded and begun our social apprenticeship?

The Art of Conspicuous Consumption and Cultural Reproduction

Burke and Gombrich pose a vital question: "How can artists check a schema against a reality if their view of reality is itself a product of the schema?" In other words, we can't see how challenged our culture may be without stepping outside the view. As Covey noted in *The 8th Habit*, "Most ailing organizations have developed a functional blindness to their own defects. They are not suffering because they cannot resolve their problems, but because they cannot *see* their problems" (Covey, p. 19). We see this "third person syndrome" at work not only in US institutions, but in US households. We have seemingly been heretofore oblivious to our cultural demise. As Covey noted, "If you want to make minor incremental changes and improvements, work on practices, behavior or attitude. But if you want to make significant, quantum improvement, work on paradigm" (p. 19). It is, in fact, the paradigm of Western culture that has been shaped, stuffed, and propped up against a backdrop of pseudo-reality. A generational mindset is being fashioned, and as Burke noted, "If each generation reinterprets the norms only slightly in the process of receiving and retransmitting them, appreciable social changes will take place over the long term (p. 133).

Thorstein Veblen, a 19th century American sociologist, coined the term "conspicuous consumption" to describe overt consumerism. He argued that "the economic behaviour of the elite, (the leisure class) was irrational and wasteful," motivated only by emulation. Burke adds that "conspicuous consumption is only one strategy for a social group to show itself superior to another." This is an important point in relation to Hollywood—by living "large," celebrities attempt to call attention to the chasm that lies between "star" and ordinary earth dwellers. "The ruling class did not rule only by force...but also by persuasion, a combination of force and consensus. The persuasion was indirect: *The subordinate classes learned to see society through their rulers' eyes"* (Burke p. 133, italics mine). In the same way, mass media rules in both word and image. It is irrefutable. And even if an error is discovered, the later retraction, indubitably buried in a tiny paragraph on page 10, is overlooked. The misinformation continues its reign of power.

Cultural reproduction' is a phrase that refers to the "tendency of society...to reproduce itself by inculcating in the rising generation the values of the past (Bourdieu and Althusser 1970). Cultural reproduction takes effort. "Traditions do not persist automatically, out of 'inertia,' as historians sometimes put it...They are transmitted as the result of a good deal of hard work by parents, teachers, priests, employers and other agents of socialization. (Burke, p. 133)" In today's generation, it is no longer the parents, teachers, priests, and pastors who are serving as the agents of socialization. It is the actors, the singers, the athletes with attitude— in short, the entertainers. And what have they "taught" us? Drink this beverage. Eat this junk food. Buy a car that you can't afford. Buy a house that you can't afford. Wear this brand, and everyone will like you. In short, we have become a nation of excess through a process of cultural reproduction in the hands of media socialization. It takes only a quick look under the hood to see that this little engine is the driving force behind much of the economic turmoil we are facing today, for excess is birthed in greed.

CHAPTER SIX

Historic Concerns: Lessons from Past Mass Media Strategies

Modern writers are not the first in history to be sobered by the all-consuming power of the media. Back as far as the 1930s, researchers were already concerned with the potential sway of this then-novel mass appeal. In an observation of 60 boys with delinquent or truant behavior patterns, Whitley (1932) analyzed the effects of the motion picture theater experience on attitudes and behavior. His goal was "not only to see the total delinquency pattern of the individual, but also to perceive the exact role of the photoplay and the motion-picture theater in problem behavior" (Cressey, 1934). In interviews with 237 boys and men, he ultimately noted that there were several compelling factors regarding the influential nature of mass media, specifically, in this case, the cinema. First, as the report showed, childhood and youth represent an "age of reception." The young child is unable to read through the social cues with great accuracy; and, as later researchers such as Strasberger and Bandura would show, the child is capable of interpreting with accuracy only very basic concepts of causation, and the links to causation may be interpreted in opposition to their initial intention. For example, Strasberger (and Singer) have shown that violence that results in laughter carries a high impact. In a child's life, and indeed in a modern adult's life, laughter is a type of social reward. Thus, linking violence with humor creates a greater level of desire for emulation of the characteristic.

Particularly among the young, the research found these early films to be quite persuasive: "While research findings show that what the child or youth perceives, remembers, and later utilizes from his photoplays is not at all what most adults would at first surmise, the fact remains that the young person, because of his immaturity, is very often more receptive to screen stimuli than are adults" (Cressey). This is not to say that adults are not receptive, but we shall return to that thought later. For now, we need simply to understand that children are highly susceptible to the malformation of the *generalized other*, and no one is completely certain as to what age in life this self-other concept develops fully.

We know from medical research that the prefrontal cortex region of the brain, the area which regulates judgment, is not fully developed until the age of 25. This immature cortex is noted as a causative factor in safe driving: a driver under 25 is more distracted (and less safe as a driver) when there are additional passengers in the car, whereas the over-25 driver, as a general rule, is significantly safer on the road with passengers, presumably because he or she bears a greater sense of responsibility for the other, or perhaps for the generalized other. Of course, if this theoretical development does not incur its fullness until the age of 25, there are serious considerations to be made concerning driving, marriage, and a host of other serious commitments. Nonetheless, it is plausible that such affectations may be cultural—that is, shaped by the prevailing generalized other as demonstrated in socio-familial roles. In that case, cinema clearly possesses a form of latent power which can be increased (or possibly decreased) according to the social and psychological context in which it is delivered.

Another phase of the cinema's potential power, says Cressey, is "the fact that it can now benefit from its many years of experience in the production and exhibiting of films especially attractive to the immature mind and to the child." This truth, of course, holds far more power today than in the 1930s. The motion picture industry employs a number of creative (or subversive, depending on one's view) techniques in order to discover themes and angles through which and from which to market its wares. As

Cressey so politely states, "Though very probably without intent and without any special pedagogical preconceptions, the motion-picture industry has actually followed the practice of producing photoplays for those of widely different cultural heritages and of varying stages of intellectual maturity." Certainly, today's tightly interwoven marketing/production systems make clear the focused methodology of television and movies, but even in the 1930s, these fledgling marketing capabilities were underway. As Cressey said, "Through its wide range of offerings, even though moralists may doubt the influence upon character of certain photoplays, the cinema provides a diet which in part is definitely attuned to the interest and mental growth of the child, and so facilitates its own educational contribution." The study found that the very format of the cinema was compelling enough to influence an individual's reality:

> (Through its) living form scenes which readily appear to the child as replicas of life itself, based upon actual life situations...(which are) made attractive and interest compelling by every device of plot, action, scenery, and acting, the photoplay possesses unique pedagogical advantages. It can command attention through the fact that it is "telling a story," an instructional advantage recognized even in early use of folklore and parables. By the portrayal upon the screen of life situations, which seem only more gripping than those the child himself usually experiences, the photoplay can readily confer upon its subject matter a sense of validity and definiteness not so easily obtained, perhaps, by any other method of communication or instruction.

The cinema, Cressey says, worked to discover basic human motives and desires in order to appeal to its audience. Consequently, "children and adults as well have, by projecting themselves into the activities and interests of the screen characters, inadvertently contacted a psychological element by which the information and general knowledge incidental to the plot could readily be seen to have meaning and could, therefore, be easily retained." This he contrasts with the scholastic environment, where motivation for learning is not internal, not sensory driven (or at least it wasn't in the 1930s when Cressey was completing his study!). In image format, learning takes place in the most powerful realm possible: the visual realm.

Finally, and most important to the interests of social psychology and influence, the prestige of the "star" in the movie is an education in itself—a how-to of social rules, norms, and behavior, of cause-and-effect relationships and wanton realities. Cressey states, "On every hand the city child meets this screen world. Even though he may not attend the cinema the urban youth is constantly exposed to ideas, patterns, and suggestions which have their origin in Hollywood." These inculcations include "garish billboards, lobby displays, and handbills telling of forthcoming attractions" as well as movie-star endorsements of the child's favorite candy or soda. Once he returns home, the child may note in the newspaper articles and ads that center on the star's lifestyle or upcoming features. In other words, wherever the cinema-goer turns, he is deluged with details of the appearance, attitude, beliefs, and happenings of the life of this "star." And, as Cressey showed, these influences extend beyond the role of mere admiration; they affect the way viewers behave, even in the seemingly-benign format of dress. "The youth, like his sister who can now equip herself from head to toe in clothing especially endorsed by actresses or modeled after clothes worn in recent photoplays, may set out upon a similar mission..."; that is, the child desires to emulate in every way the "star" with whom she has become so well acquainted. For what natural steps do we take when making a friend? We learn of the friend's interests, habits, style of dress, manner of speaking, and other superficial social behavior. A quick glance around a modern high school cafeteria solidifies for us the image: "Life" played out on the screen (whether television, movie, or computer screen) is being emulated in the microcosm. As Cressey says, "In a variety of ways, through the screen, through the play world of childhood, and through countless commercial devices Hollywood has in one way or another become intimately associated with some of the most vital interests and activities of childhood and youth."

Most important to consider in this regard, notes Cressey, is the fact that the "stars" of cinema carry with them "far greater prestige and, in the activities and thought of these young people, in many cases mean far more than do all the local political, educational, and social leaders whose activities have direct bearing upon their lives." If this was the case in 1934, when the portrayal of celebrity lifestyle was limited to cinema and street media, how much greater would the salience be today, where the opportunity for mass media marketing and product placement is virtually limitless? We are assaulted by thousands of images and messages daily, both overt and covert. Interestingly, Cressey's study also found that for people with whom a character "strikes fire" (as defined within the portrayal of interests, activities, or values the subject relates to personally), the character can serve as a "paramount influence" in the individual's life. In a few instances, researchers said, some individuals wrapped their entire personality development around the persona of the character on the screen, in essence becoming that character or adopting traits of that character into real life. This might seem extreme and extraordinary at first glance, until we relate the same trend to modern life. How many women copied the hairstyles of Jennifer Aniston religiously during the height of her "Friends" popularity? How many "fans" can answer the most remote and nonsensical trivia about the romances of Angelina Joli but cannot name the last four presidents of the United States? Like the children in Spurlock's *SuperSize Me*, who could readily identify a photo of Ronald McDonald but were stumped as to the identity of Christ, we have become a culture devoted to trivia, to nonsense, to silliness, to the mania of marketing.

Ultimately, the 1932 study found that the cinema provides a "ready basis for the acquisition of personality patterns, standards of dress and conduct, and even philosophies and schemes of life." Certainly, we can see the potential ramifications of the extraordinarily media-central culture in which Westerners find ourselves today. Our fare is not limited to 1.6 hours of cinema viewing a day, as was the extreme limit in Cressey's time. Instead, it exceeds the maximum 2-hour daily limit prescribed by pediatricians and psychologists alike by 3 times that amount. If there were serious concerns raised when the media diet consisted of a single two-hour film per week, should we not gravely consider the ramifications on our socio-emotional health in today's media-central culture?

Modern Westerners are in danger of being sucked into the undertow powered by this media deluge. Though Cressey's research focused mainly on media's influence on children, it is important to note that there is a new strategy at work behind the scenes in modern media whose audience of a more "grown-up" persuasion. Lest we think that only children are capable of being swayed by media appeals, we must understand that not all media campaigns are targeted at children, and children are definitely not the only demographic susceptible to persuasion.

As we saw in Chapter 5, there are a number of highly successful persuasive media campaigns that do regularly position themselves as change agents for the viewing population—without the viewing population's awareness or consent. The social persuasion strategy of EE is an embedded-message tactic touted by producers and lobbyists alike for its persuasive powers. The important questions modern viewers must ask EE strategists are the same ones we must ask in our churches, our synagogues, our mosques, and our homes: whose values, whose agenda, what influence?

Additional Findings on Media Influence

In the final treatment of Cressley's 1930's cinema review, the researchers found that film did indeed have tremendous latent power for individual (and thus social) change, but it required a certain "predisposition" to be most effective. The role of media had to be analyzed and understood within the context of the entire social system. In other words, if there were certain existing conditions, the likelihood for influence would be greater. As we will see in a moment, a powerful seed has been germinating inside our collective American consciousness for a number of generations, and now we now find ourselves in the midst of just such a predisposition. The researchers found the cinema's role in general conduct to be *reflexive*, that is, it takes a combination of "social-psychological frame" present at the time of viewing. The power of persuasive appeals, whether to attitude or behavior, then, rests in a number of socio-psychological factors: the person's experiences, associations, problems, interests, and the pleasure or displeasure "later experienced with this conduct" (i.e., will he be punished, ignored, or rewarded for his behavior?).

These behavioral or attitudinal alterations, then, manifest through the power of suggestion ("a release of attitudes and tendencies" already existing somewhere within the individual), through the "unwitting acquisition" of behaviors, or the conscious acquisition of behavior (Cressley, 1934)). The study found that the cinema's "net contributions" related mostly to the acquisition of social attitudes and new information rather than to overt behavior. What is perhaps most interesting about these findings is that effective persuasion requires a two-step process: we first change an attitude, then a behavior. These social training techniques are certainly resident within EE strategies, and given a long-term view of social change, a constructionist could, in effect, tailor messages to affect the population at increasingly salient levels.

As Cressley showed, "These "net contributions" are found in those areas of knowledge for which children and young people do not have other more adequate sources of information; screen representations are accepted only so long as other more "authoritative" knowledge is unavailable and only when they do not *seem* to contradict the mores, codes, and the axiomatic "truths" accepted by the subject and his group." In other words, if parents are failing to educate children regarding the interpersonal and personal roles of life, and if the media messages seem compelling, that is, sprinkled with a dose of virtually undetectable half truths mixed with a shot or two of verifiable truth, then there will most likely be a net contribution.

These findings agree with those of Cultivation Theory, a study developed by George Gerbner, dean of The Annenberg School for Communication at the University of Pennsylvania, who analyzed the effects of television programs on attitudes and behavior. For TV research to be most meaningful and effective, Gerbner and his colleagues said it must focus not on a singular effect but on an overarching, cumulative impact that television has on our view of the world (Miller 2005). Gerbner found that instead of religion or education, TV had become "the source of the most broadly shared images and messages in history...Television cultivates from infancy the very predispositions and preferences that used to be acquired from other primary sources...The repetitive pattern of television's mass-produced messages and images forms the mainstream of a common symbolic environment" (p. 18). In other words, those of us who have grown up within a media-central world have been trained under a television tutor: TV has taught us how to analyze, how to integrate, how to joke, how to look, how to feel, how to respond, and how to look—especially how to look. After all, it's all about the image. Waif-like bodies and perfect teeth are part of that image, of course, but there is much more being communicated than simply physiological elitism.

In his 1969 research, Gerbner charted the television content for prime-time and weekend programs for children. He found several significant patterns in his day, and the contrast between messages then and now is certainly intriguing. Today's TV dads are not all-knowing or well-intentioned, as they were in Gerbner's era. Instead, the vast majority of men in sitcoms are portrayed as selfish and lazy buffoons who think only about immediate gratification, whether that be in the form of food or procreation. The women of today's shows have taken on the opposite role. Women are portrayed as cool, thin, and trendy; they (and their children) outsmart dumb and disconnected dad on a continual basis. In Gerbner's day, women were the butt of jokes, and that was no better, of course. But if the initial goal of socialization was truly one of equality, we have missed that by a long shot—instead of providing greater respect to all, we have blighted both sexes with unfair presumptions and stereotypes. If this seems an unreasonable assessment, try to imagine a solitary sitcom where the husband is smart, successful, and good-looking, and his wife is a buffoon. If that sitcom exists, it is one in 100. In light of the current absence of strong socio-familial influences that might have kept a *Three Stooges* audience anchored to its intellectual moorings, today's viewer learns in a socio-familial vacuum.

Another finding for Gerbner was the under-representation of older and younger people on TV. Today, the older population is still underrepresented, as many television viewers seem to want the elderly neatly tucked away in nursing homes, where the viewer won't be reminded of the pain, the—worse, the wrinkles—that come to bear with old age. Gerbner also noted a lack in the representation of Blacks and Hispanics in televised programming, though programming has come a long way in being inclusive to ethnicity today. Finally, regarding statistical abnormalities, Gerbner found that only seven percent of TV characters represent "middle class" lifestyle (with the rest representing the lifestyles of the rich and famous) and that crime is 10 times as rampant in the "television world" as it is in the real world. These wealth and crime statistics are similar to today's TV realities, but their impact is magnified. Taken in the view of a macro-social lens, the world-context in which these modern shows are viewed is in many ways completely antithetical to Gerbner's social world.

To analyze the effects of Cultivation Theory, Gerbner and his team assessed the viewers' initial worldview, compared that worldview after TV viewing, and then made worldview comparisons between light and heavy television watchers. One of two formats of influence became clear: Media either had the tendency to override differences and promote a whitewashed, homogenized culture (mainstreaming), or it impacted viewers because of their existing real-life relation to the experience portrayed on the programming (resonance). Even in seemingly small discoveries of systematic patterns, the consequences of the impact are far-reaching (Miller, p. 286). In fact, as Cressley discovered,

The cinema has been found to influence greatly the shaping of attitudes and the acquisition of information, and even to affect overt behavior in certain situations. The *nature* of these "effects" is determined by many forces external to the motion picture but the fact of its educational and social role cannot be denied for that reason... In fields of vital interests not adequately met through other community institutions and agencies, in fields where prestige is attached to the acquisition of the "latest thing," as in fashion, popular songs, and slang, and in fields where the movie facilitates trends in standards or public opinion which are already under way, the motion picture makes some of its most distinct "contributions."

In other words, once a "desirable" social context is laid for a persuasive mass media appeal, the kindling begins to glow. It takes only a mild breeze to fan the tiny spark into a blazing fire. That gentle wind blowing through our midst at present finds itself situated at a time like no other in Western history. In the next chapter, we will analyze the ill effects of our socialization in light of our present persuasive positioning. The current generation is poised for influence like no other generation in history, for a tragic timeline has threaded its way through the recent past to wreak havoc on the unsuspecting future. But we mustn't look the other way. The events presented in the next chapter must be reviewed and rescinded before they can be reversed for the sake of generations to come.

CHAPTER SEVEN

Tragic Timeline: Social Constructionism and Persuasive Positioning

Recently, I read of an organizational leader who was denouncing another leader's call to arms over what the second leader termed an "increase in sexualized media." In his venomous discourse, the first leader accused the second leader of being over-reactionary and alarmist. "Every generation makes the same claim," the first leader said. "We all feel that the next generation is more corrupt than ours. It's just a cycle," he argued. A cycle? Definitely. Over-reactionary and alarmist? Hardly. Certainly, generational change can be tracked and traced in cyclical patterns, but such a nonchalant, even cavalier attitude toward these catastrophes is inexcusable, and, I would argue, a mark of either acute cowardice or extreme self-delusion. For when we step back to a more global view—the century perspective—the cycle hasn't been one of mild ups and relative downs. On the contrary, the current cycle represents a radical downward spiral with very few notable leaps upward.

As one small example, consider the change in scholastic environments from 1956 to 2006. My grandmother, who lived 96 on this planet, taught in the public elementary school system for most of her life. She would offer her contrast of historical perspectives and listeners would be shocked by the extraordinarily sharp disparity between the two worlds. The 50's "crimes" of chewing gum and cutting in line in school would be welcomed today in exchange for the horrors faced in the modern public school, from gang warfare to robbery to school shootings. And, to no surprise, paralleling this rise has been a steady onslaught of increasingly violent, increasingly sexualized media imagery. Gazing out from a generational perspective, the road connecting the last half of the 1900s to the early portion of 2000 seems hazy at first, but upon closer look, the twists and turns seem almost strategic in nature, as if one cultural crisis were building firmly upon the foundation of the previous one, one brick upon the other, in sinister succession. A number of sweeping changes have taken place in American culture in just the last 50 years, a time period that may prove to be the foundation for five decades of progressive decay. For at the generational perspective, the "Google Earth" level, we can observe a fascinating timeline that has availed itself over the last five decade, subtly linking itself together behind the scenes, beneath the surface.

Those of us who work and speak in Generation X and Generation Y circles often hear the argument that lewd and violent behaviors existed long before modern media assaults, and the entire culture was not swept away with them at the time of portrayal. Yes, media has held a *place* in our lives for three generations, but it has only been the *center* of our lives for the last decade or two. Furthermore, the world of 1987 was extraordinarily different than the world of 2009.

As we discussed in Chapter 1, human behavior is shaped by culture, context, and cohort. Twenty years ago, fear did not rule the hearts of the modern citizen to the degree that it often does today. A young girl could walk to school alone without fear of abduction. Children could go to the neighbor's house to spend the night with no fear (or even considerations!) of foul play. Church nursery workers did not have to undergo background checks, nor were they prevented from changing a baby's diapers for fear that they might harm a helpless infant. Toilet seats covers did not exist—and did not need to. Moms and dads could send their kids to class at the local college without fear that they would be gunned down by a fellow student on an anger rampage. Indeed, it is a new world.

No, media messages are not new, but the social context in which they present themselves is definitely unique. It is this pounding succession of events, from latchkey lifestyles, purposefully poor nutrition, missing parents, a host of new mental disease labels, virtual connectivity (and resultant familial disconnect), and a whole host of other social maladies that have created a socio-emotional foundation for a world that is more receptive than ever to media messages.

We are more "persuadable" today than ever before, stirred up by the swamp of values-free, politically-correct, nutritionally-deficient, drug-infested, familially-disengaged lifestyles. The effectiveness of modern persuasive appeals hinges on the mass of recent cultural changes that almost guarantee our receptiveness to media messages. As we shall see, the true power of the modern media is a matter of its unique recipe: a mixture of persuasion and position, biology and sociology.

The Tragic Timeline

We've already reviewed some of the underscoring for this positioning with the studies from Cressey back in the 1930s, so let's begin here with the Fabulous Fifties. Retrospectively, we are aware of a number of social undercurrents plaguing the 1950s, but for the most part, the decade is marked by its relatively harmonious, family-focused times: the "happy" days. In the minds of many, there was a pervasive innocence that seemed to define the decade. Families spent many hours together at home, eating breakfast and dinner together, listening to radio shows, and reading books.

When television first made its debut in the American home, mom and dad were there to watch with the kids. Instead of gathering around the radio together, as families had done for many years before, now families could crowd around the television in the family living room: at its early inception, the medium was unifying rather than divisive. Programming was centered on the family experience: Variety programs such as the *Ed Sullivan Show* offered familial fare: musicians, actors, and other entertainers appeared in family-friendly style at a family-friendly time. Children did not sneak upstairs to watch "their own shows" out from under the watchful eye of a parent (nor did parents hide away in the secret dens of "adult" fare). The family was a unit and television was, in many ways, just one more beam of reinforcement in the wall of familial connectivity. And then came the sixties shakeup.

The 1960s are generally known as a period of political upheaval marked by radical changes in the home and in the workplace. With the advancement of the feminist movement, women began working out of the home in droves. This movement has been documented by many writers (Blankenhorn, Popenoe, Rossi, McLanahan, Yogman, Furstenberg, and Heaton to name a few), and space does not permit explication here. However, just as television was gaining ground as a home-entertainment medium, there was a mass Mom exodus from the household.

Fortunately, television and the newly-remodeled school value systems were there to fill in the gap. While TV dispensed its "age-appropriate" diet of clever consumerism to the kiddies at home, public education underwent the most significant facelift in the history of the United States school system: The Values Clarification Movement. Howard Kirschenbaum, a leading author on Values Clarification ideology, says the movement was a mirror of the social upheaval exhibited during the radical transformations in 1950's culture to 1960's culture. Prior to 1960, as other authors have noted, the social culture underscored traditional family values. Parents did not have to counter the culture; culture was not the enemy. That all changed in the 60s. In the 1950s, as Kirschenbaum notes,

> There appeared to be a consensus among parents, religious, and society regarding values and morality, values education during this period consisted of the traditional methods of *inculcating* and *modeling*. Schools took their role in values education for granted. Children were exhorted to be prompt, neat, and polite; to work hard succeed; to respect other's property—in short, to behave themselves...Then came the

turbulent Sixties and Seventies, when traditional roles and values were seriously questioned—and in many cases rejected—by the younger generation...in one of the fastest social revolutions in human history. New attitudes toward and experimentation with human sexuality, religion, career options, lifestyles, and personal values were widespread.

Kirschenbaum explains that it was in the midst of this social upheaval that the teacher took on a new role in the lives of students. "Instead of simply inculcating and modeling values," Kirschenbaum notes, "educators were now encouraged to help students *clarify their own values*, learn higher levels of *moral reasoning*, and learn the skills of *value analysis*." Instead of providing a guide to the moral opposites of right and wrong, teachers were suddenly discouraged, even disallowed, from taking extreme positions. This moral relativity has carried through to the modern realm of course, and it now finds itself so intrinsically woven into innumerable facets of life that it is at times difficult to recognize.

I once worked with an Ivy League professor who drove this point home for me. He chastised me quite severely for a paper I had written in defense of an aspect of faith. "It is not considered scholarly," he explained in condescending fashion, "to view the world as guided by an external source. Modern scholars *write their own reality*; they do not attribute it to a nebulous god of the universe" (italics mine). When I gave a rather stinging retort quoting the educational philosophy of the school guiding our journey, and on the dividends of true diversity, explaining how unfair (and illegal) it was for him to insist that my worldview must be identical to his if I were to become a scholar, he backed down. But the point remains. The concept of tolerance and diversity in modern Western culture means thinking like the mainstream, not thinking critically or originally. These are residual effects of the sixties shakeup.

Next came the seventies mayhem. This sweeping movement built on the heightened sense of freedom established in the 1960s, and, as a result, the 1970s ushered in a decade where people suddenly believed they were free from not only the conventions of marriage and gender roles, but from all the encasements of morality itself. Morality, after all, was defined in the eye of the beholder. Educators and the children they taught were expected to define right and wrong for themselves and then live by their own individualized standards.

The tiny grassroots efforts of the Values Clarification Movement in the 1960s took deep root in the 1970s. In the classroom, these fundamental teachings evolved into an experience-based educational process, where intellectualism was subject to emotionalism. Education, it was proclaimed, "must guide the child, so that through...experience, his creativity and autonomy will be cultivated rather than stifled" (Contini). Instead of the "well-formed conscience" through which previous generations had contemplated their social, intellectual, and spiritual pursuits, students were now being released into a boundary-free realm of "valuation" (Contini).

In the early 1970s, classrooms were bursting at the seams with textbooks teaching educators the application of valuation to the classroom. In fact, according to Kirshenbaum, VCM remains the most influential methodology ever to strike the scholastic market. For 15 years, from the late 1960s to the mid-1980s, John Heenan was one of several national leaders in the values clarification movement. Heenan says that the movement garnered such widespread attention that in one decade, there were 40 books published in the 70s alone on the values clarification approach, one of which, *Values Clarification: A Handbook of Practical Strategies for Teachers and Students,* sold more than 600,000 copies-almost unheard of in the field of education (Heenan, p. 7).

So sweeping was the movement that it became a foundation for every possible scholastic subject: religious education, health education, sex education, and drug education—and its pervasiveness was not limited to school alone; in addition to public school classrooms, VCM found its way into families, scout troops, churches, synagogues, and communities (Heenan, p. 8). Though Heenan says VCM fell out of favor by title in the 1980s, he notes that "it is still being used widely and although its methods have been incorporated into curricula and training in diverse fields...Educators often employ specific values clarification methods but either do not realize they are doing so or prefer not to say so—because it might seem passé or controversial" (p. 8).

Generation X was thus indoctrinated with the idea that how we—about a matter largely governed the rightness or wrongness of the occurrence. For us, truth was suddenly subordinate to personal experience and interpretation. Truth was moldable, pliable, situational—dependent on the needs of whatever circumstance we found ourselves in. The success and pervasiveness of this ideology was rooted in the socio-political climate of the 1960s and 1970s: Give free love, do your own thing, question authority, come out of the closet, and hearken the feminist cry, "I am woman; hear me roar."

These adages became the markers for a generation steeped in egocentrism, and this self-centered paradigm paved the way for an educational reform centered in autonomy. Truly, had these theories hit the bookstores in the 1950s, who would have taken the bait? But, as they were perfectly situated instead in the 1970s, the teachings made their way to the "rebels" of the culture—who were ready for the corporate takeover.

Theorists of the day echoed the radical shift as traditional moorings were yanked from their foundations: "Value orientations from the past appear to be in a state of disintegration or collapse. Men question whether there are, or can be, any universal values"(Contini, p. 4). With the entrance of this new morality, people were free to dismiss the idea of absolute truth, creating instead a set of individual rules and laws, rooted wholly in the individual's own sense of pleasure and completely unanchored to any sense of a greater common good. "If it feels good, do it." "Listen to your heart." These became the mantras of a new generation, one that would ultimately become governed by emotion.

Values clarification itself actually owes at least part of its history to the 1890s philosopher Frederich Nietzsche, who was set on "proving" that Judeo-Christian values were imprisoning, and that values should be defined individually, not corporately. Nietzsche is perhaps best known for his announcement to the world proclaiming the "death" of God. Clearly, values clarification fit nicely inside his absolute-free worldview.

Almost 60 years later, C.S. Lewis saw the seeds of Nietzsche's philosophy beginning to take root in American soil, and he countered with a global research study in search of common values. He discovered eight such "objective values" such as honesty, generosity, mercy, and duty, and he said that without these, the body corporate will cease to function. As Lewis put it, "In a sort of ghastly simplicity we remove the organ and demand the function...We laugh at honour and are shocked to find traitors in our midst. We castrate and bid the gelding be fruitful."

Studied at face value, the idea of fluid morality is utterly nonsensical, and, in fact, it is rather difficult to comprehend how any rationally-thinking generation could have been so swept up in the concept. The entire United States legal system is based on a set of universal values: Stealing is wrong, lying is wrong, murder is wrong, taking advantage of a child is wrong, workplace deception is wrong. These morals-turned-laws are proverbial stop signs that remind us of the ultimate accuracy and the sheltering protection of absolute laws. Without an acceptance of universal values, such as the ones recognized in Burr's works in the first portion of this study, our society would collapse in a downward spiral of selfishness and stupidity. However, under the VC regime, values become the result of personal choice, and they extend from the aged to the very, very young in virtually every sphere of life. As one author said, "Values clarification teaches children to shun traditional morality and family rules. It is no wonder that even small children upon returning home from school are boldly telling their parents that they will run their own lives" (Contini, p. 7).

Though VCM scattered its seeds of discontent and disconnectedness amongst the hearts and minds of thousands, perhaps millions of readers, it was ultimately rescinded in part by its very own founders. Heenan, one of the key founders of the movement, now admits that VCM contains major theoretical flaws:

We insisted that values clarification *by itself* was sufficient method for developing satisfying values and moral behavior in young people...values clarification is not and never has been 'value free.' We acknowledged that, in its goals and methods, the values clarification approach implicitly promoted freedom, justice, rationality, equality, and other democratic and civic values. It was only on specific issues—such as politics, religion, health, personal tastes, and the like—that values clarification was value free. We suggested that young people already had enough inculcation and models related to these issues; what they needed were the skills and opportunities to reflect on all this input and come up with their own well-thought-out answers.

Even with this admission of guilt, though, VCM had already taken root so deeply in American culture that it is to this day difficult to yank it out from the root of educational processes. At the core, VCM strategists believed that "it was *better* to clarify than to inculcate values and that those who primarily inculcated values were perhaps even harming young people by denying them the decision-making skills for guiding their own lives in a complex world" (Heenan). The challenge with this idea is that independent thought is not fostered through disconnection with boundaries and laws. My college students don't learn correct writing style through penning irrational journal entries that disregard the conventions of the English language. They learn from writing a paper, turning it in, and giving me the opportunity to *correct* the paper by clearly marking the errors. Then they practice the newly-developed skill or the recognition of the "error of their ways," and they try again on the next paper.

This is learning, and while it lacks in all the flair and fancy of a create-it-yourself grammarian, the benefit of rote-memorization and application is a *correct* and ultimately beneficial end product. Interestingly, Heenan, who now writes for the New Zealand Foundation for Character Education, seems singularly focused on undoing of the values-free past, much as the star player in Roe v.

Wade, Norma McCorvey, later recanted her pro-abortion stance and made her new cause her life message. Perhaps a values hiatus has led Heenan and others to some painful self-reflection. As the saying goes, it is possible to learn in a backward glance what cannot be understood looking forward.

In the midst of the Values Clarification Movement, television programming began increasing the breadth of its specific target markets. With age-specific shows that centered on the upheaval of the era, it was now entirely possible for teens and young adults to begin identifying with characters on television, interpreting the world through the actor's eyes and emulating the character's behavior. Then, as television became a more common part of daily life, so did its influence. In essence, once we had firmly rooted two important social changes into the American psyche—television entertainment and values clarification—we were ready to hit the pavement running with a new era, the 1980s, where, in record numbers, teens were left in the care of the newest babysitter on the market: the television. While Mom and Dad took their power places in the corner office, the TV arrived on the scene like a permissive parent, ready to educate its constituents in the ways of the world.

The "big 80s" are usually known for mullets, teased coifs, and metallic-hued clothing (the latter of which, somewhat regrettably, have sneaked back into classrooms and corner stores across the nation today). In some ways, though, this era held an eerie innocence: We still walked to school without fear of gang violence, abduction, or bomb threats. We knew nothing of forthcoming diseases like AIDS and STIs. Toilet seat covers were years from both invention and necessity. Big hair and Duran Duran purses aside, though, the 1980s brought some dramatically impacting scenarios into our homes. We were aptly dubbed the MTV generation, an entire people group who were the first to claim a diet of television equal in hours to a full day's work. We knew that "Video Killed the Radio Star;" what we didn't realize was that video was slowly killing us. But more on that in a moment.

From the domestic-departure movement of the 1970s, more and more mothers had left home for work, and, as a result, a new era of childhood began: the latchkey generation. Latchkey kids were children who came home to an empty house and had to "fend for themselves" until Mom or Dad came home from work. Conveniently, just as latchkey-syndrome was sweeping the nation, two technological wonders came to the rescue of frazzled parents in need of a "babysitter": the VCR and MTV, two acronyms that would soon change the face of media.

According to Frances Alston, the director of Dependent Care Consultants, the concept of latchkey children first came into being during the Second World War. Moms had gone to work while dads were off at war, and for many families, this meant sending their children home from school with a key tied around their necks. Today's latchkey kids are not abandoned because of a human rights war; more than likely, they have been left home alone because of a Joneses war—the fight for more stuff.

Alston (2000) ranks this number relatively low: one third of all school-age children in America are latchkey kids. Statistically, this means that between five and seven million children between the ages of 5 and 13 are home by themselves for some part of the day or evening. Some researchers, such as those at the Children's Defense Fund estimate the number of latchkey kids in America to be as high as 16 million US children. The State Department of Education says that somewhere between 600,000 to 800,000 children in California fit into the latchkey category. Besides the obvious dangers of being home alone without adult supervision or guidance, though, there are some more covert dangers as well. First, a child's academic performance suffers when he has more time alone at home.

In fact, teachers have implicated latchkey status as the "number one cause of school failure" (Alston 2000). Juvenile crime peaks in the afternoon hours, when children are out of school and have no formal scholastic or familial responsibilities, so latchkey children are more likely to be introduced to criminal behavior. In addition to externally destructive behaviors, latchkey children are far more prone to internally destructive behaviors as well:

The Carnegie Council on Adolescent Development found that 8th graders who are alone *11 hours a week* are twice as likely to abuse drugs as adolescents who are busy after school....(and) teens who have sexual intercourse do it in the afternoon in the home of boys whose parents work. Unsupervised children are more likely to become depressed, smoke cigarettes and marijuana and drink alcohol (Alston, italics mine).

While 80s kids were being introduced to the precarious freedoms of the latchkey lifestyle, VC methodology stayed close by to keep the moral waters murky with "critical-thinking exercises" like the plane crash game. I remember "playing" this popular game in my high school psychology class in 1985. Sitting in small groups with classmates, we pored over a brief text given to us by our trusted teacher, a sweet but decidedly anti-establishmentarian-type, who, according to the rumors circulated by my classmates, served marijuana-laced brownies at her frequent house parties. The teacher told us there had been a plane crash on a remote island, and we, as a group of 16-year-old sages, were to determine the fate of the passengers stranded on the island. We were assured that there were no "right" answers or "wrong" answers to this exercise, only *our* answers. The food left after the crash was sparse and the likelihood of survival slim, so it was our job to decide which nine people would be allowed to live and which eight people would be forced to starve to death.

Though the exercise was touted as a didactic model for critical thinking, in retrospect, it was at best a macabre and shallow exercise in desensitization. My generation left the 80s with much more than big hair—we had sprouted big egos that rivaled our big spending habits. The MTV generation was now well on its way to creating a culture of narcissism, founded on the shaky foundation of personalized value systems and material excess.

In the 1990s, the Western world was smitten by the newest communication fad—and with nary a shred of Morse-like concern, the Internet began promulgating its wares, offering hope for restoring "lost" communities and creating "many to many" communication forums where individuals could be advised, coached, befriended, and "mentored" by someone they had never met, at least in the traditional sense of meeting. The personal computer suddenly became the personal counselor. The computer ultimately took on such a lifelike state that its Web began to connect all forms of life, all languages, all classrooms, all workspaces. The Internet has become such a vital part of modern Western life that it is difficult to imagine life without it.

In fact, a recent LiveScience survey says that 64 percent of Americans say they spend more time with their computer than with their significant other. As we passed the 2000 mark, we continued to witness the cumulative effects of the tragic timeline as we find ourselves drifting—a valueless, illiterate, familially-disconnected "community" that has been left to fend for itself. As the 60s generation comes of age, the first generation to be "raised" by the media, we are witnessing some serious social ramifications.

As parents have lessened their degree of personal involvement to more of a "supporting role" in the life of their children, the voices that rise up in influence are those of that often embrace value systems and ideologies that may not be supported by the average American family—that is, if the average American family were aware of the takeover. How has this media-centrality affected our nation? We will explore these questions in the next few chapters. Before we get to that, though, let me offer one more insight into the tragic timeline.

A Plea for Parents

In the 1980s, a great deal of emerging research began to surface in the area of maternal deprivation. It isn't a topic we hear much about today, mostly, I think, because we women have been conditioned to think that being a mother is somehow more of a hobby to our daytime job, that of earning something of true value, namely money. I see and talk with a lot of frustrated moms today, and many of them seem to believe the lie that they can do it all and still somehow have kids who turn out "all right."

Moms play a vital role in a child's development, both physiologically and socially. Numerous studies over the past three decades have linked depressive disorders, anxiety, and a lack of empathy to early life without a healthy maternal connection. It would seem that moms would instinctively know this, but just as the modern generation has been stripped of some ideals that should be fairly self-evident, I think moms, too, have been robbed of the ability to discern what a vital role they play in their children's development. As Charles Dickens' character Pip put it, they have been "robbed of their right nature."

Consider, for example, the Generation X teachings of distal parenting, where we were told to violate our conscience and let the baby "cry it out" when she was tired. This advice runs counterintuitive to a mother's natural instinct, which is to hold the baby and demonstrate the very important life message that the world is a safe and caring place. It is in the stage of trust versus mistrust (as Erikson posited) that many youngsters have been abandoned. Their lack of trust for the world around them continues to carry the past into the present.

A new field of studies on teen brains show that many, even most, of today's teenage population lacks empathy, that is, an awareness of the feelings of others. In brain scans, most teens are unable to correctly identify the feeling associated with a facial expression of fear, for example. Many researchers are citing this as a developmental phase, and it's true that we have nothing to compare it with from a neurological standpoint since functional magnetic resonance imaging (fMRI) capabilities only came of age in the last decade.

However, there may be another answer. Emerging research begs the question be answered: Is a lack of empathy, long associated with maternal deprivation, now becoming a commonplace factor in teen development? With 80% of moms working outside of the home and the vast majority leading what they self-describe as "very stressful" lives, is it any wonder that the generation's offspring is detached, confused, anchorless? There are times when a mother must work, whether she is a single mother meeting the needs of her family or whether she is the only one able. However, we perpetuate injustice when we don't give all the information. Parents must know their value, their worth, and their weighty responsibilities in childrearing. As we said in Chapter 1, knowledge is power. Let's take a look at the specific cultural transformations that have impacted Western culture—and what we can do about that influence in both an individual and a corporate sense.

EMERGE!

CHAPTER EIGHT

Media-Centrality and Multigenerational Socialization

Consider for a moment the pseudo-fictitious company Buzz, makers of one of the most popular soft drinks on the planet. The environment at Buzz is charged with excitement. Bonuses abound. Employees feel proud to be part of a corporate culture so popular with teens and adults alike. The owners of Buzz have a language that is all their own, a linguistic discipline that seeks to strip ideas completely of their true qualitative (that is, human and intangible) attributes, under the pretext of solely highlighting the product's greatest quantitative attribute—its production of profit. While the Buzz dialect adheres somewhat to the language's ideal of smiting away any true qualitative attributes of an idea, it makes no strict demand of barring qualitative language from its vernacular. In fact, it encourages qualitative idiom, especially if it portrays quantitative goals (and, especially, the means to attain those goals) more palatably than quantitative language could alone. This we will refer to as *Buzz-talk*.

A Free Market Fairytale

The workers at Buzz are shielded from knowledge about the product they sell, and they gladly accept this exclusion as part of the thrill of being part of the popular team. All the workers know is that Buzz seems to carry 100 times the buzz of caffeine, and by the rules of the free market they knew that there was a undeniable demand for superior "buzz" (and "Buzzes") and they thought that they were as good as anyone to supply it. Besides, if they didn't reap the rewards, someone else surely would. Indeed, their soda's name had always been *Buzz*, but now, at long last, it could truly deliver on its appellation.

We might imagine the effect on those unknowingly purchasing the "new" soft drink (though nobody outside of the company called it "new", because the soda company did not advertise a new formula, chiefly because, since the 1980s, everyone in the soda industry "knows what happens" when you change a soda's formula and try to market it as "new." Second, it wanted to more clandestinely test the public waters to see if the general population would respond positively to Buzz's new narcotic "*super-buzz*." The Buzz Marketing Team argued this would be a good idea just in case the general population didn't like the new formula as expected. This would undoubtedly save money in marketing costs and would also save them undue hassles (and, of course, any extra expenditures) of having to run tests to see if the additive would, potentially, have any adverse long term effects on the consumer.

The Buzz CEO agreed with the marketing team and felt if the extra buzz didn't increase sales on the general population "test-group," why put money into research at this point? "Long-term effects," the CEO said to himself, "can only be the product of long-term use." Since the national "test-group" was only a test, and not long-term partnership, no studies were needed until Buzz Soda Co. further determined if they would continue the injection of the new ingredient into Buzz.

With the new formula, Buzz began circulating even more wildly amongst the general population. It was an instant commercial success. Those who were previously casual fans of the drink became much more fanatical purchasers, and those who were already making daily purchases increased their fanaticism to twice or even thrice daily. Under this sort of purchasing frenzy, product sales tripled in the first quarter. And the company and its shareholders were quite elated, to say the least, at the mountainous surplus of dividends.

The increased prosperity allowed the corporation the financial freedom to hire on an even larger, more powerful team of executives, and many of the shareholders finally got to buy that second vacation home they had been dreaming of. All was merrymaking between company and shareholder. A huge party was thrown, attended by Buzz celebrities and decorated with Buzz fountains, which provided an unlimited supply of the drink. It was a Buzz festival complete with extensive media coverage.

At the time, things couldn't possibly seem to get any better for the soda company and its investors, but they did. They were put on the cover of prominent business journals, magazines, and periodicals. The CEO was invited to speak at business conferences around the world. And the sales and consumption of Buzz increased. Never had so many pop-music icons been knocking down its door to sing the newest Buzz jingle for radio and television (actually they never had any icons knock on their door before, but since the "new" formula had been released the celebrity-knocking was almost nonstop). Television and movie stars drank Buzz in commercials and clutched Buzz cans throughout the duration of their movies. And the sales and consumption of Buzz increased.

Buzz had always received a modest amount of fan-mail from its fanatical drinkers, but those who were previously casual fans of the drink had now become much more fanatical purchasers and were sending in letters. Those who were already frequently purchasing the product became all-out fanatics who doubled their amount of flattering fan mail. The praise mail filled the mailroom and every day President Buzz would receive the top ten fan-mail letters.

Consumption and product sales tripled again in the following quarter. If a company was in anything but the oil business during a Middle Eastern war, to have two inconceivable record quarters in a row was unimaginable. Buzz fanatics continued to expose their friends to, in their words, the liquid paradise—or Buzz—and they became fanatics. Under this sort of purchasing fury, the company and its shareholders were even more elated, to say the least, at the towering peaks of surplus in their annual dividends.

The increased prosperity allowed the corporation to take over other soda firms with respectable sized bureaucracies, and many of the shareholders finally got to buy those second vacation islands they had been dreaming of. All was merrymaking between company and shareholder. And another huge party was thrown.

At this time, Buzz executives thought that things couldn't possibly seem to get any better for the soda company and its investors, but they did. Buzz was put on the cover of *Time* magazine, *The New York Times*, and *The Economist*. President Buzz was invited to speak to heads of state and their cabinets, parliaments, and senates around the world. And the sales of Buzz increased. Never had so many special interest groups been knocking down its door for funding, and never had one company had so many lobbyists on Capitol Hill. Soon nearly every member of every Federal Branch was singing the newest of Buzz jingles (sometimes even while appearing on radio and television). And the sales of Buzz increased. The fan mail to Buzz increased. Gone were the casual fans of the product's early years. They were replaced by the fanatical fans of the moment, those whose social lives revolved around Buzz, who talked Buzz, who dreamed of Buzz, who thought in Buzz colors. The prolific praise of fan mail now not only filled the mailroom, but spilled over into the first and second floor of the office high rise, and every day the President would read the top ten fan letters from his 13th floor office suite.

Since the beginning of this great experiment, product sales had tripled, then tripled again and now tripled for the third quarter in a row. Buzz was now being consumed by the majority of the population. More than any other age group, teens were by far the most fanatic for Buzz. Buzz and was quite definitely the most consumed drink in the United States, and it also enjoyed popularity status in almost every developed nation across the globe. Nearly 75% of teens in the US now drank Buzz. This was the pinnacle of the shareholders' monetary dreams. For this US teen market was the most prized market of all in all the earth. It was the largest generation engendered in the history of America, and since American teens have more disposable income on average than any other teen in any other nation, it was easy to see why companies sought them out as a wanted demographic. Not only would this mean increased sales in the present, but as marketing executives know, brand imprinting studies show that products embraced early in life and associated with happy memories almost always make lifetime consumers. The corporation and the investors could now count on an entirely secure retirement. And the purchasing fanaticism continued until the majority of the planet was consuming the product Buzz was selling.

The increased prosperity allowed the corporation to rise to the level of the wealthiest industry in the nation and nearly the world. Buzz was making more money than all major television networks combined and more money than all US pro-sports teams combined. And then, one dissident voice rose above the din.

It was a single mother who was concerned about her son. She wrote that over the course of the previous year, her son had begun consuming more and more Buzz, and his attitude had changed quite dramatically toward her. In fact, his attitude toward everyone had changed. He was very disrespectful to his little sisters and especially to his mother. She said that she had banned him from buying any more Buzz, but because he could purchase it online, he kept drinking it behind her back.

Reports suddenly began pouring in about the drink and the adverse side effects it seemed to be having on some consumers. Letters of concern came from parents, grandparents, uncles and aunts, cousins, second-cousins and even more distant relatives who had begun noting the recent increased intake of Buzz ingested by relatives and loved ones. The writers told stories of mood swings, increased restlessness, and poor decision-making. The letters kept coming, first equal in volume to the fan mail, and then doubling it. The letters filled the company's mailroom. A mom in Milwaukee said her son had traded his entire baseball card collection for a case of Buzz, and she compared his obsession with an addiction. Buzz owners did all they could to keep the negative news to a minimum. Buzz lobbyists worked to dispel the rumors, citing studies from Buzz-drinking doctors that showed that these issues had nothing to do with the beloved Buzz, but were instead probably a result of poor parenting skills.

The corporation and its shareholders focused intently on the extraordinary financial gain they were receiving from the sales of the product, blocking out rumors about the negative effects the product was having on the health of consumers. Mainstream media and product lobbyists were working hand in hand 60 hours a week to save Buzz's image. Once, when an independent journalist somehow slipped past the radar and demanded that the company face the truth about its product, President Buzz was able to think fast, offering to open up clinics for anyone who had been born into the kind of family that might make him prone to addiction. This brilliant move labeled and then marginalized those who were unmanageably addicted to Buzz, while allowing the addicts of the general public to continue in their rabid consumption of the product. It was a bold move that made Buzz executives seem caring and responsible. That way, Buzz could continue what it did best—market the most popular drink in the world, Buzz.

After all, reasoned Buzz executives, it wasn't the shareholders' fault if the general public was addicted to the drink. It wasn't the company's fault. It wasn't the product's fault. No one was *forcing* people to drink the product. Sure, the company marketed the drink heavily to all demographics, especially, to teens who were, after all, the largest generational market the nation had ever seen, and who were in the midst of choosing the brands they would probably stick with for life. This was exactly the kind of free-market fairytale Buzz was after, just without all those villainous picketers and "concerned citizens." Those were the groups that really angered Buzz executives.

The complaints continued. Letter after letter told the story of families being torn apart when children made poor decisions while under the influence of Buzz, compounding the challenges families were already facing with the growing rate of addiction to the product. Buzz executives held their ground, saying that if there was a demand for this product, they should have the right to sell it. After all, if they didn't sell it, someone else would. They argued vehemently that they weren't creating the demand, just filling it. Buzz was simply giving the public what they were asking for. As letters continued to pour in, Buzz executives became more and more incensed by the irrational demands of parents, preachers, and a decidedly small number of politicians, who were beginning to insist that Buzz not be marketed to teens. Some even insisted that Buzz should come with a warning label. The nerve of these parents! Buzz executives gathered quotes from prominent actors, who told the public how wrong these demands were (and just how good the drink was). This, the actors read dutifully to their fawning audience, is a question of parental responsibility. It wasn't Buzz's fault if parents weren't monitoring what their children drink more closely. Clearly, parents just weren't doing their job: media and marketing couldn't possibly accept any blame for the national pandemic the culture was facing. And Buzz executives waited backstage to see if their campaign was successful. Would celebrity endorsements help save their beloved Buzz? Only time will tell. Fairytales are known for happy endings. The question here is will the happiness be directed toward the corporation or toward the consumer?

Media Speak: Messages and Methodology

Recently, I was driving home and found myself stuck in traffic behind a massive delivery truck. As I sat impatiently lamenting the two full minutes I would lose for sitting at this particular light, I noticed an interesting sign on the bumper of the commercial vehicle blocking my way: "This truck is not responsible for objects coming from the road." What an odd statement! The truck was, in essence, broadcasting to the world its refusal of responsibility. In other words, if something happens to you, it's got nothing to do with me. "We're not responsible" has become the catch phrase of the day. The challenge with this line of thinking is the disconnectedness from which it stems. These Loner Rangers forget that we are all yoked together in some way or another on this planet. Our actions affect others. Others actions affect us. It's time to take responsibility for "the objects coming from the road" as we race on furiously toward our destinations. It's time to put on the brakes, pull over, and assess the damage. We've been looking the other way for far too long—we've looked the other way regarding stewardship of the planet and its resources, we've looked the other way regarding the stewardship of our money, and we've looked the other way regarding the stewardship of our children. The cycle must stop with this generation.

As C.S. Lewis once wrote, "Sunlight is the great disinfectant." Only through the piercing light of truth can we begin to analyze the damage that's been done. The analysis may be painful. We may have to take responsibility for our actions. But it is only through awareness and acceptance that we can begin to change what is within our power to change. And much of what we face as a nation truly is within our power to change.

At the time of this writing, the most serious health concerns facing the United States are twofold, but both are related to food intake. Heart disease and obesity have approached the dangerous levels once associated with smoking. Our nation is addicted to high fat, high salt, unhealthy foods—so addicted, in fact, that the former US Surgeon General has said that if this challenge is "left unabated, obesity will overtake smoking as the leading cause of preventable death in the United States." The concept is equally fascinating and frightening, for clearly, these are diseases we are bringing on ourselves. As one study observed, they are not diseases of poverty; they are diseases of affluence. This means we are not simply unwitting victims. We have a choice. But first we must draw some implications for the projection of the current trajectory of social development.

Pragmatic Paradigms: Working Models for Modernity

As we discussed in the first three chapters, our human experience is shaped by both our inner and our outer worlds. Even the lens through which we view the world shapes our reflection of it. A continuous diet of negativity, for example, can mean that we are molding our mindset into one that is necessarily more negative. A comparison of modern headlines with headlines the day after the Great Depression provides an interesting point for reflection here. "Market still hopeful after financial challenges." The inherent message in this headline is one of hope—hang on, friends, it's going to get better. At press time, the unemployment rate in the United State is 9.7 percent (Bureau of Labor Statistics, 2009). Though it is not a perfect score, it is still an impressive one from a global perspective. It means that 90% of Americans are employed. However, the newspaper headlines do not declare daily, "90% of Americans are holding down jobs!" This headline lacks sensationalism and would be pulled from the presses for its terribly joyous mien. Instead, headlines ring out with, "Unemployment Rates Loom—Will You Be Next?"

A 90% employment rate would be incredibly invigorating news in most of the developing world, even in much of the developed world. But today's tone is different. We know it's different. We expect it to be different, for it is a different type of a package deal we've bought into unwittingly today. Ultimately, it took 50 years to rebound from the Great Depression financially, and, ultimately, it has taken 50 years for the US to slide down in corresponding depths to the negativity that now surrounds us daily.

Is there anything wrong with such cynicism? Or, if you will forgive the excessive alliteration, is a pessimistic paradigm inherently problematic? From a neural perspective, we see that cynicism breeds cynicism. However, there are also implications from a physiological perspective. Researchers at Virginia Tech and University of Pennsylvania found recently that there is a statistical significance between pessimism and infectious disease (Ayarbe 2009).

Researchers from University College London confirmed the findings, adding that regions of the brain that are dysfunctional in depressive states are active and functional during positive mental states. Thus, in this mode of social referencing, we see moral, social, and physiological decay.

Social referencing is a normal mode of learning for children, and even for adults. A child looks to a parent for social cues on how to behave: Mom, should I smile at that stranger? Is it okay to go into the nursery? The child then develops a situational view of how to act (a momentary worldview, a working model) based on that parent's response. As adults, we use social referencing when we go into a new environment and are unsure what to say or how to dress. When interviewing for a new job, we may look around at how others have dressed in order to ascertain the unwritten codes of the office and thus "fit it" on our first day of employ. When we enter a new social environment, we automatically scan the crowd for behavioral cues that will guide us in the volume of our speech, the joyous or somber nature of our topics, or the length of conversations we will engage in. These internal appeals to the culture around us give us the foundation we need to behave accordingly in any given environment.

Powered-Up Parents

In the same way, many people in modern Western culture look to the internet as a form of parent, an electronic version of social referencing. If this sounds like a strange concept, consider that in many ways, the Internet answers questions that are no longer passed on as intergenerational wisdom. Instead of seeking advice from Aunt Alice, we ask Ask.com. Instead of gleaning culinary wisdom from Grandma, we pull up some tried-and-true recipes from Food TV. The impact affects even the professional realm: Instead of calling our real MD, we check in with WebMD to make sure our symptoms are nothing serious. Strangers are a vital source of information for the modern Westerner. Review the headline stories online the day before a major holiday. How to cook a turkey, how to set your table, what to wear—these were all questions once addressed by a parent and now addressed by the computer.

For Millennials and Gen Xers alike, the computer is not just a source of information, it is a revered source, a trusted source. A Pew survey indicated that 75% of children believe Internet sources to be a consistent fount of trustworthy information (Strasberger 2002). This would not be as problematic, perhaps, if all internet sources actually *were* a source of trustworthy information, but as any researcher knows, the internet is laden with both information and misinformation. It is difficult even for adults to sift the wheat from the chaff when reading through online information. But beyond that, there is an important shift that must be noted: the trust factor. A level of trust has been established between child and computer, between child and celebrity, between child and stranger. When trust exists, so does the opportunity for influence. We tell children not to talk to strangers. Why? Conversing with a stranger gives the stranger more opportunity to harm the child—through deceitful luring, through closeness of proximity, through the power of influence.

When the source of information is trusted as true, reliable, the seeker alters not only her actions but also her mindset toward the issue. These are the paradigm shifts we spoke of in the early chapters, the combination of social referencing and the associational brain. We see this theory in action in school settings with regard to popularity. When a child who has been labeled as "popular" in the minds of the other children makes a decision that leads to action, the other children who have established an internal hierarchical relational status with the "popular" child follow suit. When the popular child makes a claim about another child, taking on the behavioral characteristics of a bully, the other children often follow suit. This example represents social referencing in some of its most frightening implications: In the case of media socialization, the potential for influence is particularly great, both because of the established hierarchy of "stars" (even their title exalts them far beyond the reach of the ordinary citizen) and because of the ubiquitous nature of mainstream media and mainstream media messages. The compelling voices are all around us. And like the water we drink, which becomes part of our cellular structure, so too, our continued sociological influences become part of our worldview, and thus, part of our biology, the associational brain that is shaped and molded through experiential factors. The change is virtually undetectable at the microcosmic level, but as we step back to that generational and global lens, the sweeping changes come into clearer focus. In the next chapter, we'll look at some of the specific statistical impacts of media centrality.

CHAPTER NINE

Hey, Mom, What's for Dinner?

We've looked at the potential for impact, but what deleterious effects are truly taking their place at the dinner table of Western culture, where the vast majority of the population pulls up a chair to sup at the table of media mania? What lifestyles are being portrayed, what messages are being sent, and who is drinking them in? In short, what's for dinner?

To a degree unlike any generation prior, today's young people are growing up in a media-saturated society, a social culture much different than any generation before has ever encountered. For the first time in history, a generation is thoroughly saturated with media influence. Youth expert Josh McDowell says, "The first generation to be more influenced by things outside the home than by influences inside." It is no wonder, when teens will sit before some sort of screen, be it television or internet, for an average of 50 hours every week (more hours than working a full-time job). How has this happened? One reason is that media conduits are now able to freely bypass the historical social defenses—community, religious institutions, and the family structure. These social defenses have previously served as filters to strain forces and entities that negatively affect the young, but today's technology has found a pathway around these important safeguards.

The majority of Americans say that the centerpiece of their dinner table is the electronic family member they have come to know and love: the television. When Ray Bradbury wrote at the dawn of the television age that one day families would sit down to eat with the television, mainstream America must have laughed at the impossibility. Yet, today, the meal that was once the therapist's couch of family togetherness, where we discussed the events of the day and connected in a very real sense, this time has been invaded by strangers, overtaken by entertainment. Instead of learning about the events of our family members' lives, we are learning about crises in far off lands or the latest boyfriend dropped by a flash-in-the-pan celebrity. Our affections and devotion lay elsewhere.

In fact, this division of the family is evident through a variety of lenses. Juliet Schor, author of *The Overworked American* (1991) says the typical American is working the equivalent of 13 months a year (Kivisto 2005). Over the last thirty years, men have seen a 98-hour increase in the number of hours worked per year (2,054 to 2,152). Women, however, have seen an even more dramatic shift: from 1,406 hours in 1969 to 1,711 hours a year in 1987—a 305-hour increase (Kivisto 2005). Family dinner time, which was once an opportunity for reflecting and connecting, has been radically altered in content, time, quality, and location. Meal preparation time has dropped from one hour (1970) to 30 minutes (1980) to the modern ten-minute "meal" (Kivisto 2005). Furthermore, the speed and variety of modern mealtime options often equate to separate dinners and separate dining rooms (Kivisto 2005). And, even when families do take the time to eat together, with 63 percent of Americans saying the television is on during mealtimes, the opportunity for meaningful connection is limited even further (KFF, 2006). From instant meals to instant messages, current trends are pulling at the family: The modern family is facing a number of demanding—and isolating—predators.

Whose News?

Let's start with one aspect of the current media deluge. If you've ever wondered why virtually every news station, newspaper, and news magazines seem to carry the same stories, the same angles, the same inherent bias, the answer is actually decidedly simple. Almost all world media is owned by an elite group of five individuals (PBS *Merchants of Cool*, 2009). And, largely as a result of their myopic media messages, our culture is becoming socialized toward embodying such unflattering adjectives as oversexualized, violent, aggressive, insecure, and isolated. We have been utterly desensitized—blinded and deafened by an onslaught of images and voices that contort, submerge, and drown out the truth.

One such eye-opening exposé of this situation is the PBS production *Merchants of Cool*, which shows a frightening glimpse of the world behind the mass marketing of "teen cool." As an expose of the secretive, highly targeted marketing techniques that retailers are using to study our teens, pre-teens and young adults, the *Merchants of Cool* video and companion website go behind the scenes to showcase the frightening, almost missive targeting through which the media is following our children with a force. The companion website reviews a list of the five media owners in the world, the tiny conglomerate of individuals who lay claim to the massive empire of newspapers, magazines, television, music, and movies throughout the world. It seems that everywhere we turn, every station, every song seems to be peddling the same wares. Sometimes the information gets close to reality, introducing just enough fact to ward off total fiction. The slant may be obvious, or it may be couched in cynicism.

The cynicism often turns to misleading omission or even misinformation. Sometimes it simply introduces a doubt in the reader's mind, a seed of pessimistic inquisition. Take a *Newsweek* review of "good books" for children (Miller 2006). The author of the article, who serves as the magazine's religion editor, provides some positive feedback on a new children's book about Noah's ark—and then pitches a loaded, cynical curveball that undermines the grace of the story itself: "Good luck, though, answering the question: why did God kill all those people?"

Sometimes the media spokesperson will introduce an argument, offer an anemic interview on the conservative side, and then drive in the last words to seal the argument, final and authoritative thoughts that completely undermine the purported objectivity of the "balanced" view. We must then ask: Is the media reporting news or creating it? Are we being fed facts or opinions? I am struck by how many supposed "news" articles have an overt bias, and increasingly, how brazen authors appear to be about imposing that bias on me, the reader. Opinions which used to be reserved for the op ed section of the paper are now stamped out in black and white as front page news. Open any major paper today and hunt for opinion words such as "still" (as in, "she *still* believes in the traditional definitions of marriage"). The connotation of the word "still" in news is often meant to describe someone whose ideologies are notably backwards, old-fashioned, archaic, out-of-touch with reality. Opinion words like these abound—subtle (or not so subtle) clues to the writer's worldview.

Sometimes the bias might be less obvious, like that in the MSN article, "Cancers You Can Catch" (Capozza 2007). In explaining why cancer-causing viruses are entering the body through the portals of mouth, throat, and reproductive areas, the author links the physiological necessities of breathing and eating to *sexual activity*, calling them all "everyday activities." Now, let's be realistic. Hollywood harlotry aside, in exactly what percentage of the population is *sexual activity* an everyday necessity akin to eating and breathing? The author goes on to advise readers to exercise, eat well, and avoid alcohol and cigarettes, with a noticeable lack of attention to the other "everyday activity" mentioned in the list. Why is this? Why does it seem that the media will go to great lengths to avoid recommendations that deal with curtailing or limiting promiscuous sexual activity? The author tells readers to wear a condom, but why not add to that advice a note to, by the way, stop sleeping around? Why not tell them that sexual involvement with multiple partners is harmful physically, emotionally, and socially? One plausible answer is that there are people or companies set to gain financially from such behaviors being modeled and emulated. We'll talk more about that later.

A common argument I hear in this regard is that every generation had its share of rebellion growing up but "turned out okay." This unequivocally denies the baggage these "normal" people have dragged into their relationships, the paradigms they've had to overcome—perhaps the string of broken relationships or the years of counseling they've had to endure to get free from the brokenness that has plagued them. Let's face it; it's not only the teens that are in trouble. Today's Western adults have a number of issues to acknowledge, from soaring rates of drug and alcohol abuse to an inability to maintain long-term relationships, as exemplified by the extraordinary divorce rate in Western culture. A lack of balanced education and community resources for parents has further exacerbated the issue.

As a result of these and other factors, parents aren't the powerful influencers they once were in culture. They've been replaced as the role models and respected leaders. Take the purveyors of junk food as a simple example. An average child is assaulted by at least 10,000 junk food ads per year. As the Yale Center for Eating disorders points out, if that child ate three meals a day with her parent, and the parent gave compelling, entertaining, captivating nutrition presentations at each meal, the parent would only have 1,000 chances at a sale. Do parents have power? Absolutely. The problem is that today's parents are outgunned. As one author put it, we no longer have the culture as part of our village, our concerned partners in parenthood. Today's voices of influence aren't the same as those of just a few decades ago, where local culture was largely shaped by the pastors, the teachers, and the civil servant heroes of the region. Today's parents can't rely on the culture; they have to counter it. The voices that are echoing through our streets and screens do not necessarily have our families' best interests at heart. Their main goal is profit, whatever the ultimate cost to society.

When Cosgrove and her University of Massachusetts team (2006) linked the writers of the Diagnostic and Statistical Manual of Mental Disorders to drug company profits, there was a rush of recognition as to the power of influence. Her team's discovery—that 100% of the panel members who wrote the section of mood disorders had financial ties to the pharmaceutical companies being recommended in the manual—resulted in social change. Happily, this led to rash of institutions and universities banning physicians from accepting gifts (lunches, cups, pens, notepads) of any amount from pharmaceutical companies. Additionally, many universities no longer allow pharmaceutical representatives on college campuses because of the potential for imbalanced influence. In the same way, we must recognize our own propensity for influence and the power we have to curtail that influence both through media literacy and through media awareness campaigns.

As a number of authors have already pointed out, more passive media use results in a lower intellectual capacity, reducing our ability to think critically. As a nation, we have lower reading scores, lower computational scores, and a host of challenges with covetousness. A material culture has bred a materialistic mindset. Consider for a moment the extraordinary lack of gratitude in modern culture. The majority of Americans, it seems, whether child or adult, are more concerned with what they don't *yet* possess instead of being grateful for what they do possess. Like the main character in Guy de Maupassaunt's "The Necklace," we spend our lives chasing after something that, it the end, is unsatisfying—a false sense of hope, security, and satisfaction. As an ancient Chinese philosopher put it, "The effect of life in society is to complicate and confuse our existence, making us forget who we really are by causing us to become obsessed with what we are not." Obsession is not too strong of a word to describe the inner frenzy most Americans claim to be experiencing on a regular basis. For many, the heart of this desire is greater material wealth.

Like the question of declining education enrollment, reading comprehension, and decreasing imaginations, many leaders have been scratching their heads in confusion, wondering what has caused such an outpour of greed and gluttony. The answer seems fairly straightforward, though, given the culture. If we are hearing 40,000 times a year that we are ugly, insipid, and in desperate need of this or that brand name, beverage, or worldly possession to make us all better, these messages are no comparison to the few little measly "little engine that could" messages with which we try to counteract those insecurity builders. The desire for instant gratification becomes overwhelming, fastening itself first as an occasional habit and then as a lifestyle. Credit card debt, gambling, excess in every area is most often the result of a desire for the instantaneous.

Filter Failure

How did mass media come to take on such a powerfully impacting role in modern culture? Inventions such as radio, television, iPods, computers, and the internet have rendered the traditional/historical social filters nearly ineffective in halting the deluge of media and advertisement influences. Through slick technological innovations, media can easily bypass community standards, religious institutions and, of course, parental oversight. Unlike a teenager of ten years ago, today's teen can upload sexually violent and degrading music onto an iPod or mp3 player from the internet in less than 60 seconds. That same teen can view and download photography and video once only obtainable to adults at a XXX store.

In the US, the average age of first exposure to pornography via the internet is age 11 (Luce 2005), and 90% of 8-16 year-olds have viewed porn online (most while doing homework), with 80% of 15-17 year-olds having been exposed to multiple hard-core porn visuals (Luce 2005). Though many citizens loathe pornography and its deleterious impact on relationships and culture, sexually degrading and pornographic adult information has remained accessible, but the pervasive power of technology means that pornography is no longer barred to the outer fringe of the adult arena. It is now more ubiquitous than ever before.

The New Center Point

How central is media in American society? More than 98% of all US households have at least one television set. In fact, American households have more televisions than toilets (Parsley 2006, p. 163). American households with teenage children watch an average of fifty-nine hours of cable and network programming a week (Parsley 2006, p. 161). Preschoolers watch an average of more than 27 hours each week—more than four hours per day. On school nights, American teens limit their television consumption to only about 3 hours per night. In contrast though, they spend about fifty-four minutes on homework, less than sixteen minutes reading, about fourteen minutes alone with their mothers, and less than five minutes with their fathers (Parsley 2006, p. 163). Teens see an average of sixty-seven full-length feature films per year—either in theaters or on video—more than one each week. Children ages 9-17 use the Internet an average of four days per week, usually for at least two hours at a time. Of those who use computers, 61% go online, and 14% of those say they see things they "wouldn't want their parents to know about" (Luce 2005, p.76) Today's teens, famous for multitasking, listen to nearly 40 hours of audio media per week, whether radio, CDs, or other sources (p. 10).

Although the amount of time teens spend interacting with media is quite sobering, the content of the media being consumed is even more alarming—especially given its direct marketing angle to young viewers and listeners. More than 25% of teen-targeted radio segments contain sexual content and 42% of top-selling CDs contain sexual content that is "pretty explicit" or "very explicit" (Luce 2005, p. 76). The "family hour" contains more than eight sexual incidents per hour. Each year teens absorb more than 15,000 sexual references, with less than 170 of those 15,000 referring to abstinence, birth control, or sexually-transmitted infections (STIs). A more recent study showed that 70% of all primetime programming depicts alcohol, tobacco, or illicit drug use. In addition to television programs, teens observe 20,000 commercials each year, with 2,000 of those selling beer and wine. A young person will see 25 to 50 extremely clever and entertaining beer and wine commercial for every solitary—and predictably dowdy—anti-drug commercial (Luce 2005, p. 37).

The most watched teen network is MTV, with an estimated 75% of teens in the US watching MTV. Given that 22.4% of all MTV videos portray overt violence, 20% of all rap videos contain violence, and 25% of all music videos display weapons, a teen will see an estimated 10,000 violent acts every year (Luce 2005, p. 37). Every week over 3,000 soft porn images are broadcast, and MTV's president publicly boasts that MTV "owns this generation" (Luce 2005, p. 12).

So what effect does this hyper-drugged, hyper-violent, hyper-sexed media have on the millions of youth who are guzzling it daily? In 2004, a study by the RAND Corporation (funded by the U.S. National Institute of Child Health), published in *Pediatrics*, shows the clear connection: Teens who watch sexualized programming are twice as likely to engage in sexual intercourse themselves. Rebecca Collins, a RAND Corporation psychologist who led the study, said, "This is the strongest evidence yet that the sexual content of television programs encourages adolescents to initiate sexual intercourse and other sexual activities. The impact of television viewing is so large that even a modest shift in the sexual content of adolescent TV watching could have a substantial effect on their sexual behavior" (Luce 2005, p. 76-77)

In addition, the Alan Guttmacher Institute lists these reveling statistics about US teenagers' sexuality:

- Average age of first sex: 15.8 years
- Average age of first sexual relationship: 3.8 months
- 24.3% of adolescents report having first sex during the same month as the start of the relationship (37.5% had sex 1 to 3 months after the start of the relationship and 40.1% after 4 months)
- 23.4% of first sexual relationships were "one-night stands" (21.2% for girls and 26.5% for guys)
- Girls reported their first sexual partner was 1.8 years older, on average; guys said their partner was 1 year younger
- 16.7 of adolescents (20.6% girls and 11.2% boys) who took virginity pledges became sexually active (BC 77)

One of the most disheartening statistics reveals that 67% of sexually experienced teens (77% of girls and 60% of boys) wish they had waited longer to become sexually active (Luce 2005, p. 78). Tragically, nearly 7 out of 10 teens who have acted out the sexual behavior modeled by current pop-media celebrities, felt afterward that their decision to engage in sexual-intercourse was premature.

Beyond regrets of wishing they would have wait longer, teens who have sex before 18 are less likely to advance in their education and career. According to one recent study, teens that do not have sex before age 18 are nearly three times less likely to drop out of high school than teens who do have sex before age 18. The statistic held true even when accounting for socioeconomic status and related factors. Nearly 22% of teens who have sex before 18 drop out of high school, while only 8.6% of teens who abstain until 18 drop out. In fact, teens that abstained from sex were 60% less likely to be expelled from school, 50% less likely to drop out of high school, and almost twice as likely to graduate from college. Remarkably, when singling out potential factors of influence, a teen's sexuality, or lack thereof, is a much better predictor of educational success than ethnicity, parental education, family income, and family structure (Heritage Foundation 2005). Now that's a statistic we don't see on the front page news.

The Heritage Foundation's 2005 study, Teenage Sexual Abstinence and Academic Achievement, also found that, because teen virgins are more successful academically, they can also expect to have incomes that will average 16% higher than sexually active teens from identical socioeconomic backgrounds. Over the lifespan, this will mean an average increase in earnings of $370,000. Also, teens that abstain from sexual activity are less likely to have children out-of-wedlock (Heritage Foundation 2005). In 2000, 240,000 children were born in the US to girls aged 18 or younger.

In fact, the US leads the industrialized world in teen pregnancy—with rates three times higher than that found in other industrialized nations. Because the vast majority of these teens are unmarried, the statistical likelihood of long-term poverty and welfare dependence is significant (Heritage Foundation 2005). Teens reap a lifetime of benefits, both academically and economically, when waiting to engage in sex until their adult years, and they can enter long-term relationships without the excessive baggage of sexual intimacy in short-term relationships.

Most adults are aware that sexually transmitted infections (STIs) have risen over the past few decades. In fact, approximately, an STI infects 8,000 teen-agers in the United States every day. This year alone, nearly 3 million teens will become infected (Heritage Foundation 2005). Beyond the physiological impact, though, is an emotional and psychological dilemma that sexually active teens must contend with as well. Sexually-active boys and girls, when compared to teenage boys and girls who are not sexually active, are significantly less likely to be happy and more likely to feel depressed: In the Heritage Foundation study, "Sexually Active Teenagers Are More Likely to Be Depressed and to Attempt Suicide," 8.3% of sexually active boys felt depressed while 3.4% of teen boys who were not sexually active felt depressed. Additionally, 25.3% of teenage girls who were sexually active felt depressed while 7.7% of teenage girls who were not sexually active felt depressed. In the same study, 60% of sexually inactive girls reported "rarely or never" feeling depressed (Heritage Foundation 2005). Clinical experience also supports the association connecting teen sexual activity and depression. In the study, Meg Meeker, doctor of adolescent medicine writes, "Teenage sexual activity routinely leads to emotional turmoil and psychological distress....to empty relationships, to feelings of self-contempt and worthlessness—all, of course, precursors to depression" (Heritage 2005).

Teens who are sexually active are also more apt to attempt suicide than teens that are not sexually active; sexually active girls were nearly three times more likely to attempt suicide, and sexually active boys were over 8.5 times more likely to attempt suicide: 14% of sexually active teenage girls attempted suicide and 5.1% of teenage girls that were not sexually active attempted suicide; 6.0% of sexually active teenage boys attempted suicide and 0.7% of teenage boys that were not sexually active attempted suicide. These statistics are troubling. Early sexual activity is a substantial factor in undermining the emotional wellbeing of American teenagers. Sadly, when teens are exposed to media messages that present sexualized scenarios with unrealistic consequences, and then those teens emulate what they see and hear—most of them experience a deep sense of regret. In fact, 7 out of 10 teens that have been sexually active wish that they had waited until they were older (Heritage 2005).

New News?

Is this the same media influence the US has faced historically? Not at all. According to a 2005 study by the Kaiser Family Foundation, the number of sexual scenes on television has nearly doubled since 1998. The study, covering 1,000 hours of programming, found that 70 percent of the top 20 shows watched by teens contain sexual content, with 45 percent containing sexual behavior, but only a very small percentage of those shows (about 10%) depicted any type of consequence for illicit sexual behavior. Kaiser Family Foundation Vice President Vicky Rideout called those high stakes, adding that the medium of television has a draw like no other: "Television has the power to bring issues of sexual risk and responsibility to life in a way that no sex ed class or public health brochure really can" (KFF 2005).

The study showed the breakdown of percentages of sexual content by specific genre: movies 92%, sitcoms 87%, drama series 87%, and soap operas 85%. Ironically, the one genre of television programming that had the least amount of sexual content was reality shows (28%). Perhaps this is reflective of an important truth: Sexual behavior is far less a component of daily life than television producers would have viewers believe!

Even more disturbing is the rise of sexual portrayals between strangers or first dates. Of the scenes depicting sexual intercourse, only half of those 53% involve long-term partners. Additionally, the percent of scenes depicting intercourse between people who have just met is up from 7% in 2002 to 15% in 2005, a more-than-double increase in a portrayal of risky sexual behavior, especially in an era of rampant sexually transmitted infections. Certainly, the rise in sexual content is disturbing on many levels. But does watching sexual content on television impact a viewer's life choices, decision-making process, choice of friends, sexual behavior? Yes, yes, yes, yes! In the book *Children and the Media*, Strasberger details the impact of media portrayals on children's value systems. We'll look at some of those compelling statistics in a moment.

With the dizzying array of media choices available today, are kids still watching television? Yes, according to the Kaiser Family Foundation. KFF says that children and teens are spending more time than ever before in front of both new and "old" media. In the study "Generation M: Media in the Lives of 8-18 Year Olds," 3rd to 12th graders reported using 8.33 hours of media a day, bringing the total media use up a full hour from just five years prior. The biggest increase came in the categories of video games and computer entertainment. Additionally, multitasking jumped from 16% of media time to 26% of media time; in other words, kids are not only disengaged from the concept of peaceful silence, but they are also increasingly engaged in multiple forms of entertainment at once. "Kids are multi-tasking and consuming many different kinds of media all at once," said Drew Altman, Ph.D., President and CEO of the Kaiser Family Foundation.

Media experts Strasberger and Wilson note that the average U.S. child lives in a home with three televisions, three tape players, three radios, two CD players, one video game player, and one computer. A full 68% of 8-18 year olds have a TV in their rooms, and 49% also have video game access in their rooms as well, and according to a KFF study, kids who have a television in their room watch an average of 1½ hours more television per day than those who do not. Outside of their bedrooms, in many young people's homes the TV is a constant companion: nearly two-thirds (63%) say the TV is "usually" on during meals (the same percentage of Americans who are overweight or obese), and half (51%) say they live in homes where the TV is *left on* "most" or "all" of the time, whether anyone is watching it or not (italics mine).

The average child in the U.S. spends at least 6 hours a day using media (Strasberger, p. 6). Nearly half (49%) say there are "no rules in their home" about how much or what they can watch on television, and children over the age of 7 said they "almost never" watch television with their parents (Strasberger, p. 7). From a macro perspective, today's youth spend one-third to one-half of their waking day with some form of mass media-and they do so in increasingly private settings such as their bedrooms or when home alone.

Additionally, the KFF study showed "media multitasking" to be the new norm for most young people, who skip back and forth from one source of constant entertainment to the next. And what are these kids filling their minds and hearts with? Most parents have no idea. While parents claim to have concerns about children's media exposure, the study found that 53% of all 8-18 year olds say that there are no rules set for TV watching in the home. Another 20% say that the rules are not always enforced. "These kids are spending the equivalent of a full-time work week using media, plus overtime," said KFF VP Vicky Rideout, "and anything that takes up that much space in their lives certainly deserves our full attention."

The KFF study also found that students with the lowest grades were also more likely to have spent more time playing video games and less time reading. Interestingly enough, this correlation was also evidenced in emotional stability and peer relationships. The 18% of the 8-18 population that recorded being sad, unhappy or having few friends also spent the most amount of time with media exposure: 9:44 hours per day as opposed to 8:07 (KFF 2004).

What marketing strategies prevail, and what mindsets have resulted? Consider a few compelling quotes from the tremendous resource of Strasberger and Wilson's (2002) voluminous text, *Children, Adolescents, and the Media*:

- More than $12 billion a year is currently spent on advertising and marketing to children in the US, doubled from 10 years ago.

- Teens directly spent $155 billion in 2000, and in 1997, children influenced another $188 billion in family spending. Absentee parents are cited as one of the main factors in increased spending.

- 45% of girls ages 4-11 feel that ads tell the truth "always" or "most of the time" (making them a defenseless target for unscrupulous advertisers).

- Most adults believe that they are not personally affected by mass media, though they believe others are. This phenomenon is present in children too; they claim that only "little kids" imitate what they see on TV (p. 9). This concept is known as the "Third Person Effect" (Gunther and Thorson; 1992, Perloff, 1993), and it demonstrates once again the propensity we have for individual as well as corporate blind spots.

- Adolescents are generally more susceptible to antisocial peer pressure when they have poor relationships with their parents (Strasberger p. 16). As discussed earlier, EE media campaigns capitalize on the power of virtual peer pressure.

- Advertisers believe in the power of advertising to convince a consumer to purchase a product, which is why a company is willing to pay 12.4 million dollars for a 30-second commercial during the Super Bowl. The company knows it's a worthwhile investment. However, while companies throw down the cash, consumers continue to deny the potential impact of advertising on human behavior. They can't both be right.

- Teens perceive celebrities as more trustworthy, competent, and attractive than non-celebrity endorsers in nearly identical ads (Strasberger, p. 55).

- Kids who watch a lot of TV want more advertised toys and actually consume more advertised foods than do kids with lighter TV habits (Strasberger, p. 54).

- 45% of 10-17 year olds would exchange personal information on the Web when offered a "free" gift (Strasberger, p. 65). Both the trust factor and the risk factor are underscored here.

- In our nation's recent past, Action for Children's Television attempted to persuade the Federal Trade Commission to ban ads targeted to children "too young to recognize commercial intent," but after several years of deliberation, and much pressure by several major corporations, the FTC decided that it would not ban ads to kids (Strasberger, p. 66).

- 75% of us adults believe that TV violence contributes to real-world crime and aggression (Strasberger, p. 74).

- 2.5 million people in America are victims of violent injuries each year, and homicide is the 2nd leading cause of death for 15-24 year olds. In fact, the United States ranks first (yes, that's right, *first*) among all developed countries in youth homicide (Strasburg, p. 74).

- The American Psychological Association says that the average US child or teen views 10,000 per year of the following: rapes, murders, and aggressive assaults.

- 70% of prime time shows contain violence; 90% of children's shows contain violence. Prime time shows have 5 violent acts per hour, whereas children's television has 20 violent acts per hour (Strasberger, p. 75).

- The National Television Violence Study, 1998, 40% of violent incidents were perpetrated by "good people" and 71% showed no remorse or criticism or penalty for the action (Strasberger, p. 75).

- A large national study by the Council of Economic Advisors in 2000 found numerous positive differences in 7-12 grade teens who ate dinner with a parent regularly versus those who didn't. Those who didn't showed higher rates of smoking, drinking, marijuana use, and fighting (Strasberger,

p. 14). Parental influence and presence are paramount to a child's socio-emotional health.

Global Shifts

Though the US spends more than 12 billion a year on advertising and marketing to children, a number of other countries have made positively prosocial demonstrations in favor of the health of their citizens, especially their youngest citizens. In Sweden, TV ads targeting kids under 12 are not permitted. In Greece, no toy ads are permitted until after 10 pm. In Belgium, no commercials are permitted during kids' programming. And in Australia, Canada, and England, there are no ads that target preschoolers whatsoever permitted (Strasburger, p. 67).

Why do these countries take such a firm stance on television ads for children? They are aware of the power of influence. In America, though, it seems that advertisers are more than willing to exploit our youngest citizens for a chance at brand imprinting or indirect expenditure. Advertisements have an overt effect on behavior. Companies will readily drop millions of dollars to help create a whiney kid culture at the grocery store or retail shop. The whine of materialism is music to their ears. More targeted advertisements mean more predictive outcomes: television ads affect beliefs, and beliefs affect behavior. In order to escape their grasp, we must be wise and cautious consumers of media.

In this media central age, the dam holding back society's destructive allowances has crumbled, and the flooding torrent of information, the good, the bad, and the sordid, is leaving no person or age group unscathed. Excessively convenient and influential media messages have formed a stagnant pool at the feet of the youngest citizens of society—and the waters continue to rise. With architectural evolution, perhaps new homes in 2020 will come complete with a table in front of the television. Dining rooms will be obsolete, replaced with TV rooms. Living rooms won't be for living anymore, as the idea of living one's own boring life will have been readily replaced with watching someone else live a more exciting one—excitement, after all, is one of the great idols of the day.

What Is Truth?

As we were working on this book, we talked to scores of children, adults, and young adults in search of quotes and experiences from people who had ventured to live in a world outside of the supreme influence of media-centrality. In addition to the transformative feedback outlined in Chapter 10, we also received a number of responses from Third Person sufferers. One very overweight young man in his late teens told us that only "soft minds" were influenced by media and that mass media was "a very important" connector to what is going on in the "real world."

Though mainstream media may be a source of information, it is certainly not the ultimate source of balanced information, and without a cross-referential approach, that is, an educated and balanced consumption from a variety of sources, it is simply not possible to avoid influence. When students are writing research papers, what professor encourages such myopic referencing? An informed mode of analysis is necessary in order to form a hypothesis. Narrow, imbalanced research stems from the utilization of sources that offer either undying support or vehement denial of the cause.

There is no middle ground. A balanced and proper paper, however, will use a cross-referential approach that examines the evidence put forth by both sides. If we only consume one brand of media, shared by the common purse strings of a handful of owners, our view will necessarily be skewed. Our research will be imbalanced. Our mindset will be myopic. From a biological and sociological standpoint, we are indeed ripe for influence.

One young mother, teary-eyed at the shattering realization that her worldview had been molded without her consent, asked me, "What is truth?" It's not a new question, of course, but it continues to be a powerful one. Echoing the heart cry of Pilate, who was faced with his own dichotomous struggles with the dissonant voices of reality, this young mother felt suddenly disconnected from reality. She had begun to feel the oppressive walls of the media cocoon pressing in upon her, and she wanted out.

The discovery of truth, or at least the pursuit of it, is the essence of the search for media literacy, of course, and we will talk more about that concept in the closing chapters. It is important to note, though, that there are still a number of non-mainstream news sources from which one can derive unbiased news on local, national, and world fronts. In fact, if you pick up a non-mainstream magazine or newspaper, you will hear stories, read studies, and be confronted with the existence of world events that you may have otherwise had no idea about. It's a whole new world, and one that is not bent on mass indoctrination through marketing mania. Again, our inherent socialization and biological wiring comes into play here. We cannot easily overwrite the influences to which we are born, but we can make a conscious effort to shape our lives in the light of positive, prosocial role models.

In northern California, we often live for months at a time without a single drop of rain. The heavens are dry, with one cloudless sky after another, day after day after day. The fields are brown (or golden, as we like to call them), and plants and people alike languish in the triple-digit heat. When the first rain comes in September or October, it's a community event. People stop to stare. Cars pull over. Students take off their iPods and walk to the windows of the classroom. There is an awakening. We suddenly remember the sweetness of the air, the smell of rain on parched pavement, the dewy feel of freshness that alerts us to the coming of fall's splendor. There is, as Alice Walker once noted in an awakening of her own, a "great and gorgeous light" that draws our attention to realities we have overlooked along our gradual path of disconnect. It is my hope that this writing will, in similar fashion, stir us to realization, that we will turn to the windows of illumination to watch the rain fall, to smell the earth, to live once more in the light of the sun instead of the faint blue haze of the electronic realm.

The Undertow of Addictions

In 1885, the world's most consumed liquid outside of water was invented—Coca-Cola. It was named for its two "medicinal" ingredients: extract of coca leaves and kola nuts. The exact amount of cocaine in the original formula is difficult to verify, but, according to "The Unauthorized History of Coca-Cola," the percentages may have been as high as 60mg of cocaine per serving. During the late 1800's many doctors and dentists prescribed cocaine in various forms and amounts to their patients, but by the early 1900's the harmful effects of cocaine—namely addiction and death—became part of the general knowledge base. Coca-Cola gradually began removing cocaine from its product until 1926 when it was deemed fully cocaine-free.

It's hard to imagine, living in 21st Century America, that highly-educated doctors would freely prescribe a deadly and addictive substance like cocaine to their patients. In modern America, the drug is not only illegal, but it is battled daily through massive sums of tax dollars as leaders attempt to rid the country of the destructive substance and its influence. And rightly so. A country concerned about its citizens' health and well-being should necessarily be responsible to educate its citizens about potential harm as well as protect citizens from further harm. If it's a drug, such as in the case of cocaine, we ban it completely or we make it available in measurable amounts, as is the case of various other prescription drugs.

When it was discovered that 2nd-hand smoke causes cancer, states began making it illegal to smoke in public buildings. This served to protect the health of the citizens of our country. Leaders felt that one person's right to smoke cigarettes should not tread on another person's rights to a healthy public environment. Smokers fought the ban, for once a person is addicted, her sense of logical analysis is overrun by emotionalism. It's difficult to think clearly in the captivating presence of addiction. When bans were sought by the general public for the safety of its citizens, addicts pleaded with the government to allow cigarette smoking in public. It took many battles to win protection for the people's health.

Now, smoking has been marginalized to a large degree, but most importantly, the public has been educated. We can't expect citizens to make healthy choices for their lives if we don't also widely publicize the facts about health and disease. Why not give people the opportunity to make an educated choice? Yes, shareholders are happy when smoking is promoted in sitcoms and movies; it means higher income. But that increase comes at the expense of the very citizens who form the base of this great country. It's a parasitic supply-and-demand relationship that will ultimately drain the life from the host. Though companies tied to financial profit in these arenas may continue to decry the accusations of influence as falsehood, respected researchers have demonstrated again and again the effect of mass media programming on human behavior. At the very least, we must educate citizens about the potential implications of influence.

How Does Media Influence Behavior

There are a number of ways that media can influence human behavior. Earlier in the book, we discussed the impact of socialization as well as the biological makeup of the human brain, an organ that makes predictions of future behavior based on an existing paradigm, and thus an organ that is ripe for socialization. A relatively new discovery in the arena of media influence, however, is that of the "virtual peer." University of North Carolina, Chapel Hill researchers (Brown 2006) demonstrated that sexual content in music, movies, and television programming can lead to sexual involvement at a younger age by acting as a "virtual peer" that influences behavior. The study, published in *The Journal of the American Academy of Pediatrics*, showed that exposure to sexual content leads to early sexual involvement, and higher exposure levels lead to greater levels of sexual activity. Brown's research was prompted by the fact that teen pregnancy in the US is three to 10 times higher than any other industrialized nation, which makes teen pregnancy and exposure to sexually transmitted infections an important area of focus.

Because there is a lack of straightforward dialogue between parents and children concerning sexual matters, media is filling that vacuum as a "powerful sex educator...providing frequent and compelling portraits of sex as fun and risk free" (Reuters 2006). Media portrayals convince teens (and others) that "everyone" is engaged in the activity seen on television or on movies or heard about in songs. In this way, the study showed, media becomes a "superpeer" chiding teens to engage in the same behavior. The findings were compelling, and the researchers related them to the findings on violence in media as a predictor of behavior, saying that it took many years to establish the connection between violent media and violent behavior, and thus to begin creating initiatives that stem the tide of influence.

Given the similarity of findings for sexual content, the researchers recommended that parents and educators begin focusing on the tremendous potential mass media has for negative impact. In other words, media plays a highly influential role in socialization. Coupled with Third-Person Syndrome as well as a general arrogance about potential for influence, however, it is often downplayed as a source. Parents would do best to evaluate modern media in the same way parents used to evaluate friends: Is this someone I or my children should be spending time with? Does he or she promote values that I want to see magnified in my own life or the life of my children? If the answer is no, then out it goes.

All of this media centrality has had a deleterious effect on our collective psyches. The clearest, most all-encompassing word that comes to mind in describing our current situation is *excess*. We have become a nation of excess, from wares to waistlines. And this life of excess has radically altered the priorities of many young adults—our paradigms have shifted toward materialism. Many researchers have been diligently and worriedly tracking the change in life goals and values from generation to generation. One such study by the Pew Research Center shows a rise in increasingly materialistic and narcissistic goals. The study showed the vast majority of 18-26 year olds-81%—citing wealth and fame as *the top priorities* of their lives (italics mine). Sharon Jayson, the author of the study, says, "Getting rich is their generation's most important or second-most-important life goal, and 51% say the same about being famous." The author quotes 22-year-old Cameron Johnson of Virginia, who clearly highlights the source of influence for this paradigm:

> When you open a celebrity magazine, it's all about the money and being rich and famous. The TV shows we watch—anything from The Apprentice where the intro to the show is the 'money song'—to *Us Weekly* magazine where you see all the celebrities and their $6 million homes. We see reality TV shows with Jessica and Nick living the life. We see Britney and Paris. The people we relate to outside our friends are those people.

Did you catch that last line? The people her generation "relates to" outside friends, she says, are the media elite. These celebrities are their virtual peers, their screen and print families. How strange it seems on paper, but how real the influence is on culture! A number of researchers have detailed this phenomenon of these strong emotional ties with "familiar" strangers, and certainly that identity factor is the heartbeat of effective EE strategies. The book *Intimate Strangers* beautifully details the false intimacy that is created between a fan and his celebrity. There is a sensation of knowing, of belonging, even though it is completely illusory and one-sided.

In addition to reminding us that these desires for fame and fortune are being fueled in large part by MTV and reality TV, the author points out that Generation Y was raised not only in the blue glare of the television screen, but also in the spotlight of their parents' video cameras. They grew up as the stars of the home, and now they expect to be treated as celebrities of the culture. "They're accustomed to being noticed, having been showered with awards and accolades," Jayson says. One of the young men interviewed for the article put it succinctly: "Society raised us where money is glamorous, and everybody wants to be glamorous." The first three words of his quote hung in the air over my head as I read them. Society raised us. We were raised by society. As a child of the MTV generation, I see myself in that phrase. Like many in my generation, I see the lingering effects of two decades spent immersed in media. Generation X must make a conscious decision to override the media messages etched on our minds and memories, and this is now a sad legacy we have passed on to the next generation.

Commercial jingles are summoned up out of the distant past when we hear a product name. The lyrics to songs sung 20 years earlier are readily accessible in the memory, word for word, though they have not been listened to for over two decades. Our view of relationships consisted of knights on white horses (a set-up for relational dissatisfaction later in life) and youthfulness that never faded (yet another setup). Everyone on television was young, cool, and hip, with perfect teeth, perfect bodies, and the perfect comeback for every putdown. These became the expectations of normalcy in the Gen X experiment. Many of us look back in retrospect at our time of young adulthood to see that we were frantically, desperately trying to live up to the ideals set forth by a media-central world, a fantasy world. Our relational expectations were built on Hollywood hype.

Psychologists say that before we can truly embrace the concept of unity with another person, we must know ourselves. We must have a secure sense of self in order to commit to a healthy relationship with another individual. These ideas are explored fully in Erik Erikson's (1959) famous *Identity and the Life Cycle*. And here's the modern-day twist. We have no foundation, no sense of self. We are told 10,000 times a year of our imperfections—by advertisers, magazine articles, and thousands of perfect faces parading across electronic screens all around us. Our sense of self has been absorbed by the strangers of the screen. One *USA Today* author put it this way: "Famous people are in their (young people's) faces so much more, and as a society, we have escalated the value we put on celebrities." In fact, the Pew study found that young people are twice as likely to admire an entertainer as they are a political leader. Many psychologists are concerned about this generational shift to center stage. Consumer psychologist Kit Yarrow says these trends can ultimately lead to emptiness and depression, as people put "their resources and energy and validation and self-worth into what people who aren't close to them think of them, which is fame."

We must take a moment to consider our own media repertoire. How many "celebrity" names are we familiar with? How much do we know about their lives? What do we admire about them? Are these traits prosocial or antisocial, beneficial or harmful? Do we see them flooding slowly into our own lifestyle, consciousness, or dreams? When I ask these questions of students and audience members at speeches, the traits they say they admire most in their "famous" friends are either material or physical. They want to look like they look or own what they own. Either way, when we focus so much energy on superficial, we lose touch with reality.

Many a young mom has lamented over her body's changes during pregnancy, when, instead of sporting a Hollywood "bump" like her favorite "star," she gained an unthinkable 35 pounds. The fear of "fat" thus overrides the joy of pregnancy, with one of the most amazing moments in a woman's life being overrun by unrealistic and superficial expectations. C.S. Lewis saw the trend emerging in 1942, when he wrote the satirical masterpiece *Screwtape Letters*: "We now teach men to like women whose bodies are scarcely distinguishable from those of boys. Since this is a kind of beauty even more transitory than most, we thus aggravate the female's chronic horror of growing old and render her less willing and less able to bear children (p. 107). In the same way, *Screwtape* reveals the plot for men's demise: "We are more and more directing the desires of men to something which does not exist—making the role of the eye in sexuality more and more important and at the same time making its demands more and more impossible" (p. 107). Now, as then, celebrities are the ever-present teachers of the modern era, educating our young in the ways and expectations of the world.

If celebrities are in fact educators in their own way, perhaps they should be called to account for their influence on society. As juries have noted in a number of trials, teachers are naturally held to a higher standard because of their potential for influence. In a Richmond, Virginia case, for example, the Chesterfield County School Board unanimously voted to fire an art teacher for his off-campus artwork. It seems the teacher was staining his genitals with paint, pressing them onto canvas, and selling them online. The school board dismissed him, saying the decision was "in keeping with court rulings that hold that teachers are expected to lead by example and be role models."

No reasonable person could argue against the fact that the teacher's behavior represents reprehensible judgment. Teachers are expected to be role models, and rightfully so. However, the truth is that today's most impacting teachers are not standing in front of a classroom of 25 well-adjusted children; today's most impacting teachers are standing in front of a camera, peddling lifestyles and mindsets and political viewpoints to naïve observers. Teachers have been replaced by entertainers. And entertainers (and producers and scriptwriters and musicians) have been cut loose from their tenuous tether of moral demands, completely absolved of personal responsibility.

As a result of media centrality, children and teens alike are rapidly shifting their focus from leaders of principle to leaders of lewdness. This begs the question: Why is the same expectation of responsible behavior not placed on the most impacting culture-shapers of our time—entertainers? Perhaps it's time we took the implications of Social Learning theory a bit more seriously. The most influential teachers of today's young people are entertainers. Who is holding them accountable? The answer, of course, is no one. Despite repetitive numbers of grossly incomprehensible acts of violence and sexual promiscuity, entertainers find themselves buttressed again and again by the nefarious graces of constitutional "freedom." Their perversion is protected. Until such time as they are held accountable for decency and honor, we have to take action in our own realm of influence—the place where change begins. If we are being educated, influenced, manipulated, and manufactured, we can shut off the source of influence.

Whose Values Prevail? Better Business for Bureaucracy

Imagine for a moment that Starbucks and Crest white strips teamed up to hatch a business plan. It would be fairly simple, really. The coffee manufacturer adds a staining ingredient to its product, and Crest adds the antidotal whitener to its product. Then both companies flood the airwaves with beautiful, gregarious young adults who are laughing through glow-in-the-dark teeth as they drink their Starbucks and polish their teeth incessantly. Is it unreasonable to think that in a society built on commercialism and materialism, that there might be covert strategies in place that benefit the company at the expense of the consumer? What if Lays potato chips added an addictive ingredient to its bet-you-can't-eat-just-one product, knowing that the secret ingredient would, over the course of a few years, cause an enlargement of fat cells around the abdominal region? Then, what if the company bought stock in a pharmaceutical corporation that targets what has now become known as "stubborn belly fat"? Both companies win. The consumer loses. Is this really all that different from company partnerships in existence today?

If these scenarios sound like science fiction, consider the details behind a statistic we mentioned earlier in this writing, Cosgrove's study on DSM writers' ties to pharmaceutical companies. When her research surfaced, major universities began kicking pharmaceutical reps out of their medical classrooms, as it became clear that doctors were prescribing unnecessary drugs out of a sense of loyalty to the drug company that sponsored research or donated gifts to the doctor. Stanford University was one of the first to say "no" to drugs, and most medical teachers are now forbidden from using pharmacological paraphernalia, even down to those subtle and seemingly innocuous coffee cups and paper pads. Later studies revealed that pharmaceutical companies had begun investing more heavily into the local doctor than into commercial advertising, for the doctor was a face the patient could trust, and if he could serve as a marketing representative for the company, sales would increase. The family doctor could step in as the pusher of the pill. All TV had to do then was to whet the consumer's appetite for it.

In a capitalist society, where money is often the bottom line, is it unreasonable to think that our lens of reality might be somewhat skewed? Is it possible that materialism might have wound its way insidiously into our mindsets, our attitudes, our parenting process, our communication styles, our ability to read and analyze and contemplate and communication and truly think for ourselves?

The question for a media-central culture is, of course, whose values will prevail? When we compare the value systems of media producers and the average American, there is a tremendous disparity between the lifestyles and the worldviews. Since the vast majority of our actions spring from habitual thoughts and behavioral patterns, it is plausible to consider that even a well-intentioned journalist would lean to his or her own worldview in thought and action when reporting a story. Let's take a look at just a few of the differences.

An Annenberg Public Policy Center survey demonstrates the differences between the views of journalists—who present the news—and the average American who consumes the news. The survey of journalists was conducted by Princeton Survey Research Associates International (2005) among 673 journalists including owners and executives, editors and producers, and staff journalists, from both local and national organizations.

Of those surveyed, 31% of the journalists self-described liberal, 49% self-described as moderates and just 9% self-described as conservative. This is quite a contrast to the average American. Among the representative sample of the general public, 24% self-described as liberal, 33% self-described as moderate, and 38% self-described as conservative. It would be naïve at best to imagine that these viewpoints would not find their way into the teachings of the media, just as a classroom teacher naturally imparts his or her own socio-political viewpoints to the class, whether overtly or covertly. There is a clear socialization effect in both instances.

With regard to viewpoints, the Annenberg report asked respondents if the government possess the right to limit the reporting of a story. Journalists' responses were 44% never, 48% rarely, and 6% sometimes. The general public view was 29% never, 17% rarely, 37% sometimes, and 14% always. Journalists were asked if they attend religious services regularly, with regularly being defined as once per week or more. Only 17% of journalists said yes, whereas 40% of the general public said yes. This is a stark contrast to say the least. Additionally, 92% of the general public rated religious freedom as "very important" and 81% of the public said it was "very important" to them "to live in a country where you can openly say what you think."

Journalists were also asked opinions on current events, including whether they supported or opposed laws permitting same-sex marriage. The percentages here were virtually opposite between journalists and the general public: 59% of journalists supported laws permitting same-sex marriage, while 20% did not. In the general public view, only 28% supported the law, while 64% did not. Whatever one's views on laws that support or oppose same-sex marriage, it is clear that the journalists reporting the news share a clear bias in one direction.

Geneva Overholser, co-editor of *The Press*, said that the study illuminates "a worrisome divide between the public's view of journalism and journalists' own views of their work" and she encourages journalists to be more effective in putting forth work that is "valuable, fair and ethically sound." The study reflected the idea "the media sample, with a median experience level of 23 years, is distinctly more liberal than the public in general" (Annenberg 2004). Certainly, if the media's values are not representative of the countrymen it serves, then there will likely be a socialization effect. Just as teens viewed the "everyone's doing it" theme in music, movies, and television programming, the news media can portray a similar "this is the worldview of everyone" concept, marginalizing those with views that differ from mainstream media.

The cocoon of mass media serves to interpret and explain the events of the world to readers and viewers. The challenge is that the interpretation is filtered through the lens of the writer, and as we see in the statistics above, there is a lack of equal representation in political and religious viewpoints amongst those who are "reporting" the news. Their opinions filter through, affecting public opinion.

For example, an article came across my desk a few weeks back. It was a story about a woman who had decided to give birth to a child with a known disorder—a decision the author of the story clearly disagreed with. The story was riddled with editorializing: the woman was called "dirty" and she "slouched" in her "sparse" apartment. These words are not news. They aren't facts. They're opinions. These are the value judgments that help the reader "know" what to think and feel about the story. In essence, it's a conscientious guide for the everyday reader, "Here's what's happening in your world, and here's how you should feel about it." If we aren't media literate, and if we don't think critically, we can easily miss these subtle notes of influence that, in the long term, can equal mass socialization and alterations in paradigm.

In the 1970s, African-Americans began to create awareness about the numerical misrepresentation of Blacks in mainstream US media. The absence of balance in representation was cultivating a sense of inferiority in many young Black viewers, and the awareness movement ushered in a fair balance concept that brought greater awareness to representation on television and other media. Today, when we turn on a children's TV program, balance in ethnicity is the norm: there is normally a representation from each of the four major ethnic groups. This balance helps create awareness and visual reminders that the whole of culture is not Caucasian.

In the same way, balance needs to be sought in media representations of political and religious views. If only 9% of journalists self-describe as conservative, and yet nearly 40% of the general public self-describes as conservative, then we need balance: 31% of the liberal journalists need to be replaced by conservatives. Let free speech reign. Let debate ensue. But let each party and policy be represented fairly and accurately.

As I write, we are passing through the slums of Hollywood, California—graffiti covered buildings huddling close together, broken windows peering out to the interstate in silent desperation. The closeness is suffocating. As we pass by one run-down street next to an overpass, a blue trash can drops to the interstate below, causing drivers to swerve suddenly in order to avoid the can and its contents. It's a fitting metaphor for the moment, I think. We swerve instinctively because we are aware of the cause and effect pattern: If we hit the can, it will, at best, dent our car and send trash flying. At worst, it could cause a crash that affects multiple cars and multiple lives. If we are aware of the danger, we can choose to respond accordingly. This, I think, has been the challenge of media centrality in Western culture. We haven't seen the trash cans barreling toward our cars, so we failed to swerve. It's time to identify some of the challenges so we can begin to seek solutions.

At the Hearst Museum in San Luis Obispo, California, visitors can view the historical background and tribute to William Randolph Hearst. On a recent visit, I was struck by the presence of a term we don't hear very often anymore, *yellow journalism.* Yellow journalism, as ThinkQuest (2009) so concisely puts it, is "biased opinion masquerading as objective fact... the practice of yellow journalism involved sensationalism, distorted stories, and misleading images for the sole purpose of boosting newspaper sales and exciting public opinion" (p. 1).

Sound familiar? It should. We have biased opinion masquerading as fact across the nation in our schools, our news stations, our government offices, and even our churches. Hearst's name became synonymous with yellow journalism because of a yellow-inked comic strip, but later the term became intrinsically connected to sensational media—media that strove to stir up emotion in order to generate sales. That tactic should sound familiar to us as well today.

Hearst hired as his newspaper editor a woman with no experience in newspapers whatsoever. Instead of news experience, she had gossip experience, and Hearst drew heavily on her role as a socialite to make his newspaper a prominent feature in American households. Today we would be hard pressed to name one news show, one newspaper, or one magazine that doesn't use the platform of sensationalism to sell news. Creating news to sell a product is big business today. As Boorstin (1969) says in *The Image*, it's the pseudo-event. News creates news to sell news.

CHAPTER TEN

State of Affairs: The Marriage of Man and Media

What happens to the social, emotional, mental, and political landscape when a generation prizes "heroes" not because of their civic leadership or academic acumen, but because of their ability to perform, to entertain? What happens to the individual in society when he or she is consumed with and consumed by mass media? What type of logic-defying, wisdom-denying paradigms persist?

Perhaps a tragic story of ludicrous sacrifice answers the question best. In 2007, a Sacramento, California radio station made the decision to hold an on-air contest to give away a Wii video game system. The organizers of the event thought it would be amusing for the general public if the words *Wii* and *Wee* shared a starring role in the title of the contest, and thus the "Hold Your Wee for a Wii" contest was born. The DJs on the program "Morning Rave" asked contestants to consume one 8-ounce bottle of water every ten minutes without relieving themselves. The childishly vile nature of the contest notwithstanding, clearly the DJs failed to exhibit both moral and medical logic: the human body is designed to take in fluids and then release fluids. To prohibit release of fluids runs contrary to the body's internal mechanisms, and overriding those internal mechanisms requires socialization, desensitization, and a dose of teenage invincibility.

That's exactly what contestants mustered up in the jeering presence of the DJs, with a tragic end to the story. Jennifer Strange, a 28-year-old mother of three who wanted to win the game for her family, died of water intoxication as a result of the contest. She unknowingly traded her life for the lure of entertainment. The Entercom Sacramento VP and market manager was "stunned" by the news and, at the time of death, said he was "awaiting information that will help explain how this tragic event occurred" (Associated Press, 2007). Was there any great mystery as to how the event occurred? It occurred as a result of irresponsibility, of negligence, of juvenile daring, and of a desire to, quite literally, *amuse ourselves to death*.

Jennifer Strange's tragic story is a metaphor for media centrality and socialization, as well as for the lack of responsibility that has been shown on behalf of those instigating the contest. Like our Buzz shareholders in the semi-fictitious story above, modern media moguls attempt to absolve themselves of responsibility with clever smokescreens and power plays and well-paid lobbyists. The fact remains, however, that in their role as authority figures, as people of influence setting the pace for those who would follow, the leaders were careless, calloused, and characteristically childish in what was ultimately a pursuit of pleasure.

The fact that there is even a question of whether or not the radio station bears any responsibility for Strange's death underscores the insanity of the situation. This is not some obscure branch of scientific research we are talking about; it's the simple biochemistry of bodily functions. It's cause and effect. If the contest involved illicit sexual liaisons, a reasonable observer might assume resultant maternity or paternity, sexually-transmitted infections or AIDS. If a father incites a child to sociopathic behavior, would the father be responsible for his actions? Of course. Why? He is the authoritative figure in the situation. His systematic socialization as a leader in the family bears directly on the child's behavior. There is no waiver of responsibility to be signed. The truck bearing the sign of refusal of responsibility does so because the potential for injurious behavior exists.

But can we simply barrel down the road, spraying debris everywhere, and announce ourselves to be absolved of responsibility? The jury on the Strange case answered a resounding "no" to that question, saying media could not and should not be absolved of responsibility in their role of the death of Jennifer Strange. The jury found Entercom Sacramento negligent for ignoring warnings of the dangers of the Hold Your Wee for a Wii contest. The Strange family was awarded $16.6 million.

The modern media mindset dismembers the connective concepts of cause and effect. This is nonsense. Our actions affect others. The denial of responsibility does not invoke healing; it invokes generational cycles of blame. But this is by far not the only case in point. Let's take a look some of the further implications of media socialization.

The Impact and Implications of Media Socialization

Though there are many available sources of media outside of the old faithful television set, TV time does retain a level of dominance in certain demographics. Despite the additions of constant internet accessibility, laptops, iPods, and always-plugged-in iPhones, Americans are still spending the majority of their screen time each day (4 hours of the average 7 hours of screen time per day) with the television (and, interestingly enough, still complaining that they don't have enough time). Just like the junk food diet we Westerners are subsisting on at present, where far too many insignificant, high-calorie, low fiber foods leave no room for healthy choices, in the same way, we are quickly becoming a culture saturated with meaningless trivia. We know intimately the marriage failures, clothing brands, and automobile choices of 15 celebrities, but we cannot name three current policies up for debate in US governmental legislation.

There are a number of ways that our cultural lens has been and is being shaped by the persistent voices of media messages. One of the functions of media centrality has been a disdain for conservatism and an intolerance for anything remotely resembling traditional values (the word *traditional* has even come to denote old-fashioned, archaic, out-of-touch). At the time of this writing, wishing colleagues a "Merry Christmas" is discouraged in the mainstream American workplace. The preferred greeting is *happy holidays* (though the word *holiday*, of course, is derived from *holy day*, but perhaps we should keep that revelation to ourselves).

Likewise, my students tell me that they are not permitted to say "Merry Christmas" to the customers who are shopping for Christmas presents at the retail stores where my students are employed, even though the stores are selling Christmas trees (and presents) and will be closed on December 25th in observance of the Christmas holiday (there's that word again). At the time of this writing, however, it *is* still legal to wish coworkers a Happy New Year. I suppose this greeting will persist until there is widespread recognition that the greeting "Happy New Year" is a representation of a calendar year, and that the calendar year is a symbolic code for the birth of a religious figure so deeply interwoven into the fabric of modern-day society that his birth is unconsciously commemorated within our Western calendar system.

Another example of the mockery of traditionalism is the double standard the media has set for discussions of sexuality. For example, in the current socio-political climate, it is considered culturally acceptable to mock and label traditional couples as "breeders"; however, if a traditional couple dares voice a procreational-biological disagreement regarding a gay couple, the traditional couple is labeled as homophobic. The art of debate is being stifled in part because we are afraid someone's feelings might get hurt, and in part because someone's political agenda might be hampered. We are captive to emotionalism, which is no surprise, given the emotion-centeredness of mass media communication. The true American spirit, however, was birthed in a climate of freedom: freedom of speech, freedom of religion, freedom to explore the vast world and form opinions that may or may not agree with those of the political powers that be. Healthy debate, an opportunity to discuss divergent views in a respectful though passionate matter, is a hallmark of a free society. In fact, historic literature demonstrates that it is through discourse and reasoning and debate that both individuals and cultures are strengthened and improved. Perhaps our lack of healthy debate has been a driving force behind our truncated growth in the many sectors where we now find ourselves failing as a country.

A pastor in our town recently began planning a message that he hoped would illuminate the harmful effects of divorce in modern society and help hearers strengthen long-term relationships. He called some community leaders around the country and asked them their advice on approaching the topic of divorce truthfully but lovingly. "Don't do it!" came the resounding collective response. "It's suicide! You'll drive everyone out of your church!" From the outpouring of feedback, the point was clear: the general tendency is to avoid discussion of cultural issues that might make people uncomfortable (i.e., cause feelings of guilt or call attention to the dangers inherent in certain lifestyle choices). Though psychologists have cautioned that fatherlessness has a dramatic influence on a child's view of the world, his likelihood of scholastic success, even his likelihood of criminal behavior later in life, community leaders encouraged the pastor to approach more "comfortable" topics in order to preserve congregational numbers. In other words, don't rock the boat. I'm pleased to say that the pastor did not succumb to the social pressure to sanitize truth in fear of making waves.

As one writer stated in a review of the jarringly insightful film *SuperSize Me*, "We have become a society of adult children. We want what feels good, what tastes good, not what is good." In an effort to deny ourselves pain and circumvent perseverance, we have, in essence, embraced the mantra of hedonism. To outrun the scorn and shame of Hester's *Scarlet Letter*, we have cast aside any connection to those terribly judgmental terms of *right* and *wrong*, falling headlong into the arms of moral relativity. A recent TV commercial underscores this idea: "Daddy, you always taught me to do what *feels* right." It seems we have become a nation led by the dubious intents of the heart, while the moral intellect atrophies beyond recognition.

In a TV generation, children don't play outside and develop creative games. All the thinking is done for them in their highly-structured play time. One student of mine took the media-free challenge in my class and went home to her 6-year old daughter with the plan. "I want you to go play outside," she told her daughter. "Why?" the daughter asked worriedly. "Am I in trouble?" When her mother replied that she wasn't in trouble, she just wanted her daughter to take some time away from the television and the computer, the daughter asked, "But what do I do out there?" Truly, the world "out there" is the world our media-central generation has lost touch with. Natural reality has been replaced with electronic fantasy. We'll talk more about this creativity-deficient culture in the last few chapters of the book.

Television culture also plays to hyperemotionalism. Over the past decade, there has been birthed a new wave of medication advertisements on television, everything from mood enhancers to sleeping aids. By taking a simple pill, viewers can discover freedom from a whole host of new maladies, and the list of symptoms for these maladies has doubled and now tripled over the last 60 years. As a recent Slate article put it, "If you spend hours online, have sex more frequently than aging psychiatrists, and moan incessantly that the federal government can't account for all its TARP funds, take heed: You may soon be classed among the 48 million Americans the APA already considers mentally ill" (Lane, 2009). Some of my personal favorites from the list of new disorders are orthorexia nervosa, an obsession with healthy eating (heaven forbid the sickest and fattest nation in the world should suffer from the perverse pathology of a desire to eat healthily! How awful!).

Other relatively new finds include mathematics disorder, sibling rivalry disorder, and the terribly annoying disease of lexical dysanhedria, which keeps its poor victims from enjoying the discipline of reading. "Put away the book, Johnny; there is no need to torture your poor lexical dysanhedric mind with textbook knowledge. Get back to your video game." Personal discipline, it seems, is a trend experiencing such a rampant decline that anyone who is not spiraling downward with it is now subject to social ridicule. There is more to write on this topic than space allows, and a number of writers have already begun public awareness campaigns and dialogue on the topic of our over-medicated America, which is an excellent start.

These ubiquitous ads, which serve to illuminate every possible symptom of real or imagined maladies in the hopes of increased product sales, do at least post warning signs. Prescription advertisements are required by law to post the potential side effects of the drug: May cause drowsiness. Do not operate large farm equipment while overdosing on this medication, etc. In the state of California, any store that carries lead crystal or sells gasoline products or was built using suspected carcinogens must be labeled with a warning sign that apprises bystanders of the dangers of exposure. In the same way, perhaps we should consider ourselves obligated to post warning signs on products associated with excessive media use: *Warning! Use of this product may cause inertia, listlessness, violence, sexual promiscuity, obesity, and anti-social tendencies. This product may be habit-forming. Use of this product may alter your paradigm and strip you of your ability to think, to reason, and to create. Use with caution and in moderation.*

Media Violence: Short and Long-Term Effects

Studies of media's violent output and resultant effects on society have been known for decades. However, one interesting new realm of study gives rise to even greater levels of concern regarding media violence—the discovery of mirror neurons. Mirror neurons were first discovered in monkeys about a decade ago, when researchers discovered that when one monkey reached for a piece of fruit, other monkeys watching him had activation in the same neural regions. When researchers applied the same constructs to the human brain, they discovered a striking similarity: Neural activity "mirrors not only the movement but also the intentions, sensations, and emotions of those around us" (Miller, 2005, p. 945). In other words, within the brain, watching is like doing. Watching parents fight is like being involved in a fight. Watching a professional sports competition is like participating in that competition, and, perhaps, watching violent acts on media sources is like practicing violent behavior.

Based on cumulative findings over the past 40 years, "the scientific and public health communities 'overwhelmingly conclude' that watching violence in any form of media poses a harmful risk to children" (KFF, 2007). We know media is replete with sexualized imagery, but just how prevalent is TV violence? In the largest analysis to date, the National Television Violence Study found that the average child who watches 2 hours of cartoons a day may see nearly 10,000 violent incidents each year, 500 of which are believed to pose a high risk for learning, emulation, and desensitization. In addition, the number of prime-time programs containing violence has increased from 53% to 67% on broadcast television and from 54% to 64% on cable networks. The latter category, cable, represents some of the most sobering statistics on TV violence: an average of 92% of cable air time is dedicated to violent programming. I realize, as one of my students once challenged, that not everyone who has watched violent programming becomes a serial killer. That's a statistical impossibility. However, even if not all people are affected, some people are affected. And it only takes some—even one—to wreak havoc on a family, a city, a culture. It was a small handful of men who destroyed so many lives in Oklahoma, Waco, New York City. It was a small group of children who imposed their violent views on Columbine and on Virginia Tech. From the influence of a handful of individuals, our nation was forever changed.

As discussed earlier with regard to Bandura's early research as well as Strasberger's later studies, viewing violence leads to predictive behavioral patterns. According to the research, viewing TV violence can lead to increased antisocial or aggressive behavior, desensitization to violence, or increased fear of becoming a victim of violence. Especially vulnerable are children under the age of 8, who are unable to differentiate between fantasy and reality; for these children especially, televised violence teaches social coping mechanisms, serving as a how-to manual for life in society.

However, as discussed earlier, the potential for socialization persists throughout one's lifetime. This point is underscored by the earlier-discussed model of the explosion of fear-driven laws in culture, from seat belts to bike helmets to toilet seat covers. It seems that fear of wrongdoing has been the catalyst for an entire generation—and most interestingly, it has been birthed in the first generation to be raised by media—the MTV, latchkey generation. Early research on television viewing showed that those who watched more than two hours of television a day had a decidedly different worldview than those who didn't, specifically regarding fear-based content. Heavy watchers developed what became known as the "Mean and Scary Worldview" model, where the fear of harm rose in direct correlation to the amount of television viewed.

What surprised researchers most in this study was that heavy viewers perceived the world as unsafe the world differently *regardless of the content* of the programming. In other words, something about the rapid intake of images, the emotion-based persuasion, and perhaps even mirror neuron behavior worked together to alter paradigms. Similarly, a recent study on teenage brains, showing a decreased ability to identify emotions, could bear interesting results if the participants were separated by amount of media use. It is plausible that continued viewing of violent acts can bear long-term effects on the human brain, perhaps even rendering an individual incapable of empathy and thus more susceptible to becoming a perpetrator of violent crime.

A few of the hundreds of examples of research on correlations between violent behavior and viewing violent programming follow. In one study, children who viewed several episodes of Batman and Spiderman were more likely to demonstrate aggressive behavior amongst their peers, whereas those who watched Mister Rogers' Neighborhood were more likely to act in a cooperative manner. A similar study tracked the group behavior of children who were shown an episode of Mighty Morphin Power Rangers. Compared to their classmates who had not seen the episode, those who did view it committed seven times as many aggressive acts, including hitting, kicking, shoving, and insulting a peer (KFF 2007). In another study, 2,300 junior and senior high school students self-described their favorite shows, and researchers analyzed the programs for violent content. The students also provided a self-described checklist of their behavior at school, including fighting and delinquency. The study showed a direct correlation between viewing violent programming and behaving in a violent and/or aggressive manner.

In another study of third, fourth, and fifth graders, a link was evidenced between viewing violent programming and exhibiting bullying behavior, including spreading rumors, engaging in excluding and insulting behaviors, and general hurtfulness (KFF 2008). Bullying has become an issue of concern in schools today, the rise of which is documented in a number of research studies. Younger and younger children are resorting to violence as a way of "dealing" with social challenges. One frightening example was the group of third grade children (i.e., 8-10 year olds) in a Georgia elementary school who conspired to bring crude weapons to class to knock out and stab their third-grade teacher, who had reprimanded a child for standing on his chair in class. Police called the setup a "serious threat," saying that the group of nine children could have succeeded in killing their teacher if police had not received a tip and intervened (Associated Press 2008). These were not college students; *these were third graders.*

Perhaps one of the most compelling studies of the impact of violent programming on behavior is a well-known University of Michigan study that began in the 1970s. The study tracked 450 6-10 year olds over the course of more than 20 years, observing preferences to and viewing of violent programming and the result on later socialization. Those who watched violent and aggressive programming in their younger years were far more likely to display violent and aggressive behavior in the teen years as well as have arrests and convictions in the adult years—especially crimes against people, such as child abuse, spousal abuse, aggravated assault, and murder. This study correlates with the idea that lifelong patterns of socialization can be set in motion when a child is "trained up" to emulate the behavior of his favorite actor, and that the paradigms persist—even into adulthood—unless their trajectory is halted. A subsequent longitudinal study showed that teens who watched more than one hour of television a day were nearly four times more likely to commit aggressive acts in adulthood. These viewing-behavioral correlations persisted even when researchers controlled for socioeconomic status, intellectual ability, and differentials in parenting styles (American Psychological Association 2003).

In July 2000, the American Academy of Pediatrics, American Academy of Child and Adolescent Psychiatry, the American Psychological Association, the American Medical Association, the American Academy of Family Physicians, and the American Psychiatric Association issued a joint statement that concluded: "At this time, well over 1,000 studies point overwhelmingly to a causal connection between media violence and aggressive behavior in some children." This extraordinary correlation should be cause for alarm. If media has such dramatic effects on behavior, why would we treat the intake of media with such casual indifference? Why would we not question the content, question the quantity, and proceed only with caution? In 1993, the APA Committee on Media and Society said, "There is absolutely no doubt that higher levels of viewing violence on television are correlated with increased acceptance of aggressive attitudes and increased aggressive behavior."

One concerning trend in recent years is the increase in violent content in adult programming. Earlier in this chapter, we discussed the percentages of violence on cable television, whose program base is now 92% violence. I often overhear men talking about shows such as "Ultimate Fighting," shows grounded not in prosocial interaction but in violent, aggressive, sociopathic behavior. What woman would want to live with a man whose conflict resolution strategy was adopted from shows such as these? Many of these men believe, quite erroneously, that their behavior will not be affected by the viewing of such programming, that watching these shows is somehow therapeutic. This is either a mark of naiveté or brazen arrogance, depending on one's view. As we discussed earlier, Bandura's Bobo Doll studies sought to disprove this very mindset. The cultural view of his day was that viewing violent programming caused a "drain" of violence in the viewer—that is, it released the tendency toward violence by allowing the viewer a chance to exert his violence vicariously without bearing an impact on the viewer. Of course, as Bandura demonstrated, this was an impractical impossibility. Study after study now demonstrates that we become like the company we keep, whether that company is sitting in our living room or emanating from our television sets. As sociological creatures working within the boundaries of our associational brains, we would be foolish to think that we are somehow above influence.

Health implications, too, abound with excessive media use. A growing body of knowledge is now drawing correlations between media use and weight gain. In the report "The Role of Media in Childhood Obesity," researchers reviewed more than 40 studies regarding correlations between media intake and childhood obesity, concluding that scientific research indicates that the more media people consume, the more likely they are to be overweight. However, it is not simply a matter of more TV, less exercise, as we might have assumed at the outset of the study. Instead, it appears that the junk food intake is significantly higher for children who consume mass quantities of media simply because 90% of the 40,000 ads seen by a typical child each year are mostly ads for junk food. Kids that watch more want more. According to the American Academy of Pediatrics, childhood obesity is now an "unprecedented burden" on children's health. The Centers for Disease Control and Prevention (CDC) have stated that since 1980, the percentage of overweight children has more than doubled in 6 to 11 year olds and has tripled in adolescents. Tragically, a child who develops diabetes before the age of 15 may limit his or her lifespan by as much as 17 years. In essence, if the trend is not reversed, a significant proportion of the current generation could be outlived by their parents.

There are over 33 million teens in the United States at the time of this writing, and they spend over $175 billion dollars a year. What do they spend their money on? They spend it on whatever is marketed the most—junk food, cosmetics, and fashion. A survey by Taylor Research Group found that the number of teen magazines more than tripled between 1990 and 2000. What are the articles about? For girls, 40% of the content centers on appearance, dating, and fashion (with a whopping 2% of the content focusing on drug/alcohol awareness, STDs, and pregnancy and/or contraception). *The Journal of Media Literacy* says that it is the combination of reality and fantasy that makes modern media especially compelling. "Today's technologies represent a startling fusion of sight and sound that frequently make it difficult for us to discern illusion from reality, fact from fiction. Special effects ...merge the past with the present, color with black and white, the dead with the living, fact with fiction in such a way that the real truth can often be confused with the reel truth" (JML 2009). Anyone who has viewed Dove's You Tube campaign on self-esteem, Evolution, has witnessed the deceptive imagery that commands the heart of teens and adults alike. These images impact the paradigms of the people.

As the Media Awareness Network puts it, "People who control a society's dominant institutions have disproportionate influence on the construction and dissemination of media messages and the values they contain." In a media-central culture, mass media disseminate the majority of the observations and experiences from which we build up our personal understandings of the world and how it works. Much of our view of reality is based on media messages that have been pre-constructed with built-in attitudes, interpretations, and conclusions. The media, to a great extent, give us our sense of reality, and whether explicitly or implicitly, mainstream media convey ideological messages.

One such ideological message should be of grave concern to parents and partners alike. Focus on the Family issued a 2009 study on another injurious form of content that often stems from excessive media use: pornography. Prior to the internet decade, the average age for a child to stumble across pornographic images was between the ages of 11 and 13. Now, the average age of first confrontation is down to 8 years old, and that confrontation usually occurs while students are doing homework online. Stories of the tragic impact of pornography abound, but one of the most chilling is the testimony of serial killer Ted Bundy. Just before Bundy was put to death for his crimes, he consented to one single interview. He didn't choose someone from the mainstream media to tell his story, because he didn't believe the mainstream media would tell the story with accuracy. Instead, he chose Focus on the Family's Dr. James Dobson, who allowed Bundy's tragic testimony to ring clear—that his pathology was rooted in an addiction to pornography that began when he was a young boy. (Bundy's chilling testimony can be heard on Focus on the Family's website.) Additionally, a recent Focus on the Family article (Jackson 2009) cites the damage done by exposure to pornography, including the power differential at work when the perpetrator is at least three years older than the one being exposed to the images. Jackson makes an excellent argument against those who would attempt to seduce our children through the ubiquitous realm of pornography: "I'm convinced that children are victims of a covert form of sexual abuse whenever they are confronted with sexually provocative materials. With this in mind, our children need us to be healthy advocates for their well-being" (Jackson 2009, p. 2)

Crazed Consumers

Another implication of media centrality is the mark of materialism, specifically crazed consumers. While preparing for the Christmas season in 2008, a Long Island Wal-Mart employee was trampled by a group of shoppers who were deathly intent on saving a few dollars. We may not know the age of the perpetrators, we don't know their gender or ethnicity; but we do know that they all shared one common trait: selfishness. What would drive a man or woman to overlook the needs of a dying human being in pursuit of a sale? At best, the crowd exhibited desensitization, a lack of empathy, a loss of connection with reality. These are growing concerns in every sphere of the Western world.

In one of my college classes a few years back, there was a curious young man whose moral ambivalence underscores some of our current cultural challenges. He was a nice student, even a smart student. He was hopeful that he might one day become a pediatrician. Numerous times throughout the semester, he would forward along to me poignant messages about how saddened he was by the country's tragic departure from faith, how we were headed down a treacherous path of immorality. He sent quotes and scriptures about the need for religion in the classroom and the need for ethical behavior in the schools and courts and households of America. I did not disagree with his message; however, I was puzzled by the unlikeness of the messenger.

There was a rather glaring disconnect—a hole, even—in his moral relativity that kept me from fully resonating with his version of truth. For, as I learned halfway through the semester, the student was a stripper, yes, a male stripper. In fact, several of the girls at the college, whom he also targeted with his morality-plugging emails, had even been to see him "perform" as a stripper. Insane, you say? How could a young man uphold ethical principles in one hand while contributing to illicit sexual liaisons with the other? Perhaps the student was a victim of VCM spinoff. Values Clarification had left him lacking a moral compass. He had never been taught a way of truth, of absolutes. He has had a vague sense of right and wrong somewhere within him, but it had been so buried by the absence of black-and-white thinking, of clear-cut right and wrong, that it was just a trickling undercurrent beneath a wall of impenetrable rock—virtually undetectable in the midst of busy modern life. In an image, he was a choir boy in a Hooter's shirt. The images are so contradictory as to be almost humorous—if they weren't indicative of such serious undertones. Yet, these are the lifestyles many modern era dwellers find themselves in—the great dichotomy birthed of freedom without guidance.

The Decline of Prosocial Behavior

A number of studies show that some of our top performers in American colleges, though they may be making more of a contribution to the work force, are making less of a contribution to society. In addition to self-injurious behaviors such as cutting and burning, discussed in a later chapter, several recent studies have indicated a decline in scholarly servitude. A longitudinal study by the University of California, Los Angeles (UCLA), found that social activism is declining among college students, and institutions of higher learning seem to be losing their ability to engage students in contemporary social issues (Astin 2002). The UCLA study, comprised of 14,021 students at 117 four-year institutions, indicated that fundamental value shifts may have influenced this behavioral change. Over the last three decades, two values in particular have changed in relation to student culture: the contrasting dreams of "developing a meaningful philosophy of life" and "being very well off financially"(p. 7). Only 40 years ago, developing a meaningful philosophy of life was deemed the more important of the two qualities by more than 80% of the entering freshmen (p. 7). "Being very well-off financially," however, placed fifth or sixth on the list; less than 45% of the freshmen called it an "important" or "essential" goal in life. However, over the last decade, these values have been transposed. Being very well-off financially is now the top value for American college students—at 74%, while developing a meaningful philosophy of life now ranks sixth place at 42% (Astin 2002, p.7). Given the glittering superficialities peddled by mainstream media, perhaps this trend is not surprising, but it is nonetheless concerning.

The Decline of Man

In addition to prosocial behavioral declines, there is also a concerning trend regarding the success of men and boys in Western culture. More men than women are born across the world (52% and 48% respectively across the globe), but once they reach school age, boys seem to take a back seat. When this book was in its inception, a headline story in *Newsweek* magazine underscored the critical changes in educational opportunities for boys. The story asked two disturbing questions: "Do Teachers Dislike Boys?" and "Is Boyhood a Disease?" In the rush to define new academic standards and attempt to gain ground in standardized testing scores, schools were looking at the behavioral "challenges" of the "disease" of boyhood, and the expectation was becoming clear: If boys wanted to do well in school, they had better act like girls. Never mind that boys and girls may have completely different learning styles and completely different physiological needs—girl behavior was being touted as the "gold standard" in the American classroom. Little wonder, then, that 90% of the elementary age boys in the US say that they dislike school.

The same oppressive message rings out clearly in visual media as well: Women are smarter than men, kids are smarter than their parents, and no grown-up, straight, Caucasian male could ever serve as a role model on a sitcom. Instead, for the past ten years, sitcom messages have told men that they sit second-string to women, who have it all together, are inherently smarter, and demonstrate more relational success and career success that men do. Males have been reminded of their inadequacies, and now it seems they are living them out in one of the decade's most disturbing self-fulfilling prophecies. For the past 15 years, we have told men that they are losers, that the family must naturally break down, that sexual perversion is normal. Shows like "Fear Factor" created a new baseline for base behavior. An extraordinary effort of not-so-subtle socialization is in effect.

Today, there are fewer boys who are successful in school, fewer men in the army, fewer male leaders and role models in general. In 2008, more women than men were heads of households in the United States (51%), and for the first time in American history, there are more women than men registered for college classes. According to the US Census, 56% of college students are women, and 59% of graduate students are women. This trend represents a linear decline of *nearly 10 percentage points in just one decade*. Men represented the majority of those seeking higher education just a decade ago, and now the tables have turned in rather dramatic fashion. Why? Though there are a number of reasons for academic decline, it seems our country may be experiencing a men's-life crisis as a result of media socialization.

Movies, sitcoms, and commercials have berated men over and over for the last 15 years, telling them that they aren't as smart as women, that women have it all together and that men, quite simply, never will. An exaggeration? Hardly. It is difficult to imagine a solitary sitcom or commercial where the wife is stupid and the husband brilliant, or where the heroic men strut around mocking a weak woman. It's difficult to recall a solitary commercial where the husband is not belittled by his wife and children because he can't cook dinner (so he orders out) or fix the computer (so the six year old takes care of it). If the roles were reversed, we would hasten to shut down such insensitive, sexist, unenlightened fare. It isn't socially-acceptable to mock women, for women have it all together today. In virtually every sitcom across the board, a beautiful, successful woman is married to an overweight, balding, "loser" husband. The husband is rarely the wise sage. That role is reserved for his children. In short, we've been telling men they aren't good enough for years, and now it seems they are beginning to believe it. They have begun to live up to the level of their socialized expectations.

A Deficit of Attention

When the World Cup rolls around every four years in our half-British household, the television gets more use than it does in the previous three years put together. The last time the World Cup entered our sociological consciousness, I noted a curious mental expectation. As I was listening to a game from another room, it dawned on me that I was waiting for a commercial. My mind had been trained to expect a "break" in programming every 10 minutes or so. A break in programming "allows" the viewer the opportunity to get up from the couch and go do something he or she had been thinking about before or during the program. It is the hallway pass, the intermission. But, in the true spirit of soccer and British television, there were no commercials on the World Cup. The viewer was forced to focus for the entirety of the game. This, I am convinced, is one of the reasons soccer has never been fully supported as a televised sport in the United States—with its anti-break structure, it doesn't leave sufficient room for commercialism.

This constant series of interruptions, this commercial mentality, has helped to spawn an ADD-like culture of people unable to focus for long stretches of time. I look around at my students, many of whom have iPod earpieces dangling from their necks and a Blue Tooth attached to their ear. They have elevated multitasking to the level of an art. Their attention is fragmented, a reflection of the on-the-go culture we've become accustomed to. Professors and preachers alike are now told to limit lecturing to no more than a 20-minute span, for this is apparently as long as the modern brain can focus. As Postman pointed out, the modern audience member could never have lasted through the 3-hour Lincoln/Douglass Debate.

TV Culture

Current FDA guidelines recommend 30-90 minutes of cardiovascular exercise a day to maintain a healthy sense of well-being. The vast majority of Americans, however, say they get almost no cardiovascular exercise at all—in the past week, most have had 0 to 1 day of exercise. The number one reason cited was a lack of time. Ironically, this is the same percentage of citizens who have been consuming screen time in the equivalent of seven hours per day, watching life instead of living it. As we saw in the earlier studies, it is the influence of advertising, and not necessarily the inertia, that makes TV watchers more overweight.

In the *Abolition of Man*, C.S. Lewis writes of the importance of stepping outside of one's "generational lens." When we read only the literature of our day, he posits, we get caught up in the minutia of the moment. When we read only of statistical percentages over the last 10 years, we begin to feel that the current social malaise—suicide, depression, road rage, drug abuse, weight gain, depression, laziness, legal drugs, illiterate college graduates, junk food addicts—is normal. But when we step outside of the "generational lens," we see a completely different picture. Educators of the 1950s were faced with the emotionally wrenching acts of disobedience such as gum chewing and talking out of turn. Today, as other authors have pointed out, the consequences of today's educators are considerably grimmer: rape, robbery, gang violence, and the list goes on.

As former *Washington Post* author Pete Hammil once noted, there are many remarkable similarities between a television addict and a drug addict: the unearned high, the vacant gaze, the powerlessness, the working of one's schedule around a particular "drug" need, and the behavioral changes, mood swings, dependence. Most importantly, both are supported by a culture that reinforces their dependence. Like a crack addict strung out with his addict "friends" in a hole-in-the-wall crack house, the television addict excitedly discusses plots and characters and marriages and divorces and adulterous relationships with like-minded addicts. A generation that has been formed, fashioned, shaped on the television is one that has a unique set of value systems, ideals, and a paradigm that often eschews reality.

Because of Third Person Syndrome (discussed in detail earlier in this text), there is often a denial of one's potential for influence, a resistance to the acknowledgement of potential socialization. People think that the rules and consequences apply to others, but not to the individual observer. This syndrome affects adults as well as children, and this, it seems is where the effects can be most deleterious. For example, nearly 65% of the adult population in America is overweight, yet only 1/3 of adults say they are personally overweight. Young children say that movies can be influential, but "only for babies." Imagine a whole segment of the adult population watching a show where married women are regularly engaged in extramarital affairs. Will their behavior eventually begin to mimic that of the celebrities they admire? Will they become numb to the consequences of their actions and so begin to seek out elicit relationships? Third Person Syndrome eradicates the humility needed to acknowledge and thus protect oneself from the deluge of media socialization.

Crude and Crass

A number of authors have observed that one of the results of media centrality is an increasingly crass culture. Instead of the respectful tones communicated in past years, today's Westerners speak to one another openly and unabashedly in rude ways that would have brought a scornful glance from community members just a few years back. It only takes a brief visit to a grocery store or one of the nation's theme parks to hear and see the rudeness of many children in the modern generation, who push and shove their way to the front of the line, begging for this toy or that snack, persisting in their discourteous, demanding displays until the weary parent finally gives in. These out-of-control kids are often carted around by out-of-touch parents who wink at the prospective monsters they are raising. If a lack of self-discipline is unattractive in a four year old, how much more menacing will it be in a 14 year old? These parents often dine with their offspring in front of the television set from which profanity and perversity flow at an alarming rate, blanketing the family in a snug cocoon that spins them wildly from silliness to coarseness to rudeness to smug complacency. The parents are then utterly mystified when their children display these same qualities in magnified quantities in public. In the absence of cause-and-effect programming, there is an absence of connection to the reality of if-then plausibility in real life just as there is in screen life.

Humor in mass media today seems to have lost its wit, its intellectual edge, and has settled instead on a baseline of pre-adolescent humor. Regardless of the age demographic targeted by the marketing campaign or the movie or the sitcom or the "reality" show, the jokes mainly center on sexual content and bodily functions. There is nothing witty or clever about the humor, no thought process required. Instead, it simply appeals to the desire for disconnect from reality—an incessant laugh track that rolls on in predictable waves from production to production to production.

A New Educational Venture

Meanwhile, in the midst of our national academic slump, it seems the public school system has taken the socialization message to heart by venturing into a new land of questionable quagmires with opportunities that allow schools to promote preteen promiscuity. The American Center for Law and Justice (ACLJ) organization reported in 2007 that middle schools in Portland, Maine voted overwhelmingly to begin distributing prescription birth control pills and patches to students in grades 6 to 8—students as young as 11 years old! The students were free to obtain these contraceptives even without their parents' permission—despite the fact that the law in Maine prohibits anyone from engaging in sexual relations with a person under the age of 14 (ACLJ 2007).

Since the vast majority of these children are watching sexualized content on television and in movies as well as hearing songs promoting a lust for intimacy over their school intercom system every day, it is not surprising that they would seek entrance into the adult world of "romance" themselves, as developmentally unnatural as that desire would normally be at this stage of life. They have been socialized by their "superpeers," as UNC Chapel Hill researchers explained the phenomenon. It is surprising and saddening, however, that school officials would not only permit but also promote such behavior.

Another parent told me she had been "voted" into a specialized club at her daughter's high school, where her daughter's male friends had decided the mom was worthy of sexual conquest, a MILF, as the sordid acronym explained. I tried to imagine the terribly conflicting images and messages that must have been running through the poor daughter's mind as her mother was chosen as a sexual interest by the daughter's peers. The perverseness of the concept notwithstanding, inherent in these cultural base points are messages of personal unworthiness, of familial destruction, of boundary-crossing at its most extreme. This is the unfortunate fare of the lewd and ludicrous behaviors of Hollywood. This crassness and oversexualization of the modern culture is no secret, except to those who have denied the oncoming reality since the 1970s, to those who refuse to believe that the values-free era of the 1960s and 70s has ushered in a culture that epitomizes freedom from restraint of any sort. What messages about relationships and love and honor and integrity are being sent and received by America's children?

Another parent told me of a shocking revelation she had made about a party her daughter was invited to attend. The daughter, a 15-year old student at a public school in California, was invited to attend a "rainbow party" with her friends from school. After asking enough questions of enough people, the parent was finally able to discover the definition of the term (before the child's attendance, fortunately!) and learn exactly what a rainbow party really entailed. It certainly had nothing to do with prancing ponies or leaping leprechauns. Instead, the teenage *rainbow party* consists of a number of young female party attendees wearing different colored lipstick, who, while the lights are turned off, engage in oral sex with the young men at the party. When the lights are turned back on, the party goers try to guess whose lipstick "rainbow" was left behind on the young man's genitals.

Shocked? I certainly hope so. This is quite a leap from "spin the bottle," which of course had its own set of challenges, but let's not forget that these young people carry within them a socialized mindset about sexual intimacy; after all, a former leader of the country stood before the American people and denied his involvement in an extramarital affair—based on his definition of the type of intimacy he was engaged in.

Rainbow parties are taking place all over the country, teaching young people that sexual intimacy with multiple partners is just a game, one that will bear no consequences on their present life, and no negative ramifications on their future. But the sad truth, of course, is that every young girl who gives away her body in a social exchange such as this one gives away part of herself. She will live with a sense of fragmentation, experiencing great difficulty attaching in a true love relationship later in life. Every young man who takes selfish advantage of a young girl in this manner will bear equally compelling ramifications in later relationships. May our shock at these trends propel us out of complacency and into action!

The Rise of the "Prostitot"

I recently visited the home of an acquaintance who had a prepubescent daughter. Plastered all over the young girl's wall were pictures of female singers wearing sassy, come-hither expressions, pushing the fare of romantic love and sexual relationships. I stood in the doorway in shock for a moment, wondering what on earth could be going through a mom's mind when she stood in line to purchase this prepubescent propaganda. The answer, I suppose, is nothing. Mom couldn't have possibly been thinking, or at least she couldn't have been thinking clearly. What parent in his or her right mind would be pushing a daughter barely in double digits toward such a sexualized view of the world? Well, to answer bluntly, the parent who is blinded to the hazards of media socialization, or, perhaps, the parent who is living out her own emptiness through a tragic and selfish style of vicarious existence. That parent has put the OK stamp on the behavior.

So, the little girl heads out to school wearing shorts that fall two inches below her underwear, and she hangs out with the boys at lunch instead of the girls. How likely is it that she will be sexually involved and/or sexually infected within a few years? It's highly likely. At the time of press, nearly 60 percent of girls in the US who are over the age of 14 have tested positive for a sexually transmitted infection—yes, 60 percent. Doctors from the Indiana University School of Medicine in Indianapolis and colleagues weren't surprised by these findings: "It was something that we sort of expected to find based on the incidence of other sexually transmitted infections in this population," one doctor told Reuters Health (Reuters 2006). Doctors may not be surprised, but if you are a parent, I hope you are both surprised and shaken by these findings.

One LA writer addressed the social trend toward oversexualization head-on by calling parents to account for why their children were dressing as "prostitots": mini-versions of seductive adults. The author questions the ultimate end of these decisions to dress young children in such revealing adult clothing, whether the kids are tweens or just-out-of-diapers-tots.

What are these parents encouraging in terms of behavior? In terms of self-worth? In terms of identity? This question parallels Postman's address of the "adultified" child: the barriers that once separated adults from children have been razed. The lines are blurred. When children dress like adults and watch programming for adults and have conversations like adults and attend parties with extraordinarily questionable "adult" themes, there is simply not enough of a deep well of either character or logic or self-control for most children to draw upon to protect themselves from themselves. If a parent abandons the throne of parental responsibility, whether through negligence or ignorance, the child has few protective resources left at his disposal.

The Evolution of Conspicuous Consumption

Thorstein Veblen, an American sociologist at the end of the nineteenth century, coined the term "conspicuous consumption" to describe the behavior of someone who was "living large" for the impress of others (Burke, 2005 p. 66). He believed that the economic behavior of the elite, or 'leisure class' was irrational and wasteful, motivated by undercurrents of emulation. Certainly, wastefulness categorizes the recent history of Americana, from the waste of time (7 gratuitous hours of media use a day) to the waste of food (a University of Arizona study tracked $75 billion in US food waste each year), and, it could be argued, money—given the propensity toward conspicuous consumption that is now so tragically evidenced in the crash of the housing market. Burke (2005) adds that "conspicuous consumption is (a) strategy for a social group to show itself superior to another." This principle may be seen in operation on shows like *Cribs*, where Hollywood elites show just how much money they are capable of wasting on useless furniture and toys. But the elitism stirs up the desire for emulation, as we learned in the EE segment. So viewers want what their "idols" have—and will often go to great lengths to obtain it. In today's tumultuous economy, an interesting (though likely temporal) shift has taken place: the elite are being careful to maintain a superficial balance between elitism and realism, for alienating fans through flamboyant financial upstaging is simply not in vogue at the moment.

The Sad Deduction: Cultural Reproduction

Cultural reproduction refers to the "tendency of society...to reproduce itself by inculcating in the rising generation the values of the past" (Bourdieu and Althusser 1970). Traditions do not persist automatically, out of 'inertia,' as historians sometimes put it, but they are instead "transmitted as the result of a good deal of hard work by parents, teachers, priests, employers and other agents of socialization" (Burke 2005, p. 67). Today's cultural reproduction is not being driven by parents or priests but instead by media, peers, and educators (after all, the vast majority of children in the United States spend more time with their peers, teachers, and TVs than they do with their parents).

In speaking of understanding cultures, Burke says there is a "need to take symbols seriously, to recognize their power in mobilizing support." Drawing together Singhal's theory with this concept, we see a tendency toward subconscious socialization. Periphery is partly a matter of psychology, not just geography; it's a form of consciousness. "Provincials" often feel inferior, suffering from what Australia (1958) called the Cultural Cringe. "They believe that their knowledge is out-of-date, just as their clothes are out of fashion." This is similar to today's insecurities, a nation of insecure people who wear an outward bravado but believe inwardly that everything they do is less than good enough. Could this social stigma be birthed of a diet of 10,000 commercials a year? What does a commercial do? It tells us that we aren't enough: not pretty enough, not handsome enough, not tall enough, not smart enough, not well-dressed enough, not endowed with a cool enough car or house or boat or bank account.

Commercial people aren't real people; they are perfect people—an elite class created to illuminate the sharp differences between your life and theirs. The latest Old Navy commercial displays eight stick figures dancing around in sheer joy over their exciting new skirts. In a perfect representation of the microcosm of culture, the stick figures would swell to represent 6.4 heavy people, some of whom would not have perfect teeth, and another 4 that would range from high BMI to anorexic. But this is not the case for most advertisers, for the role of commercials is to keep us all on the periphery. Otherwise, why would we be interested in joining the club? If the leaders were just like us, what would be the persuasive power, the sway?

We noted earlier that our paradigm is shaped by the company we keep. I once heard one Hollywood elite congratulate another Hollywood elite on his long marriage—of five years. "Five years," I thought to myself, "is still the honeymoon phase." I thought of the relational fortitude exhibited by friends who had been married 30 years, and of my own marriage of 19 years. But this person lived in a fast-paced world of constant seduction, where the turnover rate of marriage is as frequent as the burgers being flipped at her local In 'N Out. To her, five years was a long time. Her standard was different. And it was her influence, the company she kept, that created those standards for her. In her mind, a marriage was to be "endured," and this remarkable man had endured for an impressively long span of time—of five whole years. After all, televised lifestyles don't show the dailyness of daily life. Daily life, with its occasional drudgery, is not good TV fare. TV fare is built on hyperemotionalism. And this diet of constant imagery and emotion, with nary a nod to logic or critical thinking, can do little more than paralyze one's capacity for rationale thought. The heavy dose of conflict and sensationalism in the news provides the model, the necessary underpinnings for constant conflict and stress in the home. And when people do experience a conflict, they expect it to be neatly tied up in 30 minutes, or worse, 30 seconds. That's the TV way, after all. There are very few realistic cause-and-effect relationships on television. Why, then, should it surprise us that children and teens are engaging in increasingly risky behaviors and not imaging the possibility of consequences?

Piaget noted that the child's world is one of egocentrism, of self-centeredness in thought and word. What he called autistic thought, or undirected thought, is "not adapted to reality, but creates for itself a dream world of imagination; it tends, not to establish truths, but to satisfy desires (p. 16). It is a world run "chiefly by images, and in order to express itself, has recourse to indirect methods, evoking by means of symbols and myths the feeling by which it is led" (p. 16). In the same way, today's young adults often seem arrested in this stage of half-development. The PBS documentary *The Making of Cool* calls them "mooks" and "midriffs," social chameleons mesmerized and hypnotized by the image of cool.

Further, Piaget said that children lacked introspective abilities (p. 24), said 44-47% of a preschool child's talk is egocentric (26), and the egocentric child, he says, does not communicate, for there is no true exchange of messages, only parallel play. I cannot help but think of the newness of the virtual world and its impact on social depth and narcissism, how it has created a world where people, especially the Internet Generation, seem to have lost their grip on social skills and appropriate levels of disclosure, where they are simply spinning out filament into the air (to cite Wordsworth's poetic reference) hoping that some ethereal concept, some gossamer thread, will cling somehow to someone, and a "connection" will be forged. The young have grown less capable at the subtle arts of listening, turn-taking, and nonverbal communication in general. The rapidity with which they seem to develop "true friends" online fosters a surge of disturbing behaviors, such as disclosing personal information far more readily than is deemed healthy for the relationship. If "speech is an expression of that process of becoming aware" (Vygotsky, p. 30), then learning how and when and why and when to speak is a vital component of that process-and a vital component to our own health as individuals and as a culture.

TV Kid Culture

"TV Kids" are easy to spot. If you visit the home of a TV kid, you will not be acknowledged. They eyes of the viewer are glued to something far more important than the presence of an actual, real person; they are glued to the view of an illusion, a pseudo person whom they no doubt admire. If you are the parent of a TV kid, you may be unaware of these prevailing TV kid traits, or perhaps you have been a TV adult, and until this moment, you were unaware of the multigenerational, anti-social traits being transmitted right under your roof. But if you happen to recognize your child's behavior (or your own) in any of these statements or characteristics, you may want to consider the media diet of your family. The intake levels may in fact be toxic.

The most common vernacular for a TV kid is "I'm bored" or "I want." They are rarely satisfied unless their lives are moving 60 miles an hour, like an action movie. And unless they are the star of said action movie, getting all the perks they desire along the way, they are equally dissatisfied. TV kids must be constantly entertained. Never tell a TV kid to enjoy "looking out the window at the scenery" on a long road trip, as many of us were forced to do when we were children. Oh, no! The natural surroundings have nothing to offer the TV kid. He wants action-packed entertainment, and he wants it now. His teachers had better be funny. His preacher had better be armed with a good joke or two (or ten). Otherwise, the TV kid will be checking out in search of something that will captivate his attention and transport him out of this dim world of reality.

The TV kid has been targeted by upwards of 30,000 commercial advertisements every year of his life. Little wonder that he is a selfish, blubbering blob of materialism, consumerism, and emotionalism. And what will become of these Veruca Salts and Violet Beaureguards, these Mike Tevees and Augustus Gloops? The truth is that bratty kids don't just round out on their own. They become bratty teens who become bratty, self-seeking adults. And honestly, don't we have enough of those gracing the planet already?

If I discover that my child gets sick from eating a certain food, what kind of parent would I be if I did not moderate his consumption of that food? Responsible parents do not allow their children to persist in harmful practices. And yet, many parents are blinded to the importance of their role in the formation process. The parents of a 12 year old told me recently that they didn't want to influence their daughter's thinking too much, as they wanted to allow her the freedom to make her own good choices. They said they wanted her decisions to stem from her own desire to do right, not from the mandates of the parents. At 18, this might be an effective strategy. At 12, it is nonsense. The 12-year-old brain lacks the full recourse of balance between logic and emotion. The 12 year old is still a child in training to be an adult. She is not an adult or even a young adult. She needs parental guidance, direction, oversight, influence. If she jumps from the nest at 12, she will more than likely break a wing.

Psychologists define *addiction* as a repeating behavioral pattern of harmful activity that the addict finds difficult to stop. In other words, the litmus test of addictive behavior is the inability to change or cease in that behavior. Given this definition, I do not believe it is too strong a phrase to say that we are a nation of TV addicts. When I talk to most people about the subject of viewing cessation, they experience the same physiological responses as that of a nicotine or crack addict: Sweaty palms, racing heartbeat, panic. They laugh nervously. "But what else would I do with my time?" they wonder aloud with a visible sense of dread. That question will be answered in the final chapter. For now, let's take a moment to consider our own individual responses to the question.

Perhaps the gentle reader would be surprised to learn just what it takes to make a "couch potato." Eight hours a day? Five?

No—just two. Anyone watching more than two hours of television a day is considered a couch potato by national standards. And, statistically, that's the vast majority of the culture. We will talk about the habit-breaking strategies in the last few chapters, but if you can't go *cold turkey* yet, at least consider reducing the hours of use. Cut back from that pack a day down to two a day, to follow a smoking metaphor. And then mark the behavioral changes. Mark the physical changes. Mark the emotional and relational changes. All of these fall under the insidious realm of influence.

If we turn a blind eye to the scale, the likelihood of weight gain is virtually imminent. If we ignore our checking account balances and continue to write check after check, impending doom will fall upon our finances. Likewise, if we continue consuming the same media messages day after day without giving thought to their purpose, their philosophy, or their power, we will drown in the deluge of media centrality.

Predictions of the Past

In 1953, a young author named Ray Bradbury began looking around at his world, piecing together in a fiction story the trajectories for the social changes that were beginning to be unleashed in the oh-so-idyllic era of the 1950s. At the time of his writing, people yawned at the book. But as the changes he predicted began germinating in the culture at large, people began to take notice. Forty and fifty years after Bradbury wrote *Fahrenheit 451*, teachers began adding it to their booklists. Sales began to rise. Why? Because of the eerie accuracy with which he was able to predict the trajectory of two generations of public change. Bradbury described a world where the main goal of U.S. citizens was happiness. He wrote of a world where entertainment was king, where people spent long hours with their television "family" in the parlor, a room designated to television viewing, with screens so large they took up the entire wall (just imagine that!). The firemen were the "thought" police, regulating intake and keeping people "happy" by destroying any thought-provoking materials, namely books and magazines that might cause people to think or question or analyze (and thus become unhappy).

Bradbury's book made a number of striking predictions whose oddities are heightened by the fact that he saw them before they came to be. Most of us wouldn't blink twice at the thought of a TV the size of a wall today. Most wouldn't shudder at someone eating dinner with the TV or knowing all the names of characters on a show (as well as their favorite colors, songs, and other useless trivia about their real or imagined lives). Most wouldn't be shocked that a viewer had memorized the times a show came on or had scheduled events around the viewing of a show (if that person were unable to prerecord, of course), but these were all completely foreign concepts at the time of his writing.

Bradbury's characters wore "seashells," tiny electronic devices that fit snugly into the ear to provide constant mobile entertainment to the listener—and shut out the annoying realities of human interaction and personal introspection. Fast-forward to today: In school hallways, at bus stops, in cars, in bedrooms, children and adults alike are found wandering vacuously from place to place, eschewing interpersonal interaction in exchange for personalized entertainment, whether it's that modern "seashell" (the iPod) or its not-so-distant cousin the cell phone.

In Bradbury's world, the lack of literacy led to the nation's downfall. The characters stopped caring about reality, choosing to live in the cocooned comfort of a fantasy realm instead. In modern culture, TV has become a mainstay, a virtual best friend, in the American household. Though psychologists warn that TV can cause stress and depression in children as they are "groomed for a lifetime of consumerism" which breeds in them "anxiety, increasingly lower satisfaction with themselves and their lives, and poorer relationships with others," still Americans tune in daily (Scanlon 2007). Though psychologists are urging parents to consider who is "forming" their children (Scanlon 2007), parents continue to take the advice with a pinch of salt. And though UK psychologists have even found that "excessive television viewing by children under three can lead to problems with mathematic ability, reading and comprehension in later childhood," (Guardian 2007) parents are either uneducated about the need for change or unmotivated to make a change.

Then there are corporate conundrums to contend with as well: Though pediatricians say that children under the age of two should not watch any television at all, there are entire venues devoted to baby viewing. It's the ultimate trans-fat metaphor: valueless, devoid of nutrients, potentially harmful in the long run. As Stephen Covey so wisely puts it in his book *Living the Habits*, kids are like water, which manifests itself in its various possible states of liquid, ice, or vapor depending on the pressure and temperature surrounding it (p. 66). Perhaps we all resemble H20 in some ways. Who among us has not felt ourselves soar under the guidance of a teacher or coach who seemed to care or believe in us? Who among us has not had those relationships that seem to "bring out the worst" in us?

Without a doubt, we are products of our sociological environment. As we find ourselves hurtling away from orality, away from literacy, and into the new realm of visuality, these discoveries will help us navigate the ship through stormy seas. Postman says we need to ask some questions, and we need to ask them now. In what ways is new media altering our ways of learning, our conception of reality, our definition of happiness, and our conception of God (p. 19)? Postman proposes an overhaul of the entire educational system, with a renewed focus on history, specifically the history of technology in both its science and its art, and the addition of religious study. Let us make every effort to ensure that his dreams do not die here on the printed page.

If I pick up an apple, I am aware that it may have been exposed to one of two types of contaminants: external and systemic. I can wash off the external pesticides, but the internal pesticides, the systemic ones, are present throughout the entire fruit. They cannot be systematically separated from the apple itself. In the same way, individuals are systemically imbedded within the context of a society. Whatever the child's upbringing, parental influence and participation, social challenges, mental and emotional wellbeing or lack thereof, these basic foundations affect and indeed are resident within the individual. So, the question of formation from childhood becomes a very important one: The role of the parent and the system of education and socio-cultural forces—these all become vital considerations for those who wish to help facilitate positive social transformations.

What are the current systemic values of society, how are these being inculcated, and what are they producing in the system as a whole? Certainly, given our standing in the timeline, we must admit that having been lured away to some degree by half truths is within the realm of possibility. Despite Americans' propensity for Third-Person Syndrome and its resultant functional blindness, it would be difficult for even the most ardent media addict to deny the medium's impact on our social and even physical worlds. The question is not whether or not we are being influenced. The question is how much are we being influenced, and whose values are shaping our conscious and subconscious choices.

How does a culture steeped in visuality live? It runs up credit cards, seeks cosmetic surgical alterations, and buys houses it can't afford, sending ripples of panic throughout financial institutions across the globe. In fact, in the great state of plastic, home of Hollywood hype and hyberbole, the numbers on these three superficiality indicators are through the roof: Credit card debt is skyrocketing, cosmetic surgery was the number one requested *high school* graduation present in 2006, and home foreclosure rates (many of which are linked to people buying homes well outside the family budget) are some of the most dramatic in the region. But it doesn't stop there. This year's headline stories reflect the decline of Western physiological, emotional, and intellectual wellbeing. The Associated Press says Americans are clinging desperately to the 42nd rung of the ladder of physical health, with the lowest life-expectancy rates in 20 years. *US News and World Report* says our brain power may be sinking even faster than our muscle power. In 1995, US students ranked at the bottom of the world hierarchy in math and science, beating only two other countries participating in the global contest of wits (or lack thereof): Cyprus and South

Africa. And in 2006, *Newsweek*'s stinging study revealed that 50% of our nation's four-year college *graduates* and 75% of its two-year college grads cannot read or compute mathematically at the college level.

Postman speaks of the grim future possibility that mankind would one day come to love oppression, to "adore the technologies that undo their capacity to think." Given its date of his writings—in the pre-AIDS, pre-Columbine, pre-toilet seat covers, pre-9-year-olds-getting-vaccinated-for-STIs 1980s, there is an eerie sense of alarm to his quotation. When we watch the news or listen to a broadcast on the radio, what we are listening to is actually someone else's opinion and interpretation, for it is the human voice that infuses these words with "deeper shades of meaning," as poet and author Maya Angelou once put it. It is only when I read the words for myself—reader to reading—that my own intellect can dissect and digest it. No one puts it in more piercingly poetic fashion than Postman:

> A written sentence calls upon its author to say something...the reader must come armed, in a serious state of intellectual readiness. This is not easy because he comes to the text alone. In reading, one's responses are isolated, one's intellect thrown back on its own resources. To be confronted by the cold abstractions of printed sentences is to look upon language bare, without the assistance of beauty or community. (50)

As Cassini so succinctly observed, modern society has become so cocooned within the world of media that man can no longer "see or know anything except by the interposition of (an) artificial medium"(Postman, p. 10). In other words, we are ill-equipped for the task of having to judge it and weigh its worth with the scales of our own intellect. Without the wildly clapping audience and the deafening laugh track, we lack the capacity for appropriate response. Furthermore, with our modern propensity for entertainment indulgence, from car TVs for the kids to iPods for the teens to iPhones for the parents, we find ourselves in a position of sensory overload. And undoubtedly, this never-ending drive for never-ending entertainment is going to have consequences—in the home, in the classroom, in the workplace. It is my position, and the position of many other researchers and authors, that we are training the human brain to crave something that it was never built to handle: constant stimulation. As Postman puts it, the rapid decline of print and the corresponding rise of televised entertainment is causing us to grow "sillier by the minute" (p. 24). In fact, Postman says, perhaps silly is too benign a word. This media shift has created a discourse of "dangerous nonsense" (p. 16).

In the early years of our nation's history, intelligent men found themselves pressed between the rocks of compromise and conviction. The North and South tried endlessly to comfort the growing national distress through a series of weak-kneed compromises, adding slave state and free in an attempt to balance the desires of men; meanwhile tensions mounted, with blows breaking out in the very Senate Chamber (Boorstin 1987, p. 170). Compromise was not enough. The bloodshed and hatred continued until one man was willing to stand up for what was right: Though the Civil War would be the bloodiest war in the entire 19th Century, with over 600,000 dead (p. 175), it was the proverbial line in the sand that drew a nation together in a firm stance of equality. It took one man to stand up beyond the spirit of compromise and label slavery for the exploitative practice that it was. Abraham Lincoln became the voice of freedom, and even though he is long gone, there are voices today that echo his call to arms, his unwillingness to compromise, his desire that all men would be free. That hope remains.

As Postman puts it in *Technopoly*, "The effects of technology are always unpredictable. But they are not always inevitable" (p. 24). We must begin a serious conversation on the issue of media-centrality and its effects on our lives. We must begin to teach the next generation how to argue and how to think critically; otherwise, there will not only be no movement toward change, but there will be no *desire* for it. If we fail to hearken the call of wisdom, embracing instead the continuous summons of the media siren, we will be left with a skewed paradigm. Our lives and hearts will be entirely focused on trivia, on fantasy, while we are blinded to the real world with real people and real needs. As we are drawn deeper and deeper into the maddening myopia of media-centrality, we lose our focus, our sense of direction, our awareness of reality. As Edmund Burke once said, all that is necessary for evil to prevail is for good men to do nothing. The next chapter brings to light one of the most serious ramifications of media-centrality, one with such far-reaching implications as to render it worthy of a chapter all to itself. We are swift becoming a nation of illiterate masses.

EMERGE!

CHAPTER ELEVEN

Land of the Lost Literacy

In the 15 years that I have worked as an educator, I would say without hesitation that my best students are almost invariably the strongest readers. I find that there are fewer and fewer of them as the years progress, but inevitably, my strongest, most well-versed, academically superior students are those who read books. It is a struggle to get many of my students to read now ("Professor Dunne, do I *really* need to buy the textbook for this class?"), but there are occasional exceptions. I had a student recently who became smitten with the lost art of reading during a power outage. The power had gone off at her house over the weekend, and she was supposed to be finishing a book for a class project. The student was overcome with frustration, and having no idea what to do with her preteen children during a power outage, she lit some candles and got out the book she had been assigned to read. Tentatively at first, because as she said, "They love TV," she began to read aloud to her children. To her amazement, her children sat silently for an hour as she read aloud from a 19th century literature book, reveling, no doubt, in both the time with mom and the opportunity to awaken their imaginative powers. "I'm a reader now," she said to me later. "I'm sold on it."

One of the tragic effects of media centrality has been the drop in literacy rates and literacy usage at the national level. The average US child today spends 7 *minutes* a day in silent reading versus 7 *hours* a day in screen time, in front of a computer or television, where reality is interpreted for her. The movie *Walle* portrays the trajectory of this future life best—a world of overstimulated, oversaturated, overweight adults who live passive lives devoid of any connection to reality. If the train keeps speeding down that track, we too may be increasingly incompetent and utterly immobile in a few short decades.

In the insightful book *Orality and Literacy*, Ong says that in this time of radical change, "modes and categories inherited from the past...no longer seem to fit the reality experienced by a new generation." These words have a striking poignancy today, for as we launch into another successive generation, we see ourselves poised at the dawn of yet another era. The transference is completing its cycle: We have moved from orality to literacy and now to the new monster: visuality, an image-central culture where the package matters more than the product in every realm from dish soap to delegates. The shift in mentality is heaving a sigh of exasperation, as we leave behind once again the complexities of organized literate thought and enter the dark ages of a newfound hieroglyphic illiteracy.

Through the analysis of such linguistic components as phonemics (the manner in which language is nested in sound) and the grapholect ("a transdialectal language formed by deep commitment to writing"), Ong shows how literacy offers a power far exceeding that of any purely oral dialect. Modernists would cast off this latent power in exchange for the leisure of being read to, of having someone else do the interpretation. However, as Maya Angelou once observed in her tribute to "Sister Flowers," it is the human voice that infuses words with the "deeper shades of meaning."

In our case, we have grown tragically contented to allow ourselves the vacancy of thought processes-to function, as we do in so many areas of modern life, on auto pilot. After all, as Ong points out, the grapholect of Standard English has a vocabulary of no less than a million and a half words, whereas an oral culture can retain only a few thousand words, "and its users will have virtually no knowledge of the real semantic history of any of these words."

What a striking resemblance this bears to our own culture of literate illiteracy! As an educator, I have witnessed the surreptitious decline of the intellect—paralleled with the maddening rise of knowledge concerning all things trite and Hollywood. It is said that the average vocabulary of today's adult mirrors that of a 14-year-old boy in 1940s America. As mentioned earlier, *Newsweek*'s 2006 study of the drastic educational decline facing the US is a case in point: 50% of four-year-college grads and 75% of two-year-college grads in our country today cannot read at the college level!

"Literacy," says Ong, "consumes its own oral antecedents, and, unless it is carefully monitored, even destroys their memory" (15). A point of interest here is the fluidity of the Internet, with its odd cross-breeding of ubiquity, anonymity, and changeability. It is a chameleon in the true sense of the word. When I began hearing from text book publishers that we teachers might soon wish to leave behind our books for the more "convenient" format of online texts, I did not leap for joy. Already, it seems college texts are beginning to cross the bridge into online oblivion; it seems that nearly every textbook I've taught from in the last year is now offering a companion CD for students, and in some cases, like that of a recent public speaking textbook I reviewed, the true text is "complemented" by an oral reading of the entirety of the text on CD—presumably in the event that the college population it addresses is unable to read. Given the statistics mentioned earlier, national illiteracy is not a farfetched concept. But there is a point not to be missed: College textbook publishers should necessarily be in the business of preserving readership, not undermining it.

Textbook companies, however, are a symptom of a much bigger problem, one that illuminates the fluid culture of orality and visuality. As part of their blend-in-to-make-money appeal, textbook publishers have recently found themselves in the business of rewriting history, of marketing fiction as fact. I refer specifically here to the disappearance of Christ. In the mid 1990s, academic authors introduced a fascinating change in terminology. According to the *Washington Times*, the terms BC and AD have now been "shunned by certain scholars," who have decided to rename BC's

"Before Christ" as "Before the Common Era" and ADs "anno Domini" (Latin for "in the year of our Lord") to "Common Era." Despite objections from the global intellectual community, the US team decided to proceed with the change. Now, virtually all US textbooks explain the division of eras as centering on time instead of personage. According to Peter Daniels, a linguist from Cornell University and the University of Chicago, CE and BCE terms are used not only in textbooks, but they are also found in materials published by the College Board, the National Geographic Society, The United States Naval Observatory, and the Smithsonian Institution to name a few.

Essentially, the challenge was this. Textbook publishers wanted to make money, and they feared that noting the calendar's central figure as the center of the historical timeline was akin to acknowledging both his existence and his deity. This made secular historians very uncomfortable. As we have noted in the context of non-literate cultures, it is the practice of such cultures to rewrite any historical events which are in any way discomforting to one's current view. Modernity rules, and history is, apparently, history.

But the change was not universally supported. In fact, at the time of the change, a number of voices from both the UK and the US spoke out against it. According to the *New York Times*, the use of BCE in Australia prompted protestations in 2005, with individuals appealing to the chambers of the State Parliament, where "the State Education Minister stated in Parliament saying that the change should not have been made" (NYT 2005). In 2002, BCE/s introduction into the English National Curriculum resulted in a flurry of letters. In Canada, complaints were printed in the national press. According to the *Washington Times*, Candace de Russy, trustee for the State University of New York, said that the change in language is more than just a "mere verbal tweaking"; instead, she saw it as a "concerted attack on the religious foundation of our social and political order." In the same article, the director of the American Textbook Council and president of the Center for Education Studies, Gilbert Sewall, was quoted as saying he found the change "distressing" and that it could pave the way for other modern social movements to rewrite history for the sake of their own cause. According to the *Times*, "most major textbooks" have now adopted the terminology.

In a 2005 article in the Phi Delta Kappan, Sewell explains that textbook publishing is a lucrative business which often focuses on quantity instead of quality. The four main companies that own the "elhi" (elementary and high school) textbook terrain in the United States are subject to the whims of every interest group with an active lobby. This, says Sewell, who holds a Ph.D. from Harvard, is resulting in whitewashed literature that has been bleached of its historic stains and controversies:

> The four major educational publishers are no longer confident about how to represent the nation, its civic ideals, or the world. Nor are they interested in deciding how to do so. They are willing to leave content to standards committees and focus groups. But they are deeply interested in selling instructional materials, and, after the history wars of the 1990s, they are warier than ever of content disputes. Without concern for consequences—or perhaps deluded into thinking that their revisions constitute a thematic correction and a step forward—history textbook editors continue to give the nation's students a misshapen view of the global past and a false view of the global future.

This misguided aim, he says, has resulted in a number of potentially (and presently) damaging changes. Publishers, he says, are playing to the itching ears of schoolchildren:

> Textbook makers are adjusting to short attention spans and nonreaders. Too many children cannot—or do not want to—read. Nor are they eager to digest concrete facts or memorize events, principles, and concepts. Among editors, phrases such as "text-heavy," "information-loaded," "fact-based," and "nonvisual" are negatives. A picture, they insist, tells a story and takes the place of a thousand

words...Textbooks across the curriculum are being transformed into picture and activity books instead of clear, portable, simply designed, text-centered primers. Bright photographs, broken formats, and seductive colors overwhelm the text and confuse the page. Type is larger and looser, which results in many fewer words and much more white space per page. The text itself can get lost. And what text remains is dense and often unintelligible.

The challenge with this scholastic scenario is twofold. First, we have the sanitizing of history, the removal of any historical context that might offend or embarrass certain segment of society, as decided by the textbook editors. This does not teach us to think critically. Instead, it reduces history to a 30-minute sitcom with a happy ending. And these plastic alterations teach us nothing about truth and life and the reality of conquest. Second, we have the discomfiting practice of replacing text with images, further removing our non-literate culture from its literate potential. We give the people what they say they want. Textbooks have become the MSG of the national eatery. People crave the taste, so we happily dispense the goods, looking the other way when confronted with the statistics on forthcoming obesity and degenerative disease—or, in this case, illiteracy and ignorance.

Textbook inauthenticity is noted by other authors as well, including Harvard Ph.D. James Loewen, who writes extensively about the erroneous historical accounts proffered by the elhi textbook marketers. His book *Lies My Teacher Told Me* criticizes the one-dimensional accounts of history in the United States. On his homepage, Loewen notes his two-year stint at the Smithsonian Institute, where he dissected twelve leading high school history textbooks. The analysis left him with the feeling that our students our offered little more than what he calls "an embarrassing blend of bland optimism, blind nationalism, and plain misinformation."

Likewise, historian and author Howard Zinn says that textbooks have focused on the view of the establishment instead of the common man or woman. In a 1998 interview, Zinn said that he hoped to achieve a "quiet revolution" with his book *A People's History*, "...not a revolution in the classical sense of a seizure of power, but rather from people beginning to take power from within the institutions."

Whatever one's religious viewpoint, it is difficult to deny conscientiously that history is being rewritten. Instead of embracing religious figures, as we claim to do through cultural diversity, we continue to bury their names, eradicating from the annals their messages and memories. Though the reasons for such behavior may be complex, the act itself is simple and easily verifiable. It is rumored that America remains a democracy, but I simply cannot recall having the opportunity to vote on this change in the historical calendar, any more than I recall voting for the governor of California to prohibit the use of "Mom" and "Dad" from the school classroom (SB777 2007) in order to keep teachers from offending students from single-parent households.

Recently, I read that the most recent edition of the *Oxford Junior Dictionary* has dropped hundreds of "useless" words from its pages: Apparently, a number of words relating to monarchies (*emperor*, *duke*), Christianity (*sin*, *devil*), history (*decade*), and nature (*oyster*, *spaniel*) are simply not used enough to justify their continued presence in the dictionary. Instead, they have been replaced by the ubiquitous gems of *analog*, *blog*, *celebrity*, and *chatroom* (Drake 2009). With such alterations, we make history fluid. We make value judgments about the past. In a non-literate culture, history is remembered only in the manner that it serves our present reality well.

Earlier this year, my family and I were visiting one of our state's many rich historical sites. As we stood in line to await the next segment of information from our tour guide, a member of the audience asked a question pertaining to a large book in the back of the room. The tour guide explained that it was a book of religious reference, similar to a Bible. A little girl standing behind me grabbed her father's arm and asked aloud, "Daddy, what is a Bible?" The man laughed nervously and looked around as if to see what the onlookers were thinking of him, expecting of him.

"You really don't know what a Bible is?" he asked with tempered incredulity. She shook her head. "It's, well," he looked around at all of us again. "I'll explain it later." The room was quiet. The irony was palpable. So many conflicting thoughts ran through my head at that moment that I'm ashamed to say that I said nothing. Here we stood on the grounds of a historic site, and this seemingly knowledgeable and literate man, who had been answering trivia questions and pointing out artifacts throughout the tour, had failed to discuss with his daughter, even from an academic standpoint, the most historically-accurate, best-preserved piece of ancient literature in the history of the world. I sincerely hope he went home and explained to her the richness of the history, the mysteries, the worlds that were shaped within the pages of those 66 books. I hope he did, but I cannot say that I have great faith that he did. As in many modern households, it seemed that religious writings had been moved to the periphery, replaced by cynical humor and meaningless trivia.

When the Pilgrims first came to America, one of their primary goals was maintaining the renowned standard of intellectual capacity for reasoning and analysis to both the present and future generations. They believed this intelligence was developed through the discipline of reading. In *Landmark History of the American People*, renown historian Daniel Boorstin says that the pilgrims' predominant rationale for launching Harvard University in 1636 was for the establishment of a literate colony that would continue to read, dissect, and teach the doctrine of the Bible to the rest of the country. The Pilgrims were one of the most literate populations on the planet at the time: 89-95% of the men and 62% of the women were able to read, whereas the mother England sported a literacy rate of only 40% (Postman 1985).

Today, the literacy rates have declined from that level rather dramatically. In the aforementioned *Newsweek* story, we became acquainted with the dismal state of the nation's college students (not to mention its less-educated populace). Let's break the numbers down even further: 50% of four-year college graduates and 75% of two-year college graduates could not read or compute at the basic college level, and, according to the 2006 US Census, the majority of US states boast a populace where 20%-30% hold a Bachelor's degree or higher. This means that, even on the generous side of 30% with college education, we have an enormous literacy problem on our hands. For the 70% of the population that hasn't darkened the hallways of a classroom, and the 50% of 4-year grads who did, reading comprehension is an unlikely offshoot.

Statistically, this means that the vast majority of the population is unable to conceptualize a text such as, say, the Bible. And, in fact, when I ask people who identify themselves as Christians if they have read the Bible, they almost always say, "Well, not all of it." When people can't understand, they don't read, and when they don't read, they can't understand. And thus the downward spiral begins. If our modern literacy rates are anywhere close to that of 17th Century England—40%—we must seriously consider the future implications of a materially wealthy but literarily impoverished people. I find the weight of this revelation staggering. Of the more than 6,000 languages in the world, 3,000 (roughly 400 million people) do not have a Bible in their language (Hathersmith 2002). Westerners have the privilege of information access, but it's combined with a lack of motivation, interest, and self-discipline.

When we contemplate the rapidity of this decline, the facts are even more staggering. The language of the great debates of Abraham Lincoln and Stephen Douglas, which took place only 150 years ago, would be challenging for most modernists to listen to, let alone write. In fact, just sitting through these 3-4 hour debates attentively would be a remarkable quest for our ADD culture. This era, as Postman points out, was the pinnacle of literary genius. Living at the time were Mark Twain, Emily Dickinson, Walt Whitman, Henry David Thoreau, Herman Melville, John Greenleaf Whittier, Henry Wadsworth Longfellow, Nathaniel Hawthorne, and Ralph Waldo Emerson. In Lincoln's day, intelligent citizens were inspired by intelligent leaders. Lincoln's lack of education did not keep him from being educated. Today, the vast majority of our leaders are known more for their gilded performances and sex appeal than their character or intelligence or societal contributions.

For those in our culture claiming religious affiliation, an inability to read and comprehend has serious implications. "In comparison with the citizens of other industrial nations," says Anthony Giddens (2006), London School of Economics professor, "Americans are unusually religious" (p. 330). The overwhelming majority "believe in God and claim they regularly pray" (p. 330). Given that each religious sect has a book of teachings to be followed, there are dramatic implications for a people of any religious affiliation who cannot or will not read the historical writings, the guidelines, of their own religious history. Let's take a look at Christianity, the majority religion in the United States. As Giddens says, there are some important implications of transformative potential within the Christian religion. For Christianity, as he puts it, has a "revolutionary aspect" that generates "a tension and an emotional dynamism essentially absent from the Eastern religions.... Whereas the religions of the East cultivate an attitude of passivity or acceptance within the believer, Christianity demands a constant struggle against sin and so can stimulate revolt against the existing order" (p. 326).

However, this beneficial upheaval, this progression toward growth and development, is dependent upon the carriage of the written word from one generation to the next. Can an illiterate mass sustain that demand? According to well-known religious pollster George Barna, the vast majority of Christians in the United States today have not read the Bible in its entirety, nor do they read it regularly. This stands in striking contrast to earlier generations, even in our own nation's history, where children read and analyzed and memorized scripture as part of the academic process. They were free to think and reason with history because they were granted the liberty of access to history. Such readings were not forbidden from view in the public sector then in the way they are now. Perhaps this lack of connection to the teachings of moral law is one reason that ethical challenges such as infidelity, gossip, greed, and divorce in the Christian culture largely mirror those in secular circles. Certainly, a generation that has not read the Bible would likely display a general lack of knowledge about biblical principles.

A logical choice for this comparison is the core system of values for the Judeo-Christian religions, The Ten Commandments, which of course played a leading role in the development of the American legal system. Despite their controversy in the public school classroom, they are nonetheless an important foundation to the mores and values of our nation. Postman makes a fascinating observation about the Decalogue, or Ten Commandments. As others have observed, TV offers conversation in images, not words. And, as Postman, says, "The forms of our media are rather like metaphors, working by unobtrusive but powerful implication to enforce their special definitions of reality (p. 10). He notes that the 2nd commandment brings an interesting address, "a strange injunction to include as part of an ethical system," unless, he says, the author knew something we didn't—that there is an innate connection between the "forms of human communication and the quality of a culture." Perhaps, as Postman suggests, "The God of the Jews was to exist in the Word and through the Word, an unprecedented conception requiring the highest order of abstract thinking" (p. 9). Let's look at a handful of these ten straightforward statements, these foundations for living in society, and see how Hollywood fares in "keeping the law." How do the values systems of our new virtual peers compare to our traditional religious heritage?

These ten ancient laws can be broken down into two categories, loving God and loving one's neighbor. The second law says that people "must not make for themselves an idol in the form of anything in heaven above or on the earth beneath or in the waters below." The five-year run of the popular show American Idol brought the term "idol" into the forefront of the American conscience. An idol is defined as something that one "bows down to," which, in essence means something a person reverences or worships. Another definition of worship is what one spends one's time contemplating, thinking about, talking about, what one is consumed with. As we discussed in the chapter on parasocial interaction, the constant presence, the blitzing of media personalities, serves to create a stronghold in the viewer's mind, an ever-present image of the "star" to be studied, discussed, obsessed over, emulated, worshipped.

The third commandment says that followers should not misuse the name of the Lord their God, for the Lord "will not hold anyone guiltless who misuses his name." The most common references to God, well over 94% of them, are associated with frustration or anger or "like OMG" Valleygirl-esque talk. They are not, primarily, references to calling on the name of God, they are examples of misuse, of using the name of God as a catchall phrase for frustration, anger, mock surprise, or defiance.

The fifth commandment is to honor one's father and mother. A few definitions of the word *honor* include showing great respect or admiration for someone, recognizing someone publically or elevating someone's status, paying tribute or public praise to someone, or giving prestige or dignity to someone in a public setting. Parents are not revered or even mildly respected by our virtual Hollywood peers. It is difficult to name three commercials or sitcoms or modern-day movies where a child is honoring his father or mother. Why? Because it's not considered "entertaining" to watch children behave. *Entertainment* has come to mean watching families who are so off the charts with their issues that viewers feel *normal* by comparison. The lower the standard, the better our chances are of looking good ourselves. Our virtual peers are mocking and despising their parents, not honoring them.

The sixth commandment is not to murder. As we covered in the media violence segment, murder is a commonplace theme in mainstream media. The swollen river of violence and disregard for human life has swept over the banks of the city streets and is pushing past adults and children alike with a fury. The massive consumption of violent media cannot be discounted for its impact on declining rates of empathy, on the rise of fear-based behaviors, or the paralleled rise of violence in culture in general. We cannot overlook the fact that the US "boasts" some of the highest homicide rates of any industrialized nation. The invocation to violent and murderous behavior is disseminated through a vast array of programming, from the 20 violent acts per hour in children's shows to the 92% violent content of cable programs.

The seventh commandment is not to commit adultery, that is, not to engage in sexual relations with someone who is not your spouse. Need we even run a tally for this overtly disregarded commandment? There are entire shows devoted to adultery today, broadcasting their siren song from morning till night. The vast majority of sexual relationships displayed on mass media are not between committed, married couples; they are between one-night stands and extramarital affairs, between teenagers and young adults unashamedly giving their bodies to one another in full public view. Though Ricky and Lucy weren't even allowed to be seen in the same bed together at the dawn of the television age, today, viewers are hard pressed to find anyone in Hollywood who *isn't* in bed with someone (or *everyone*) else. There are no social, physical, mental, or emotional consequences shown in these situations—just an abandonment of logic for the pursuit of pleasure. As we saw with the UNC Chapel Hill studies, watching (or listening to) this subject matter has a clear and direct effect on human behavior.

Lastly, commandment ten tells readers not to *covet*, that is, not to yearn for the possessions of someone else. The airwaves are bulging with shows that are intended to fuel the fire of jealousy and covetousness. Some shows promote unrealistic lifestyles of wealth and fame lived by people working in minimum-wage jobs, while others simply take viewers right in the doors of the "stars" to ooh and aah over the fruits that their hard labor (memorizing script lines) has earned them. The elite class, as Burke and others have noted, rules by proving itself better than its underlings, creating a system of covetous, greedy, obsessed followers.

Whatever our individual religious convictions may be, we can likely agree that the rules governing civil society have been and are continuously being undermined in the current media climate. This illumination begs the question of both personal and corporate responsibility. If we know our virtual peers are influencing antisocial, personally injurious behavior, will we persist in spending all of our time with them? If corporations are alerted to the fact that their real-life "buzz" is contributing to the declining psycho-social health of the citizens of this great country, will they persist in unscrupulously seducing the members of society, especially its youngest, most vulnerable members?

From Worrier to Warrior: Lessons from History

When speaking with historical experts through the years, I have asked about the era of oppression under the rule of Hitler, and how so many millions of people could have suffered so tragically without revolting, without fighting back, succumbing to the evil demands of the country's leadership. History experts and those who lived during the era all tell the same story: The Jews were manipulated by fear, convinced they weren't strong enough to fight back. The governing rulers oppressed the Jewish people to such a degree that they felt unable to retaliate, despite the fact that their basic human rights, and ultimately their lives, were taken away. The horror of the Holocaust is so dramatic that there has been a movement to forget it, to wipe it from the annals of history. But the history of the Holocaust carries within its heartrending pages some vital lessons.

The laws in the United States have transformed radically in the last 20 years, spiraling from parental control to social control. A cursory glance at the laws governing the educational system in our country yields some shocking discoveries at just how un-diverse and how intolerant our educational laws have become. The rules do not simply *omit* or overlook religious discussion, even discussion of the commandments that inspired our very Constitution; the rules go out of their way to be certain that the roots of faith are not winding their way into any heart or mind of any student in the public educational system. The education code does not say that a *variety* of religions will be introduced and overviewed (for that would be true diversity!) and it does not say that religion can be expressed and spoken of freely (for that, of course, would *tolerance*). Instead, the law expressly prohibits any religious education whatsoever.

At the time of this writing, there are a number of laws on the docket that seem intended to silence, intimidate, and even oppress those who would hold to a Judeo-Christian value system. If that oppression continues, if good men and women do not stand up for not only their own rights but for what is right, then we may find ourselves with another cultural tragedy on our hands.

There is a chilling parallel here to a beautiful story in historic Jewish literature. In the book of 2 Chronicles, Chapter 34, King Josiah had employed a group of men to rebuild the ruins of the temple. As the men worked along diligently, suddenly one man discovered a remarkable find—an ancient book that had been tucked away and forgotten by the previous generations, its guiding wisdom lost in the darkened rubble of the temple. When the book was brought to Josiah, there was a somber moment, still palpable in the historical accounts thousands of years later. When the words from the book were read aloud to King Josiah, he tore his robes, and cried aloud, saying, "Great is the Lord's anger that is poured out on us because our fathers...have not acted in accordance with all that is within this book." Josiah recognized that the decisive disconnect from the wisdom of the past had created an anchorless present. He and his generation were bearing the consequences for the folly of the previous generation. If we think we may not one day find ourselves in a similar fashion, disconnected from spiritual anchors and living in a world fraught with pain and suffering as a result of our forefathers burying the truth in a massive heap of minutia, we delude ourselves. Let us not be guilty of the same crime.

The War of Words

I once attended a marriage seminar taught by a gentle and joyful couple in their 70s. The woman mentioned a time early in their marriage, where she learned to be aware of her "competition" at her husband's place of work. In her story, she referred to a "young divorcee" who sat at the front desk, poised and "ready to strike." When she said the word "divorcee," there was a palpable sense of discomfort in the room, similar to what one might feel when someone says the word "retarded." We want to rush over and whisper in the speaker's ear, "We don't use that word anymore. Instead, we use a homogenized, more sanitized term that won't hurt people's feelings." We've been trained to shudder at words that carry stigmas for certain people groups, and it seemed *divorcee* had fallen into that category too. As we learned in the Values Clarification segment, removing the label from a group is a way of removing the value judgment from them.

Willful Illiteracy

As oral traditions replace written ones, we face a loss of context, a lack of connection to the historical foundations of the written word. In the illiterate eras of early England, the common man was unable to read the news of the day or the Bible, so he had to have it translated for him into sounds he could comprehend. Today, it seems we have enslaved ourselves once again to illiteracy, and we've replaced our own valuable insights and interpretations with ones viewed through the lens of the priests of our culture, the media moguls. We have become willingly illiterate.

When we watch the news or listen to a broadcast on the radio, we are listening to someone else's opinion and interpretation. It is only when we read the words for ourselves, reader to reading, that our own intellect can dissect and digest it. No one puts it in more piercingly poetic fashion than Postman:

> A written sentence calls upon its author to say something...the reader must come armed, in a serious state of intellectual readiness. This is not easy because he comes to the text alone. In reading, one's responses are isolated, one's intellect thrown back on its own resources. To be confronted by the cold abstractions of printed sentences is to look upon language bare, without the assistance of beauty or community. (p. 50)

As one author so succinctly observed, modern society has become so *cocooned* within the world of media that man can no longer "see or know anything except by the interposition of (an) artificial medium" (Cassini). In other words, in order to understand it, we have to judge it, to weight its worth with the scales of our own intellect. Sadly, we have grown pathetically ill-equipped for the task. Without the wildly clapping audience and the effervescent laugh track, we fail to comprehend the meaning.

In his comparison of movement within oral and literate frames, Ong says that sound cannot be stopped and still exist. It must be moving, living, to be sound. "All sensation takes place in time, but no other sensory field totally resists a holding action, stabilization, in quite this way...We often reduce motion to a series of still shots to better see what motion is. There is no equivalent of a still shot for sound. An oscillogram is silent. It lies outside the sound world" (p. 32). We now live in a transient realm, impermanent and constantly shifting, and this impermanence often makes truth fluid. "In the total absence of any writing, there is nothing outside the thinker, no text, to enable him or her to produce the same line of thought again or even to verify whether he or she has done so or not" (Ong, p. 34).

The same fluid possibility exists for the Internet savvy world. An online employee handbook, for example, can be changed at the will of the employer, an action over which the employee has no control. An online news source that erroneously reports a death in an automobile accident can cover its tracks by correcting the article upon realization of the error. Or, in a more subtle and dramatic example, a writer can begin asserting that history has been written from fallible perspectives and should therefore be questioned, and then that history can be altogether rewritten (actions that the president of the American Textbook Council claims are already taking place). If this sounds like a science fiction storyline, consider the recent battle over whether the Holocaust *ever took place*. One of the key arguments for the younger generation, even in our own country, was the *lack of compelling living eyewitnesses*.

Sadly, our cultural expectation for truth is a convincing sound byte on a news program. If we didn't see it, we can't bring ourselves to believe it. Media shape our consciousness. Consider the brief organ donor crisis brought on by shows giving organ donorship a negative portrayal, specifically a soap opera where doctors "killed" patients to harvest body parts. After the show aired, donor rates plummeted. People responded to entertainment *in* real life as if entertainment *were* real life. To avoid future mishaps such as this one, EE appointees representing every imaginable facet of society have now taken their judicial stance aside Hollywood producers, making sure no group (or no vocal, lobbyist-savvy group, at least) is misrepresented on the screen.

Ong speaks of the primary oral culture's desire to preserve knowledge through the wise sages of the region, those who are highly regarded for the wisdom that is birthed through longevity. Ong's argument was that the print culture allowed societies to store information outside of the mind, eventually leading to a point where print will "downgrade the figures of the wise old man and the wise old woman, repeaters of the past, in favor of younger discoverers of something new" (p. 41). These words have an eerie and oppressive ring to them, and once we dissect their matter, we find that we are living within this exact system of age-despising, youth-worshipping, truth-eschewing culture. What is true has been exchanged for what is comfortable.

Oral cultures, says Ong, are homeostatic in nature, living "very much *in a present* which keeps itself in equilibrium or homeostasis by sloughing off memories *which no longer have present relevance*" (p. 46, italics mine). In an oral culture, words acquire meaning through use, not printed foundations. They are anchorless, moored only to the moment. As Ong puts it, "Words acquire their meanings only from their always insistent actual habitat, which is not, as in a dictionary, simply other words, but includes...the entire existential setting in which the real spoken word always occurs" (p. 47).

This transference of meaning and depth is so serious, in fact, that it often leads to the death of the word. "When generations pass and the object or institution referred to by the archaic word is not longer part of present lived experience...its meaning is altered or simply vanishes" (p. 47). Once a word is deemed unimportant—or uncomfortable—it falls from use. The same is true for historical events. When it is easier not to recall them, such as the removal of the Holocaust from a historical textbook, a non-literate culture will call these into question. As Ong puts it, the "present (has) imposed its own economy on past remembrances."

There are additional benefits to the written word. Written discourse, says Ong, has a more elaborate sensitivity to grammar because the punctuation and other devices serve as cues for the reader. In oral presentations, these cues are readily effused to the hearer. There is no need to think, to analyze, to weigh and consider the author's context when listening to news on a television broadcast. The thinking, the analyzing, has already been done. The context has been decided. In reading, grammar gives the intonation, emphasis, and pauses provided in speech, but the reader must possess the tools to excavate the meaning himself. (The breaking of the gender pronoun rule in this previous sentence is an example of our socialized lens and the rule of the generalized other. This lens tells me I "should" add *herself* to my reflexive pronoun list to make sure that I let the reader know I don't mean to exclude either gender; however, as this continuous pressure for political correctness seems, at times, tiring and pretentious, here I have silenced the generalized other and proceeded, albeit somewhat sheepishly, with the forbidden masculine terminology. When we are aware of the looking glass lens or the generalized other, we can at times choose psychology over sociology, though not always without a nagging sense of guilt.)

"In a primary oral culture, where the word has its existence only in sound, with no reference whatsoever to any visually perceptible text, and no awareness of even the possibility of such a text, the phenomenology of sound enters deeply into human beings' feel for existence, as processed by the spoken word" (p. 231). Truly, a word brought to life by the human voice has a unique entry point into the heart. It feels alive, vibrant, meaningful—and thus valid.

The spoken word, being only momentary, adheres us to the present moment. In the same way, a culture that is not built around literacy is capable of viewing and considering only its own present existence, which limits it to an egocentric, myopic view of reality. "For oral cultures, the cosmos is an ongoing event with man at its center. Man is the *umbilicus mundi*, the navel of the world" (Eliade 1958). This idea of a "belly button culture" is extraordinarily descriptive, both for the "midriffs" our fashion-conscious society models and for the me-centricness in which we find ourselves adrift. Today's culture is one of narcissism, where the world revolves around the individual, and all choices that are made are reflective of the self-centeredness which has become so intricately interwoven with modern human "nature."

In "Writing Restructures Consciousness," Ong attributes the invention of writing to a transformation of human consciousness, and in the case of early Western history, this seems to have spawned a highly literate, creative, critically thinking mass of US residents. As Ong says, the book is consummate in its ability to both educate and convict, which is why it has been burnt and censored and tortured to death. It is a bleak reminder of the world that may not be the way we want it to be. It is a *Truman Show* caller voicing painful reality. It is unwanted sunlight spilling over into a forgotten corner of the soul.

Of course, it is much simpler to avoid all of this confrontational literacy, to live with one's head in the sand. As Ong says, "A text stating what the whole world knows is false will state falsehood forever, so long as the text exists" (79). The Ray-Bradbury-esque idea of burning books and making television ubiquitous in order to control the thoughts and behaviors of a culture doesn't seem as farfetched today as it may have 40 years ago. Textbooks, says Ong, are inviolably rebellious, obstinate, disobedient, insubordinate. They don't speak to itching ears. They offend. They do not sanitize. They stir up, provoke, infuriate. But they force us to think. For this reason alone, they must be preserved.

Like their counterparts around the country, many of my college students squirm under the syntax of 19th and early 20th century English writing. To offer an allusion, a reference to history or literature, classic writers could reference a Greek tragedy, the Bible, or a historical event. Today, if we want our "audience" to understand our comparison, there is but one sure-fire allusion available to us: the sitcom. We can't assume that our hearers have read any text of value; however, we can assume that they will most certainly follow along with our illustration if we reference the one cup from which they've all supped in the previous 24 hours: the television.

Television is one of the main purveyors of a product called *information*. In fact, information commands our attention to such a degree today that researchers have dubbed the current era the "information age," where we buy and sell in a "knowledge-based economy." And the amount of information available in this age of knowledge (not to be confused with an age of wisdom) is simply staggering. It has been noted that the amount of information in a regular Saturday edition of the *New York Times* newspaper contains more information than the average 17th century Englishman would have come across *in his entire lifetime*. Knowledge in some fields is said to be doubling daily. And yet, for all of this information, do we find ourselves better or worse civilly, intellectually, morally, socially, physically?

Intelligence-wise, there seems to have been little positive effect. In fact, the average adult vocabulary today is said to be roughly the equivalent of a prepubescent boy of the early 1900s. Civic-engagement-wise, the effects are dimmer still. The majority of what we hear and see has little impact on the course of our lives. It is interesting, certainly, but ultimately meaningless. The rock star on her fourth marriage, the public official quietly embezzling funds for a decade—these are curiosities, but they are not life-altering chunks of information on an individual level. The truth is that the information we are gaining today in the "information age" is largely trivial, meaningless, unsubstantial in its ability to allow us response or change. As Postman (1985) asks, "Of all the information you take in today...will any of it influence a decision you will make today on any important fact of your life?" For most of us, the answer is no. And yet, day in and day out, we continue to fill our minds with information that is far more life-draining than life-giving.

When the astute writers of the Declaration of Independence said that they held certain truths to be self-evident, I can have no doubts in their intellectual capacity for analyzing and recognizing truth in its "self-evident" certainty. Of modern readers and writers, I cannot make the same claim. Historical documents, from Moses to the U.S. Constitution, make numerous references to "natural laws" and "self-evident truths." These historical writings assume a reader's knowledge of history as well as an innate ability to reason, analyze, and interpret reading material. Today, however, the idea of self-evident anything seems to have gone the route of not-so-common sense. The skill of reading between the lines is a discipline nearing extinction. In fact, the skill of reading itself seems to teeter perilously on the shoreline of survival. Our intellectual prowess has been drained and replaced instead with nauseating levels of cute commercialism.

Text, says Ong, is paradoxical. Despite its state of "deadness," it is inexorably alive. Writing "assures its endurance and its potential for being resurrected into limitless living contexts by a potentially infinite number of living readers" (p. 80). What a powerful and beautiful conception! Writing lives and transcends time through the continued availability of the text itself. Additionally, it heightens our consciousness, plucking us out of the automatic pilot function where we often drift vacantly within our motorized lives. Finally, writing provides a balance to life. "To live and to understand fully, we need not only proximity but also distance. This writing provides for consciousness as nothing else does" (Ong 81).

Havelock (1976) said that the transformation from sound to sight gave the Greek culture the intellectual superiority it needed to trump its ancient illiterate neighbors. Now, as we leave behind high rates of literacy, migrating toward image-centrality, we find ourselves sinking rapidly down the worldwide corporate ladder as well as the scholastic ladder. Perhaps a return to literacy is more than a desperate plea from English teachers. Maybe it is a gateway to greater levels of success on a personal as well as a global scale.

Ong notes that when printed text became available, suddenly two texts didn't just make similar arguments; they were exact duplicates of one another—identical textual twins. Thus, their persuasive power was doubled. In the same way, magazine covers duplicate, multiply and mass communicate the images of perfection they hold up as a standard embodied by only 2% of the world's population. In early cultures, visual art was seen through the lens of the artist. The artist would interpret the picture through his own lens, and thus his view of reality would become our view of reality. In a media-saturated society, where image is king, our view of reality is skewed in the same way.

An excellent example of the artist's lens is shown in the YouTube video "Evolutions" by Dove skincare. The video is an "exposé" of sorts on the fashion/beauty industry (yes, the industry Dove belongs to), showing how fake, how unrealistic, and superficial the pictorial world has become. The video shows an average-looking woman sitting in a make-up room, where she is "made over" until she is virtually unrecognizable. Then, her photo is submitted to that malevolent morphing machine, the computer, where all of her human flaws are brushed away, lengthened, lightened, and distorted into robotic perfection. This pseudo-human image is then plastered on billboards throughout the nation to help young impressionable girls see just how imperfect they are in light of true perfection. This media image is inarguable. It is not up for debate. It does not say, "Draw your view of reality here." It stands, firm and immovable, like a plastic Statue of Liberty, proclaiming her brand of physical perfection to those huddled masses of youngsters yearning to breathe free (and popular).

Face-to-face human communication is based on give and take. You talk. I listen. I talk. You listen. The media model, however, is quite the opposite. It is dominating, foreboding, one-to-many. It overshadows our wimpy "I'm okay" talk with its dialectical despotism. The image reigns supreme. And, as a result of this absolute authority, this systemic socialization, a wave of cinematic contagion has swept across our culture. What are the socio-emotional ramifications for a culture where the court jester has become the king, where the elevation of "celebrity" status has reached such a dizzying altitude that being funny commands a bigger salary than being wise? What if image-centrality is spiraling us into peripheral routes of thinking that engage only our lower nature and not our higher intellect? What happens when a society devoid of parental involvement permits virtual peers with questionable moral status, not to mention materialistic motives, to offer advice in the spirit of a rebellious big sister?

If the sound culture is invasive, the image culture is even more so. The image is disturbingly salient, drawing deep into our psyche and implanting its pseudo values and half truths deep within. In various ways, both overt and covert, cultural sociology influences our personal psychology. We would thus do well to be aware of our surroundings and their potential for influence, choosing our electronic "friends" with caution. Though we may have limited cognitive awareness of the inner workings of our own minds, one thing is certain: We possess both the ability and the responsibility for making responsible choices regarding the socialization of not only our own lives, but also for the lives of the most vulnerable citizens of our planet-our children.

Call it idealistic, but I have hope for change. As long as we have breath, as long as we have vision, personal and social transformation lies within the realm of possibility for us all. As Postman so poignantly stated, "Like the fish who survive a toxic river and the boatmen who sail on it, there still dwell among us those whose sense of things is largely influenced by older and clearer waters" (p. 28).

CHAPTER TWELVE

F2FMIA: A Nation of Isolation

In 1609, John Donne lamented the state of disconnectedness and discontent infecting his inner and outer worlds. "No man is an island, entire of itself," he chided his hearers. "Every man is a piece of the continent, a part of the main." Though today's technological advances have made possible communication strategies far beyond the imagination of the 17th century mind, 21st century dwellers nonetheless often find ourselves in a state of virtual isolation. Though we may come in contact with hundreds or thousands of people daily, there is a sense of disconnect, a sense of isolation in the midst of a crowd. Master teacher and author Parker Palmer calls this a serious cultural ailment.

"Human beings were made for relationships: without a rich and nourishing network of connections, we wither and die. I am not speaking metaphorically. It is a clinical fact that people who lack relationships get sick more often and recover more slowly than people surrounded by family and friends." But the true connectivity of our modern-day communities has been called into question by the communicative processes that have so radically transformed our culture.

Redefining Relationships

In the 1995 movie *The Net*, Angela Bennett was a freelance software analyst whose only connection with the outside world was through the internet. She found herself completely separated from human relationships, and in her time of greatest need, there was no one to vouch for her existence. No one in the "real" world knew her—the only identities she could call on were the fluid connections of her online realm.

At the movie's inception, in the dawning of the internet age, few of us could imagine the world this character lived in: ordering dinner online, talking to strangers online, a world virtually devoid of face-to-face contact with anyone. In fact, when the movie debuted just over a decade ago, the idea of being completely unattached from society seemed an improbable Tinseltown trauma, but today, in many ways, Hollywood fantasy has become an American reality. Author Andy Stanley has observed that whether it is the gym, the mall, the grocery store, or the coffee shop, Americans are increasingly "together but alone." George Gallup echoes this sentiment: In the midst of increasingly overcrowded cities and frantic personal schedules, he says, "Americans are among the loneliest people in the world."

Researchers have noted that even architecture has begun to reflect a resistance to community: houses are now intentionally built, as Putnum puts it, "to promote privacy and seclusion, not connection." The American front porch, once a zone for interacting with neighbors, has been replaced by the walled fortress of the community-eschewing garage door. We pull into our driveways, cross the moat, and quickly shut the drawbridge behind us, locking out the world. Over the last 100 years, we've gone from a nation of 80% agricultural regions, where we knew everyone in our city, to a nation of 20% agriculture where we don't even know the person living next door. We travel from place to place in our castle-like cars, a universe in themselves, complete with Global Tracking Systems (so we don't have to stop and ask a person for directions) and DVD players (so we don't have to talk to each other along the way). And the number of us who eat our meals at home around the dinner table on a regular basis (sans TV) is decreasing by the minute.

As if to replace these physical structures, online communities have exploded on the scene. At the time of this writing,

Meetup.com boasts 1.5 million community-seeking members in 612 US cities. Friendster.com claims 13 million members, Britain's Friendsreunited claims 11 million members, Classmates.com another 38 million, and E-Harmony calls itself the #1 *relationship site* in the world—a moniker that strikes me as paradoxically bizarre. The trend appears to be gaining unprecedented momentum. In 2001, the Pew Internet and American Life Project found that 84 percent of Internet users go online with the singular goal of developing deeper social ties. What we once said face-to-face, we now say and do in a virtual world. We are "together but alone."

This absence of face-to-face communication has etched its warped linguistic structure into every facet of modern life, plowing its way into the classroom, the living room, and the boardroom, with progressively deleterious effects. A few years back I found myself standing before a humanities class where I had to ask students not to parrot information, but to think for themselves. They were dumbfounded, completely unnerved. "Do you mean paraphrase what you've said? Put it in our own words?"

"No," I said, "I want you to *analyze* the content. Tell me what *you* think. Interpret for yourself." They stopped me in the hallways, rough drafts in hand: "Is this what you mean?" They emailed me: "I don't understand the assignment." They turned in paper after paper that regurgitated the theme of the story, devoid of personal analysis or insight. Without a script, many students seemed to find it difficult to act. Improvisation does not come naturally, and imaginative insight and analysis are decidedly problematic. Invariably, with one or two exceptions, each student in the class repeated, paraphrased, and summarized either the story line or the class discussion.

Original observations were seemingly extinct. "Critical thinking" is an educational buzzword and purported objective in nearly every academic circle in the United States; however, today's students often seem less creative and insightful, and even less clear about their goals and direction, their purpose for school and life.

The New World Isolation Breeds Distress

"Personal accountability in today's world goes beyond 'watching out for Number One.' It means personally accepting some responsibility to create and to nurture ideas which can make this a better world" (Cook, 2000). We live in an increasingly complex society, one with multiple difficult for adults, let alone young adults, to conquer. Over the last twenty years, our social, emotional, familial, and physical worlds have undergone radical changes of every possible scope. As the Internet Generation has come of age, Boomers and Generation Xers have awakened to an onslaught of pandemic post-modernity. Parents must now battle messages from junk food ads, overly sexualized media, violent video gaming, media centrality, and increasingly unnerving peer behavior. In short, it is a maddening quest, a bewildering battle, a race to counter the culture.

College educators who have been in the game for more than a decade have witnessed these subtle but profound cultural shifts and their application to the life of a student. A few years back, Cornell psychologist Janis Whitlock published a study on the "rampant self-mutilation at Ivy League schools," where she said that 17 percent of Cornell and Princeton students are purposely cutting or burning themselves. When I tell parents of these statistics, they are shocked. When I tell teens, they yawn. It's a commonplace component of culture. It's the *norm*. The Indiana University School of Medicine recently reported that 60 percent of the population over the age of 14 carries *at least* one sexually transmitted disease.

Add to these statistics the burgeoning rates of US homicide, (the second-leading cause of death for 15-24-year-olds), the tripling of obesity rates in teenagers, the rapidly escalating rate of consumer debt among college students (1 in 5 carry $10,000 balances), and the fivefold increase in antipsychotic prescription drug use—and we have a recipe for socio-emotional disaster. The feel-good 70s have collided with the virtual 90s—and as Dorothy once observed, we're not in Kansas anymore.

The reason for these challenges is complex, of course, but a number of recent social overhauls have begun to present potentially negative ramifications for both the domestic and educational sectors. First, we have changes in the workplace that continue to wreak havoc on the family structure. As noted earlier, Schor (1991) showed that the typical American family is working longer hours, with men working almost 100 hours more per year and women working over 300 hours more per year than in previous decades. Family dinnertime, which was once an opportunity for reflecting and connecting, has been radically altered in content, time, quality, and location. Meal preparation as an activity of togetherness and conversation has been radically altered, and mealtime space has been reduced to separate dinners in separate rooms—often while working, connecting with friends online, or plugging in to some form of entertainment. Even when families do take the time to eat together, 63 percent of Americans say the television is on during mealtimes, which means the opportunity for meaningful connection is limited even further (KFF, 2006).

From instant meals to instant messages, current trends are pulling at the family: The modern college student is facing a number of demanding—and isolating—predators. Though numerous studies (as discussed later in this paper) demonstrate the role of familial accountability in a student's personal, social, and academic success, modern life breeds enemies to this foundation. One such nemesis is the continual encroaching of government and post-secondary institutions on the private lives and structures of American families. Though there are numerous examples of ineffective government interventions, such as the current ruling on the UN Rights of the Child, which is racing through our legal system in an attempt to give governments the right to supersede parental rule in matters such as education and religion.

Known Benefits of Familial Connectedness

A number of studies underscore the importance of family connectivity, openness, and disclosure. The Life Skills Training Center has found that "self-disclosure reduces levels of rage, substance abuse, deviancy, divorce, and criminal behavior: "People have a basic need for emotional closeness...(and) problems increase in persons as they move away from close, intimate and trusting relationships" (Frankin, 2006). When a person is experiences low levels of emotionally intimate connections, he or she may become withdrawn, have decreasing levels of self esteem, turn hostile or mean, or turn to self-destructive behaviors (Frankin, 2006). A lack of accountability relationships can lead a student to behavioral patterns that are not sufficient for full mental health, let alone academic success. The reverse, however, is also true.

Close, personal relations are proven to yield health benefits. Documented benefits range from lower blood pressure, greater feelings of gratification, an ability to cope with stress, stronger feelings of certainty to greater longevity (Frankin, 2006). Research has shown that even under extreme financial duress, people with strong relationships maintain a stronger level of happiness. "Intimacy is one of psychology's optimum lifestyle factors" (Frankin, 2006). Additionally, healthy relational ties lower a number of risk factors. The University of Minnesota's Minnesota Multiphase Personality Inventory (MMPI) found healthy socialization to be the number one "moderating influence in the whole realm of mental illness problems...reducing both risk and severity" in nine forms of mental illness: hypochondriasis, depression, conversion hysteria, psychopathic deviancy, masculine-feminine identity, paranoia, schizophrenia, and hypomania (Frankin, 2006). In an era of disengagement and disconnection, these findings are important considerations.

Sidney Jourard, former professor of psychology at the University of Miami and author of *The Transparent Self* (1971), also presses the importance of closeness: "Being heard and touched by another who cares seems to reinforce identity, mobilize spirit, and promote self-healing" (Franklin, 2006). Accountability and openness engender physiological benefits as well. For example, several studies have documented the success of positive behavior training, such as weight loss, when people committed to their goals together. Karen Miller-Kovach (2005), Chief Scientist at Weight Watchers International says, "Friends who diet together have a greater success rate than those who diet alone...They are more effective at staying motivated and beating obstacles." The importance of these support systems was explored in another weight-based study published in the *Journal of Consulting and Clinical Psychology* (Wing 2006). Researchers discovered that of those who dieted alone, 76% completed their program and 24% maintained their weight loss, whereas those who dieted with support saw a 95% completion rate and a 66% rate of weight loss maintenance" (Wing 2006).

In addition to physiological factors such as weight loss, other areas of life are impacted by openness and positive socialization; for example, research demonstrates that the marriage relationship dramatically impacts mental and physical health. "The benefits are better physical health, more resistance to infection, fewer infections, and a reduced likelihood of dying from cancer, from heart disease, from all major killers," says psychologist and author John Gottman, PhD. (Hope, 2006). Longevity is another offspring of marriage: "People live longer if they are in marital relationships, particularly if they are in good, satisfying relationships." Other benefits include fewer instances of depression, anxiety disorders, psychosis, posttraumatic stress disorders, and phobias. Some of these benefits are explained within the realm of relationship.

For example, "Married individuals have lower rates of alcoholism than their unmarried counterparts because they tend to offer encouragement, support, and protection from daily problems that could otherwise lead them to using alcohol and other drugs (Hope, 2006).

Additionally, married individuals display lower suicide rates, lower rates of illness, accidents, and murder, and they are less likely to die from heart disease, stroke, cancer, car accidents, and murder. They spend less time in hospitals, have higher recovery rates, and stronger immune systems (Hope, 2006). Finally, they are better at handling stress, more motivated to do well at work, and more determined to persevere in times of stress. "On the whole, married persons are more likely to report feeling hopeful, happy, and good about themselves" (Hope, 2006). In the media-central culture of today, marriage is mocked more than it is supported. The vast majority of relationships on television and movies are between unmarried individuals, often one-night stands.

Central to the replication of positive behavior is the type of influence surrounding the individual. As discussed earlier, Albert Bandura, professor of psychology at Stanford University, addressed these concerns in a number of studies. Social Learning Theory, for example, demonstrates that our view of our world, our interactions, and ourselves is largely shaped by our socialization; in other words, we mirror the company we keep.

One such example of the importance of positive socialization in the development of prosocial behavior is a study published in *The Journal of Studies on Alcohol* and led by researchers from the Johns Hopkins Bloomberg School of Public Health. The study links the connectivity and accountability found in faith-based communities to the greater likelihood of prosocial behaviors (Bowie, Ensminger & Robertson, 2006).

Through this pervasive, longitudinal study, researchers determined that the voluntary accountability inherent in regular church attendance results in lower rates of alcoholism and depression, especially among young Black men. As the researchers tracked participants' progress over a period of 30 years, they found that the positive socialization was an important link to behavior: "Collaboration with religious institutions may be helpful in developing research and interventions linking religion and health" (Bowie, Ensminger & Robertson, 2006).

Familial Socialization Needs for Students

The family-centric model of education, embraced for thousands of years before the current era of media-centralization, remains the primary system of educational health. According to Dr. John Wherry of the Parent Institute, children with involved parents are more likely to earn higher grades and test scores, attend school regularly, have better social skills, demonstrate positive behaviors, and adapt well to school. "The research evidence is now beyond dispute. When schools work together with families to support learning, children tend to succeed not just in school, but throughout life...In fact, the most accurate predictor of a student's achievement in school is not income or social status, but the extent to which that student's family is involved in the child's education" (Wherry, 2006).

In the more than 30 years of research on parent involvement, researchers have consistently found that parent involvement produces positive results for children (Decker et al., 1996), and the Manitoba Department of Education and Training (1994) notes that, "Parents are more significant than either teachers or peers in influencing educational aspirations for the majority of children," including improved academic performance, improved school behavior, greater academic motivation, and lower dropout rates. When we look behind the scenes at schools were new programs are hailed for increasing student performance, we almost always see a common factor—though not one commonly pointed out: Parents have been invited into the mix. In other words, it's not the social system that is improving grades: it is the inclusion of family in the process.

In 1994, the importance of parent involvement was designated as one of the National Education Goals in the "Goals 2000: Educate America Act." The U.S. Department of Education (1997) noted that "research over the past 30 years has consistently shown that greater family involvement in children's learning is a critical link to achieving a high-quality education." What is most interesting about these findings is that the benefits are not confined to early childhood or the elementary level; a number of studies demonstrate the importance of family ties in post-secondary education as well Many parents today seem unaware of the powerful role they play in the lives of their children. Perhaps this is a result of the continued mockery of authority that is promulgated on entertainment media today; perhaps it is the result of a disconnect between this generation of parents and the former generation. Either way, parents seem to believe that someone else can to a better job of inculcating values, but this is simply untrue from a statistical standpoint.

I overheard a group of moms talking recently about the changes in the local school system. Because of budget cuts, the schools had added a number of minimum days and "furlough" days to the calendar, which meant students would not be in classes. "What are they thinking?" one mother asked aloud in frustration. "Who's going to watch them on all those half days? I have a job!" Instead of welcoming the extra time with their children and recognizing the vital role they play as parents, these moms were bemoaning the fact that their own lives were being inconvenienced for the sake of the child.

Another example of this "what-do-we-do-with-them" mentality can be found in headlines at the start of summer break or those dreaded two long weeks of winter break, where school is not in session. The headlines give pseudo support to parents who, apparently, have lost touch with the joy that is found in childrearing. Articles abound along the lines of "how to keep kids out of your hair during those torturous long weeks of vacation." This type of advice could only be possible in a culture where parental connectivity has been severed and, most likely, replaced with a prosthetic version of leadership—electronic parents and virtual friends.

The Harvard Family Research Project (2004) found that the positive impact parental involvement bears on academic success does not stop in adolescence: In fact, parent participation is equally relevant in post-secondary academic achievement. The lead researcher in the project, Evanthia N. Patrikakou, professor at the University of Illinois, Chicago, found that parent involvement tends to decline as children reach the upper grades. Some reasons for this, she says, are the complex structure of school systems, fewer schools requesting help from parents, and curricula that can leave parents feeling intimidated. According to the National Association of Secondary School Principals (1992), the majority of parents express an interest in being involved in their children's education. "Family requests for involvement are constant" (Epstein, 1988); however, many parents feel unable or uninvited when it comes to their children's education. Movements like the UN Rights of the Child, which seeks to overthrow parental rights in favor of child rights (i.e., a child has the right to decide what is best for herself without parental "intervention") make these messages even more confusing for parents. Many parents, out of a supportive but decidedly uneducated desire to help their children, hand over the reins to someone else.

Harvard's (2004) extensive longitudinal study followed a cohort of students from the eighth grade through high school, college, and into the workforce. The study found that parents' expectations and, essentially, their belief in the students' academic capabilities, were predictors of the students' success: "The further in school parents believed their adolescents would go, the clearer the adolescents' perception of such expectations, the higher their own academic expectations, the higher their academic achievement" (Patrikakou, 2004). And that marker did not diminish as students aged. "The long-lasting effects that parent involvement variables have on the academic achievement of adolescents and young adults indicate that parent involvement during high school and beyond still remains an important source of guidance and support for the developing individual" (Patrikakou, 2004). The Harvard study also stressed that schools need to initiate relationships with parents in order to secure the much-needed support. "We should also recognize that school-initiated communication for specific students tends to take place when adolescents misbehave or face academic problems...By encouraging parents to be involved in developmentally appropriate ways, schools can maximize the benefits for all students by gaining an important ally in their effort not to leave children behind" (Patrikakou, 2004).

Psychologist and author Dr. David Walsh explains the need for parental guidance well into young adulthood. The brain, he says, develops in spurts until the age of 25. Until this quarter-of-a-century mark, the prefrontal cortex is still "under construction," and since this is the area that regulates impulse control, aggression management, emotional control, and self-regulation, it is important that adolescents have a good grounding in parental oversight. Dr. Ruth Kraus, assistant professor of clinical psychology at the University of Chicago, agrees. "Adolescence is a time when everything is out of kilter, and nothing is stable in the body or mind." Parents, she adds, must step in as the "designated prefrontal cortex," offering common sense, guidance, and advice.

In many ways, instead of incorporating family and school, it seems the modern educational environment attempts to decentralize the family unit from the child's life at 18, despite the fact that these vital components of judgment and self-regulation are unformed and inconsistent in the developing adolescent's mind. By the time a non-familial intervention has taken place, the student may have already dropped out of school (or worse). According to the American College Testing Program's 2006 data, the average retention rate for two-year public college students across the nation is 52 percent. This means that nearly half of the students who begin college do not make it to the finish line. Furthermore, only 26 percent of those who stay in college actually complete their degree program. These are staggering statistics. Replacing safeguards such as greater ties to family accountability may offer students the needed boost to help them succeed. "We cannot look at the school and the home in isolation from one another; we must see how they interconnect with each other and with the world at large" (Wherry, 2006).

If we desire for young adults to progress socially, scholastically, and emotionally, we must support this growth by providing access to a healthy foundation—instead of defaulting to options that essentially sever the ties that bind. At present, a number of institutional and governmental regulations that were designed to protect students are, in truth, actually working against them.

One such example of academia positioning itself against the structure of family accountability is through the Family Educational Rights to Privacy Act (FERPA). The U.S. Department of Education defines FERPA as a federal law "designed to protect the privacy of student education records." In effect since 1974, the law applies to all schools receiving funds through the U.S. Department of Education. FERPA requires that the control of a child's education records be transferred to the student at and beyond the age of 18. What this means to the average college student (and the student's parents) is that the student now controls the access to all records pertaining to the student's education: These include grades and academic standing, attendance records, financial standing with the college, results of any disciplinary proceedings involving the student, hospitalization, treatment for any emergency or life-threatening medical or psychological conditions, missed classes, and disruptive or erratic behavior.

It is a fascinating shift from parent-centric to other-centric models of education and accountability, and the poor performance of most American schoolchildren today should cause at least a raised eyebrow at some of these strategies. Only through a written release from the student can a parent gain access to a student's file—even if that parent is funding the student's education. Neither the instructor nor the administrator has the "right" under FERPA's regulations to speak to a parent about the student's records. In a number of recent cases, this has been problematic, even life-threatening.

Thomas Baker, associate dean of students at the University of Iowa, notes the increasingly dramatic number of college students engaged in self-destructive behaviors and the challenges FERPA regulations have presented in some of these cases. In his discussion of a rash of tragic suicides on college campuses—and the administrative decisions not to notify parents of prior suicide attempts—Baker argues that violating a student's privacy rights may be a necessary step in protecting the student's well-being. In a 2002 court case, a college dean had learned of a student's suicide intentions. The dean then met with the student and required him to sign a "statement pledging not to hurt himself." The student committed suicide two days after signing the pledge (Baker, 2005).

Obviously, most parents would recognize the futility of asking a suicidal patient to sign a note promising he wouldn't hurt himself. This is a naïve oath at best. Yet, as schools are increasingly called upon to take the parental mantle upon themselves, such faulty decision making is likely to be more the norm than the exception. To this end, Baker says he desires to see parental notification as part of the overall strategy in suicide prevention and mental health. "Protection from harm includes the ability to influence the student's behavior, and...parental notice influences the behavior of a troubled student" by reinforcing positive feelings that exist between the student and his or her family members. Inherent in this system of disclosure is a belief in the value of accountability: "Sending a copy of the parental notice letter to the student encourages the student to refrain from self-destructive behavior in the future." Ideally, Baker says, a more open relationship with the student's family will prevent further self-destructive behavior as well as address and heal any existing dysfunction within the family." At present, though, FERPA regulations continue to "protect" a troubled student from the prying eyes and ears of his parents.

In addition to medical records, grades, and attendance, FERPA also protects the records of a student's financial accounts, so while a student may have developed a habit of making frivolous expenditures, thus tightening the noose of long-term indebtedness, her parents are unlikely to know. According to the Consumer Federation of America (CFA), nearly 70 percent of undergraduates at four-year colleges possess at least one credit card, and the majority of students have at least five credit cards. The vast majority (over 81%) receive their first card by the end of their freshman year. Most of those students are carrying $2000 this year (up $1000 from one year ago), and one-fifth of the students are carrying balances of over $10,000.

Upon completion of their undergraduate degree, most will owe at least $14,000 in school debt, though with rising tuition rates, many will owe five times that amount. The CFA says that more and more students are experiencing financial challenges because of overextended credit, and university administrators have begun to link these massive debts to more dropouts, defaults, and self-destructive behavior. One administrator put it succinctly: "We lose more students to credit card debt than to academic failure."(CFA). Alas, once again, student records are protected from those prying parental eyes, and thus, a parent might not know until it is too late that her son has dropped out of school and is working at a fast-food restaurant to pay off his debts.

But what if the rules were different? What if there was a greater level of financial accountability encouraged between parents and students? What if student privacy rights defaulted in favor of greater familial support instead of offering a refuge from self-disclosure? With a trend toward parental intervention, would students be less likely to drop out, less likely to be overcome by everyday problems, and more likely to finish the proverbial race?

Children need guidance—and not in the mindless words of a distraught singer, a superficial celebrity, or even, predominately, at least, in the transitory connection with a governmental education system. They need parental support, community support. The road is not easy, and young adults are often ill prepared emotionally, socially, physically, and mentally for the challenges ahead. Some children have great difficulty dealing with the interpersonal issues bound to arise in student settings: peers they dislike, instructors they fear, courses they don't understand, the complex challenges of relationships, stress, and overactive hormones. Instead of relying solely on peer feedback—which, though it can useful in the simpler cases, can be woefully inadequate in the more serious cases-students should be encouraged to maintain open relationships with parents, and, at the very least, FERPA laws should default in favor of accountability, not isolation. A peer's friends or mentors may do their best to assist struggling students, but a mentor is not a mother, and a faculty member is not a father. Forcing pseudo-parental status is an unfair burden on our educational system and, more importantly, on our student population.

Faulty Foundations

In discussing the "major shift in attitudes" that has recently occurred in the culture at large, Peter Burke says, "There is a tendency to take structures less seriously, associated with a dizzy sense of liberty and also of uncertainly and precariousness...We live in an age of fluidity...where even personal relationships seem to be less constant than they used to be" (2005). In reviewing the role of a student's right to educational privacy, her right, in essence, to be "protected" from her parents (who may, ironically, be footing the bill for the very college experience from which they have been legally severed), we would do well to consider this anti-family march toward an era of "fluidity," examining the vast number of challenges American society is currently facing as a result of the decentralization of the family.

To do so, we will need to become self-aware enough, as a society, to view the appreciable changes that have taken place in culture over the last three decades. As Burke says, "How can artists check a schema against a reality if their view of reality is itself a product of the schema?" As "products" of the culture, we must examine both our packaging and our waywardness. As C.S. Lewis once offered, we must step outside of our "generational lens" and consider the way it was, the way it is, and the way it will be if society does not apply the brakes to some of these potentially destructive "safeguards."

In essence, FERPA was the spawn of an educational "freedom" movement in the 1970s, the era that brought us Values Clarification as well as a number of other authoritarian-eschewing ideologies. During that phase of anti-establishmentarian sentiment, a number of "creative strategies" washed over all things educational, governmental, and domestic. Though these educational support strategies were designed to help students stay afloat academically, in retrospect, many parents and educators have realized that the strategies were—and are still—submerging our students in a violent undertow. Creating an automatic escape route directing students away from accountability, especially at a time when they remain vulnerable to poor decision-making tendencies, is a disservice to students, to educators, and to families. In fact, perhaps the greatest irony of the Family Educational Rights to Privacy Act is its own internal enigma: FERPA isn't protection *for* families; it's protection *from* families.

FERPA's spirit continues on today, even in fledgling programs. President Obama recently announced that he favors longer school days and longer school years, government programs that offer up to 300 more "instructional" hours of school (Quaid 2009). At present, it should be noted, United States school children spend approximately 1,146 hours in school, which is far more than the Asian countries that regularly outscore their US counterparts in science and math. Singapore, for example spends on 903 hours per year in school, and Japanese children spend 1,005 (Quaid 2009). Disadvantaged children represent the greatest concern, for as the Associated Press has noted, these children often make little to no academic progress in the summer; whereas wealthier kids are read to and played with regularly, disadvantaged children often find themselves alone. "Those hours from 3 o'clock to 7 o'clock are times of high anxiety for parents," Education Secretary Arne Duncan told the Associated Press (Quaid 2009), adding that parents "want their children safe" and are working "one and two and three jobs now to make ends meet."

This, however, is circular logic. Who is paying for these pricey programs, for extra school hours and extra meals to make up for the lack in familial support? That would be the taxpayers—the families themselves—who are working one and two and three jobs to provide for their children. Why would we not instead invest the money directly into families? Why not educate moms and dads on parenting, on nutrition, on reading skills, on self-improvement? Teachers—as well-intentioned as they are—are actually a short-term solution. A teacher gets a child for a year. A parent has a child for a lifetime. Pouring more money into a system that is already failing is like putting a Band-Aid on a gaping wound.

From a statistical standpoint, the sad truth is that the public school system in the United States has been on a downward spiral since the 1970s. It's no surprise that 65% of a public teacher's school day is spent in classroom management, when students have not been required to demonstrate respect for the teacher's authority or even for the intrinsic value of their own classmates. Parents regularly defend their truant and defiant children in spite of wrongdoing, further undermining the teacher's already eroding foundation of respect and authority. Values clarification continues to rear its ugly head in the modern classroom as well as in the home, and little has been done to turn that tide in either realm. One has only to compare the statistics to see that the current public school methodology is not working and that the school environment is not even a close runner-up in the contest for the most impacting predictor of socio-academic success rates. In fact, some of the most successful children in the country from an academic standpoint utterly defy the nation's current educational mindset.

In a recent study of almost 12,000 home educated students, researcher Dr. Brian Ray (2009) confirmed what the public schools have denied all along: home-educated students outperform their public school counterparts by almost 30 points on national, standardized tests such as the *California Achievement Test* and the *Stanford Achievement Test*. Even when accounting for parental education and gender, the studies remained consistent. Whether a parent had a college degree or not, the home-educated children scored in the 84th to 89th percentiles in reading, language, math, science, and social studies. This statistic held true—even (gulp) when the parent did not hold a college degree. Clearly, the study illuminates the need for a paradigm shift. We have been attempting to sail on a flat planet, not realizing all along that the symmetry of the surface may be considerably different than our existing paradigms have allowed us to believe.

As Burke says, "Change is often a result of conflict," and if we are to begin an educational overhaul, the journey must begin with one small, seemingly insignificant step. If we, as educators and parents, truly desire to transform the educational process for society's young adults, we would do well to begin evaluating and addressing the ironies inherent in America's educational system. Without significant changes, we will continue to foster a false sense of independence, and thus, a lack of accountability, resulting in continued personal loss to students as well as the society they were intended to thrive in. The bell, as Donne so aptly stated, tolls for all of us. Lower rates of passage (and higher rates of self-inflicted injury and/or death) will have profound implications for the family, the corporate sector, the economy, and the nation itself. We must begin the process of restoring parents to their rightful place of rule, educating them as well as supporting them in this all-important venture of childrearing.

EMERGE!

CHAPTER THIRTEEN

Hope for a Breakthrough: The Winds of Change

Peter Burke once said, "If each generation reinterprets the norms only slightly in the process of receiving and retransmitting them, appreciable social changes will take place over the long term." Other authors have likened this gradual change to the slight adjustment of tracking radar on an airplane—just a degree or two of change can have a tremendous impact on the final destination. This adage can work to our advantage just as effectively as it has worked to our disadvantage. As Newtonian law explains, to every action there is an equal and opposite reaction. Knowledge is power if we act upon it, and recognition of our propensity for influence is a starting point for us all, as individuals and as a culture. We must ask ourselves few vital questions: When we follow the current trajectory of our personal and collective destinies, do we like what we see? From the trends of personal violence such as cutting and drug abuse, to the issues of mass violence and homicide rates, is the spiral moving closer or further from socio-emotional healing? Do we enjoy the fractured lives and fluid relationships exemplified in current lifestyles? Is this the world we want to pass on to our children? Many people would agree that America has been headed not only for financial ruin, but for moral bankruptcy as well. The good news is that, as we learned earlier in this writing, the possibility for personal and social transformation rests within every person, no matter the age.

In the last chapter, we highlighted some of the incredible challenges facing the public school system in the United States. The government has continued to throw money at the problem in the same way we threw money at developing countries in the 1980s: We didn't teach skills; we simply alleviated our own guilt by assuring ourselves that "we gave at the office." However, winds of change are blowing. An encouraging story appeared in the National Education Association magazine in October 2009, highlighting a new trend for a handful of public schools in Oklahoma, Boston, and Chicago: "Intersection of Church and State: How public schools are welcoming religious help, and why there hasn't been a lawsuit." The article says that for the past three years, the Oklahoma Education Association has been "talking about melding religious values and working with students" because, as OEA President Becky Felts says, "the church family can be a natural place for many" to find help (p. 32). In Oklahoma, this means that church members volunteer to help with reading, writing, math, and art after school. The responses have been phenomenal as individual lives have been impacted, and students are turning from purposeless to purposeful as a result of this unlikely merger. Kudos to both organizations for displaying the courage to change-and for setting aside personal differences in order to facilitate prosocial transformation.

After a recent talk I gave on the concept of this book, a couple rushed up to me excitedly. The man, woman, and their 8-year-old son had just spent two weeks without television. The reason for their fast was simple: they wanted to know how much of a role TV was playing in their lives and how much of their time was being invested into it. At the end of the two-week period, the parents expected that the child would be begging for reinstatement of the electronic entertainer. Instead, though, the son begged his parents to go another two weeks! He was having the time of his life, interacting with his parents, being listened to (instead of suffering those "uh huh" responses uttered by a TV adult or child engrossed in a show), playing games, and being creative. For this child, pulling the plug on television meant an opportunity to grow closer to his family. Without the din of minutiae and the constant whine of commercialism, the most important matters came into clear view.

What a beautiful picture was etched in my mind from that conversation! What would our own collective worlds look like if they were people-centric instead of media-centric? What if we knew more about our neighbor's struggle or triumph than we knew about the latest celebrity lip enhancement? What if we knew more about our own children's hopes and dreams and fears than how many muggings took place in the 4th Street district of New York last week? What if we didn't know who won the Amazing Race because we were too busy winning our own race to care? These are important questions, because in reality, television causes us to be caught up in a world that isn't reality. It causes us to watch life as observers, as spectators, instead of engaging in life as adventurers, explorers.

This type of real-life living has begun to spring up in grassroots movements across the United States.

In addition to corporate change, many individuals have shared with us their own stories of triumph and emergence from the cocoon of media-centrality.

Jamie wrote to us that she had recently made some changes in her viewing habits. "I have stopped watching (crime investigation shows) and have seen a huge difference," she said, adding that she realized she was watching lifestyles that contradicted her faith. As Jamie put it, "It's not just about turning the TV off as much as it is turning your spiritual discernment on. We shouldn't let the world rate our shows and movies for us; the word should be our rating scale. We shouldn't watch sin as entertainment."

Carrie told us that she and her husband to give up screen time for 40 days. They felt that their constant exposure to all of these media outlets was keeping them from connecting with the real world: "It was not only stifling our creativity and relationship, it was also numbing us to being present with one another, our community, and most importantly, God." The first week, she says, they were at a total loss, having no idea what to do with their time. "We didn't know how to unwind or relax, " she said. "Our thumbs ached to surf our Blackberries and check email. It felt compulsive. Slowly, we emerged from our fog and began to reconnect with Life." Carrie said that she and her husband began to talk more, to cook together, to have friends over for games, and to connect on a whole new level. "We remembered that we were not only husband and wife, but also best friends! Neither one of us realized how much we had been checking out emotionally and spiritually," she said. "We also didn't realize how we had been missing out on the real pleasures of life. We had been too busy filling up on the constant media inundation to be present in our own lives," she said, adding that the experience without media has helped them both create balance. "Now, we have made it a point to unplug, with great intention, at least once a week," she said. "We needed the drastic withdrawal in the beginning; it was the only way to kick the addiction."

Rachel told us that she and her husband decided to give up television five years ago. They had only planned to disconnect the plug for a year or two, but once they saw the change in their lives, they decided to keep it off. "We most likely will never go back," she said. "You see, once you break away from it, you are shocked by how much things have changed when you end up seeing it again. We have become sensitive to what we see...we also are not locked into a TV schedule, so we never feel like we are missing something," she said. "I believe media has a purpose and that it is hugely powerful, unfortunately, the mainstream is so perverted that you have to wade through so much to find what it truly good," she added. "The main benefit for our family has been the fact that we are at ease and full of peace in our home."

Another respondent said that while he believed there considerable merit to a media fast, he wants to maintain a mindset of being media savvy. "How we manage our intake of information is important," he explained. Many leaders have taught their followers to reject but not to discern, he added. "Making space for stillness is wonderfully healthy. It helps provide a broader vantage point," he said. "The challenge isn't to simply leave the grid, but rather, not to get tangled up in it."

Rich told us that he grew up surrounded by media. "I grew up having every gaming system there is, remembering my love for playing Atari, Nintendo64, and Playstation," he said, and "movie upon movies growing up was what fascinated me...my dad had his own "Blockbuster-In-The-Bedroom" that I loved to look at often and pick the movie of the night," he said. "My happiness was found in those things and the community that it also brought with it, whether with friends or sitting on the couch, with my family, 'bonding' (not really)." Then, five years ago, he took on a media fast that gave him a new perspective in life. "The fast shifted my life in significant ways," he said, "defrosting" his heart and changing his focus. When he was able to "overcome that powerful draw to the numbing venues of media upon my heart," he said, his passion for life "went to a whole other level." His relationships became more focused, more intentional, which surprised him at first. "The normal functions of life continued, but they didn't stay 'normal' long wherever I went," he said, adding that his priorities in life have since changed dramatically. "If we believe that our heart is what will matter in the end," he said, "then we must do all we can not only to protect it, but to keep it alive."

Christina told us that she and a friend had decided to take a break from music for 40 days. "We realized that nearly every minute of our life was 'tuned' into some sort of music," she said. "The alarm clock in the morning was set to music, we had music as we prepped for work, and we listened to it on the way to work, while at work and during the return trip. Once home and cooking dinner, yep we listened to music, and then we fell asleep listening to music." In the absence of music, she had to learn to find new ways "to fill the silence" and express herself creatively and spiritually.

Another respondent told us that he stopped watching TV over three years ago, with the exception of presidential debates. "I now have a more positive frame of mind," he said. "I attribute this to the fact that I am not inundated with the negative stories on the news. Also, I no longer get mentally or emotionally involved in TV dramas. I did not realize, until I stopped watching TV, how irritated or excited some shows made me," he said. "My mental and emotional energy is now directed toward more constructive endeavors. The time freed up by not watching TV allowed me to spend more time with friends and doing other things that I find enjoyable and fulfilling."

Steve told us that he and his wife had decided six years back to cancel their TV service. "It was a sacrifice for me," he said, "as this meant giving up sports as well." Now, he says, "we have a TV, but we control what goes in the DVD player." He has seen a difference in their children, he adds. "Our children could care less about TV. I notice how much they use their imagination and how caring and compassionate they are compared to their peers. They have not been desensitized to mindless killing. They do not know how to curse or use foul language." Steve said that his family now spends more time talking and engaging in activities the family finds meaningful. "I don't know how we would even fit TV into our lives because it would mean sacrificing the things we have gained." To those who argue that mainstream media is the only way to stay in touch with current events, he added, "Don't believe everything the liberal media throws your way. Think for yourself." He challenges others to "step away from the propaganda for 30 days" and see "how ridiculous things sound from your friends who are quoting the (mainstream) media."

Jennifer, now 18 years old, told us that when she was a young girl, media took a central role in her life. "When I was in elementary school, that's when girls like Britney Spears was on the scene," she said. "Sometimes I would come home crying because I just wanted to be like the other girls. I would look at magazines like *People* and *Us* at ten years old and see all the women they called beautiful. I began to realize at that point that I would never measure up to these girls." This sent her into a downward spiral as she made one desperate attempt after another to fit in to what media was telling her, at a very impressionable age, was the norm. "When I was 13, because I wanted to be like these girls, most days I wouldn't eat all day. I just wanted to be skinny. I started to dye my hair and wear tons of make-up. All through high school I was like that, looking to magazines and movies for a false (definition) of beauty." Jennifer said that she realized one day that she didn't seem to have any true friends, and as she began to contemplate this, she suddenly realized that her insecurities were driving others away. "I realized that it was because I was not respecting my own beauty," she said. "I finally decided to stop reading the magazines and watching TV and decided to find out what God said about me. I found out that I was fearfully and wonderfully made, a daughter of the king." This realization of worth, of personal value and inimitable beauty gave her a sense of freedom she had never experienced before. "Now I no longer read magazines because the image of beauty to them is a woman who is air-brushed," she said, "a woman who doesn't respect herself, a woman who commits herself to tons of broken relationships."

Like the stories of Jennifer, Rich, Steve, Rachel, and Carrie, there are many more stories to tell: stories of refocusing priorities, of reestablishing relationships, of connecting once again with life, real life. More testimonies of media literacy and media fasting like these can be found on the *Emerge!* preview page at www.4genpress.com.

During a recession, just as during a funeral, we have the opportunity to refocus our priorities. A recession is like death in many ways, for it means a loss of something familiar, something comfortable. If we put our hope in the almighty dollar, yen, franc, or deutschmark, we are likely to be gravely disappointed. If we put our hope in a false image of unattainable beauty, we will be profoundly insecure. But if we hope in things that matter, then our hope cannot be shaken, despite the tumultuous economy, despite the shifting ground beneath our feet.

The point is illuminated in one of my favorite of Shakespeare's poems, Sonnet 29:

> When, in disgrace with Fortune and men's eyes,
> I all alone beweep my outcast state,
> And trouble deaf heaven with my bootless cries,
> And look upon myself and curse my fate,

> Wishing me like to one more rich in hope,
> Featured like him, like him with friends possessed,
> Desiring this man's art, and that man's scope,
> With what I most enjoy contented least,
> Yet in these thoughts myself almost despising,
> Haply I think on thee, and then my state,
> Like to the lark at break of day arising
> From sullen earth, sings hymns at heaven's gate
> For thy sweet love remembered such wealth brings,
> That then I scorn to change my state with kings.

Where our treasure is, our heart follows. It is our cultural tendency in a capitalistic society to wrap our hearts around money or fame or beauty or other markers of physical or material wealth. This of course, is one of the reasons we have been so shaken as a culture by the news of a recession. When we have emotional stock invested in material goods, we have a great deal to lose. When our treasure is, there our hearts and minds and hopes and dreams will be also. The hummingbird hovering at the bird feeder on my porch is not troubled by the recession. Our puppy is no more troubled than the hummingbird. Our children, too, are shielded from the emotionalism of recession because they do not belong, as my son put it once, to "the adult world of worry." They belong to the here and now, and the most important thing to them is that they are loved, supported, encouraged. As adults, it is time to refocus our priorities, to become media literate, to assess the damage, and to emerge unfettered from the cocoon of media socialization. This requires a paradigmatic shift, a new framework of thinking.

Consider for a moment a paradigm you once embraced that you now know to be inaccurate-and how that inaccurate paradigm can so dramatically shape your existing view of reality. Maybe it was the discovery that Santa was really Dad, or maybe it was something more compelling. I remember attending a function once where someone had been seriously disfigured in an accident, injured to such a degree that the top half of his face was literally missing. I knew I would be meeting the person at the event, and I wanted to show respect and warmth and humanity to him. Try as I might, though, when I shook his hand, I could not force myself to look him in the face. I greeted him warmly, but my face would simply not obey my commands for eye contact. I went home absolutely drenched in guilt, feeling terrible for how I must have made him feel because I couldn't look at him. After two days of wallowing in the guilt of this experience, I had a sudden realization that shattered my paradigm. The man was blinded by the accident. He couldn't see me looking at the floor! He knew only my warm handshake and words of commendation. The tremendous burden of guilt was a product of my faulty paradigm.

If you've ever been trapped in a paradigm, emerged from it, and looked back in retrospect, you too have probably experienced a sense of amazement that you could have been so misled, so deceived by something that was ultimately not even real. It seems that many of us live our lives like this today—caught up in a world that is more of an illusion than a representation of reality. There are imaginary pressures and imaginary milestones to reach and imaginary deadlines and imaginary people to impress when we meet them. It's a world of illusion and delusion.

With so much that devastation behind us, it may be difficult to look out through the rubble and scan the ground for a ray of hope. But, as the modern poet Adam Zagejewski reminds us in "Praise the Mutilated World," there is a gentle light that strays, even vanishes, but in the end, that light returns. At times, we must push aside the decayed leaves that have formed a veil over truth for so long, just as King Josiah's servants dug through the rubble to find that forgotten book of law that had altered the course of history. The hope of a generation is housed within the individual in transition, and, as we will see in the next section, we are fully equipped to usher a powerful movement of both personal and corporate transformation.

It's time for us to rejoin the communicative dialogue that has been lacking since the 1970s Values Clarification tornado swept through our educational and familial systems. If we desire social transformation, and if we are eager to be proactive and not simply critical, then we must begin with our first line of defense: self. If we see that moderate to excessive screen time decreases our intellectual ability and our interpersonal skills, if we see that it increases our propensity for violence and laziness and materialism and selfishness and idolatry, why would we then not modify our lifestyles to facilitate a personal transformation? What if the germination of that transformation was as simple as evaluating and reducing our intake from that source?

Thankfully, there is a growing focus on personal and social responsibility today. We see this at the micro level with regard to weight issues, and we see it at the macro level with concerns over better stewardship of the planet. For the first time in decades, Westerners are actually asking questions involving personal and social responsibility. Instead of pursuing litigation against our enemies, we are facing them in the mirror. Our physical health has been a great starting point; now it is time to spread the focus to our socio-emotional health. What if we rejected media-centrality at the local level, our individual realm of influence? What would our social worlds look like if they were people-centric instead of media-centric? What if we knew more about our neighbor's struggle or triumph than the latest celebrity lip enhancement? What if we didn't know who won the Amazing Race because we were too busy running our own race to care? What price has media centrality exacted from each of us individually, corporately? What functional blindness has developed, and what can be done to create greater awareness for self and others?

These are important questions, because in reality, television catches us up in a world that isn't reality. Its entertainment-driven modality teaches us to *watch* life as observers, as spectators, instead of *engaging* in life as adventurers, explorers. Whether we have been lulled into a narcotic stupor or incited to rampant materialism, the ultimate detriment is the same. Massive mass media consumption has impaired our ability to think correctly. We've named the enemy: Now it's time to fight. As Peter Burke says, "If each generation reinterprets the norms only slightly in the process of receiving and retransmitting them, appreciable social changes will take place over the long term." Such possibilities for cultural transformation rest with those who still remember Postman's older and clearer waters. Truly, these may just be the anecdotes to our cinematic contagion.

As some of our respondents encouraged, we must begin to contemplate both the quality and the quantity of our media diet. We must begin to ask ourselves some pointed questions. What is the purpose of consuming and being consumed by seven hours of media intake per day? What is the purpose of entertaining ourselves with mindless fare that runs contrary to our belief systems and the prosocial behaviors necessary for the survival of a civil culture? What is the purpose of "amusing ourselves to death"?

As we saw in the first three chapters of this book, our sociological and biological propensity for influence, along with the timeline of persuasive positioning, have laid the groundwork for personal and societal impact. Like our food intake, a media diet should be managed through portion control and nutrient density. Too much "dangerous nonsense" will skew the behavioral scale. Media use needs to be tempered, purposeful, and literate in nature. In the final chapters, we will look at some strategies for staying afloat in the media deluge, and then we will look at some preventative measures for ourselves and our future generations.

EMERGE!

CHAPTER FOURTEEN

Strategies of Healing: Socio-Cultural Perspectives

When I was 17 years old, I moved from my small town of 2100 people to the city of Miami to attend college. I was completely unprepared for the assault on mind and body that ensued, and there are many tales born of that experience. One such tragic tale is that of a friend I met my second year of college. Chris was an insecure young man who always tried to go out of his way to get people to like him and to laugh at him. He was awkward in many ways, unaware of his strengths and blinded only by the weaknesses that must have loomed large in his eyes. He always had a story to entertain whatever audience showed up, and his stories were always arrogant in that paradoxically insecure way that so many teen boys tell stories today. I had the sense that most of his stories were complete fabrication, but I said nothing of this revelation.

Despite cautions from his friends, Chris became involved with a young girl. He was very needy, very smitten, and very dysfunctional in his attachments, including his attachment to her. Still, no one saw it coming. One day, the young girl decided it was time to break off this needy, suffocating relationship, but Chris refused to let go. He tried unsuccessfully to maintain her affection, to keep his hold on her, but he could not. Out of desperation, anger, and probably a profound fear of rejection, he took her to a hotel room and shot himself in the head in front of her. Undoubtedly, the scars from this tragic experience remain etched on this young girl's mind, even 20 years later. In retrospect, the community around him could see that Chris was emotionally frail, insecure, utterly dependent on the approval of others for his own self image. Before the tragic incident, though, we had no idea just how dangerous that lack of self would prove to be.

Though his story is extreme, it does not represent an impossible trajectory. The rate of self-induced violence in Western culture is rising on a terrible curve today. Students in the best schools in our country are cutting and burning their bodies in an attempt to deal with the pain and uncertainty they feel inside. Children are joining gangs and committing atrocious crimes in order to experience a pseudo sense of belonging, a connectedness to a community—however vile, however dysfunctional. These aren't pleasant truths, but they are necessary ones. As C.S. Lewis said, "Sunlight is the great disinfectant," and we must allow that sunlight, the piercing rays of truth, to scour the darkened corners of our cultural souls so that we may emerge free.

May we take a lesson from these tragic accounts and do all that we can to help raise confident, kind, respectful, emotionally-balanced children who firmly believe not only in the value of their own life but in the value of the lives around them. These confident children do not grow on television trees. They do not sprout from sexualized MTV video seeds. They are birthed of loving families who balance grace and truth effectively, teaching the art of humility and respect as an act of deference, teaching love of the self not in an inflated and egocentric fashion as so many seem to do today, but in the sense of personal value, individual worth, unconditional love. These are the ingredients for a new generation, and they won't be birthed of an electronic parent.

Strategies of Healing: Socio-Cultural Perspectives

American author Frederich Buechner once said that it doesn't matter where else we succeed if we don't succeed at home.

The home front, he said, is our most important contribution to the world; we are the only parents our children will ever have, and we will shape the future for better or worse through what we create in them. Schore (2003) and his colleagues are laboring to create a developmental context that promotes just such a healing intervention: "The mental health field must move from late intervention to early prevention in order to address the problem of violence in children...the most recent embodiments of our expression of hope for the future of humanity" (Schore 2003, p. 148). He calls for a joint effort from a lengthy list of professionals—to which I would add parents, for it is clear that parents continue to exert not only sociological but also biological influence on their children throughout the lifetime. Ultimately, it isn't the job of the government. It isn't even fully the job of educators. It is the job of parents, and to disconnect this power source is to do a great disservice to children and to the society in which they live.

When a "working model" or paradigm goes unnoticed and unquestioned, it can affect every aspect of a person's life. This process creates a response to the worldview, which may be represented as "the misinterpretation of innocuous stimuli as potential threats" (van der Kolk, 182). In other words, it creates a worldview of fear where fear is not warranted. For example, we discussed earlier the tendency of the modern generation of parents to be overprotective and overly-anxious. This hyper-vigilance may indeed be due to a fear response that was birthed in childhood and strengthened by heavy doses of fear-inducing media. When 83% of the stories on the nightly news focus on the most sensationally terrifying crimes committed in nearby neighborhoods, one's worldview begins to be affected. In the next chapter, we will look at some statistically significant markers of this theory, the "mean and scary worldview" study.

Our ability to create meaning out of life experience is influenced by circuitry, for better or for worse, but we don't have to remain in those systems, trapped within that circuitry. "Systems that are able to move toward maximal complexity are thought to allow the most stable, flexible, and adaptive states to occur."

(Solomon 2003, p. xvi). In order to move toward maximal complexity, we must adapt. Systems that remain stuck in isolation, or blinded by problematic paradigms, are susceptible to cultural reproduction and multigenerational socialization. As the adage goes, the apple does not fall far from the tree. Hesse et al (2003) describe the challenges of second generation, or transgenerational, trauma: "As minds become integrated within attachment relationships, impairments to balanced forms of self-regulation can be transmitted from one individual to another" (Solomon 2003, p. xvi). In other words, if we don't begin to assess and address some of the problematic cultural paradigms within our midst, we will persist in transmitting them to the next generation.

This description offers a clearer understanding of the impact the familial experience has on a developing mind. A parent who has not assessed the socialization strategies of mass media and their collective impact on the family psyche can continue to pass along the inheritance. Thus, a parent can be a carrier of the dysfunction without being aware of its existence in his or her own life. Parents play a vital role in the health and well-being of not only the current generation, but of the generations to come.

The road to transformation will begin with truth, acceptance, courage, and restoration. It's like the aforementioned stream of obesity flooding our nation today. Left unchecked, millions will suffer or die from complications stemming from diabetes and other weight-related debilitations. However, with a lifestyle change that embraces whole grains, fruits, and vegetables as well as more cardiovascular exercise, these physical manifestations can be not only halted—but also completely transformed. Just as a diagnostic test might show a liver in disrepair, so a brain scan might show an emotionally-challenged patient as completely debilitated. The exciting news about both of these organs is that they are capable of change. Nutritionists have told us for years that the body is a self-healing mechanism. Why have we been hesitant to believe the same about the brain? The brain, too, is self-regulating, self-healing. So often, though, the brain is labeled with that proverbial permanent marker and people spend their lives (and their wallets) living out those labels.

In terms of media intake, children and teens have the highest volume of media. Often when children become teenagers, parents feel that their children are "old enough to go it alone" in this realm, but the teen years are not the time for parents to take a hands-off approach. The adolescent years are a time of rapid and often uneven brain development (i.e., logic and emotion regulation do not develop in predictably stable patterns). Thus, teens would be better served with more guidance and direction in this season of life, not less. Yes, they need autonomy, but the responsibility must be progressive in nature. The radical neural pruning they undergo is shaped experientially, and like the statistical accounts of second marriage, if the message isn't learned the first time around (in childhood), the same emotional baggage may be carried into this developmental period as well.

Parents' behavior is not simply socially impacting; it is neurologically impacting, for the family is the first social unit any of us experience—and this early experience can shape future ones. Thus, as visionaries and parents, we have a responsibility to speak truth to the next generation. Moms and dads must be fully enlightened and engaged in the areas of parental responsibility if they are to make the best choices for those that are looking up to them as role models. Additionally, we must continue to educate adults on the possibility of personal transformation. Multigenerational socialization can be un-created the same way it was created. Through education, re-socialization, and positive modeling, we can begin to turn this statistic around, and, in just one generation, we could begin to see a radical transformation in culture.

We know that our biology influences our sociology, that is, our genetic heritage causes us to seek out an environment that "fits" us as individuals. What many of us perhaps have not realized, however, is that our sociology also impacts our biology. At both the meso and the micro levels, there is a constant situation-induced fluctuation in the body and brain. Both our heredity and our environment play important roles in who we become, but only one of these two is controllable.

The family structure is the relational foundation that sets the pace for every other relationship in life. When we fail at this most basic system, we task the next generation with the challenge of having to devote excessive time and resources to healing that infected segment of society. There is a great deal of talk today about our carbon footprint, the imprint we are leaving on planet earth. I don't dispute the importance of this vision. But I think we need to ask ourselves an even deeper soul-searching question, and that is, what kind of relational footprint are we leaving for the next generation? Family must be restored to its rightful place as the main facet of socialization. Not media, not government, not peers, not even educators. We see at the neurological and biological levels that we have been wired for connectivity with our biological offspring, and to this sobering responsibility, parents and family members must remain true.

Obligations for Future Generations

I was talking with an American friend this week who told me about a trip he made to China several years ago. He was struck by the focused determination of the Chinese people to overtake the status quo and become world leaders. Their eyes were set on the prize. The adults worked tirelessly. The children soaked up knowledge for 12 hours a day. They were focused in their pursuit of purpose, not pleasure. Though these are extreme measures of dedication, their diligence was clear. While their next generation of young people was sitting in environments designed to boost their brain power, their American counterparts were sitting in front of TV screens boosting their game power.

Each generation will ultimately decide for itself, and for the next generation, the direction of the nation. As former Illinois Governor Adlai Stevenson once said to a group of recent graduates,

"Over the coming decades, as in the past, you will be the pacesetters for political and social thought in your community. You may not accept this responsibility but it makes no difference, it is inescapable. If you decide to set no pace, to forward no dreams and to have no vision, you will still be the pace setters. You will simply have decided that there is no pace."

Life is much more than a narcissistic, egocentric adventure. It takes a conscious effort not to get so caught up in our own microcosm that we miss the bigger picture. It takes a conscious effort to push out of the inertia-inducing arm chair of media centrality and embrace life with all its ups, its downs, its rawness, and its dailyness. But these are necessary steps to becoming a free society once more—unencumbered by the lens of mediocrity, of vulgarity, of violence, of silliness, even. In this last and final chapter, let's begin to envision the ways in which we can leave a positive imprint on the world within our influence, whether that circle extends around the neighborhood or across the globe.

EMERGE!

CHAPTER FIFTEEN

Staying Afloat in the Midst of a Media Deluge

In the 1993 movie *Groundhog Day*, Phil Connors finds himself trapped within an endless cycle of repetition as he awakes again and again to the same wintry day in Punxsutawney, Pennsylvania. Through conversational trial and error, Connor slowly begins to realize that his words shape the turn of events not only in his own life, but also in the lives of the people within his realm of influence. Though Connors' experience is birthed in Hollywood fantasy, there is a ring of possibility to the storyline. The main character has tapped into what Pearce (2007) calls bifurcation points, moments of conversational opportunities that enable us to turn the trajectory of the conversation—for better or for worse. These meditative moments, these opportunistic offshoots, call us to account for the content of our communication methodologies in both a personal and a collective sense.

Like Phil Connors, we too possess the potential for shaping our social worlds through the words we speak and the inferences we make out of the words spoken by others. We too have the power to change the focus of the mass conversation, eliminating the idle, hurtful words that bring relational death and transforming them instead into life-giving conversations that build up individuals, communities, and cultures. Much of what we see and hear through the lens of mass media is negative, stereotypical, cynical, vengeful, seductive, hurtful—not constructive but destructive.

We've spent sufficient time in this text smelling the poison, but what is the antidote? There are a number of proactive and prosocial steps that can be taken to manage the influx of mass media messages. Awareness of our potential for impact was the first step. In this section we'll look at some creative strategies for building "new social worlds."

Pearce's (2007) co-created CMM, the coordinated management of meaning, offers "a set of concepts and tools focusing on the process by which...events and objects are made. It functions to discipline and enable inquiry into specific moments of that process for the purpose of understanding, acting wisely, and intervening to improve the process" (Pearce 2007, p. 78). CMM offers insights that are both preventative and healing, building and rebuilding, throughout all ages and stages of life. It will benefit us tremendously to begin giving thought to what Pearce calls the "afterlife" created by our media conversations, by our resulting actions or inactions, and by the wasted time and energy that has literally "gone down the tubes" as we sit in front of the television.

It's time to look back in the rearview mirror of our own lives to begin to draw out the hard lessons, to demonstrate how "what is said or done in specific moments prefigured the realities in which we live now" (Pearce 2007, p. 3). Better still, if we turn from the rearview mirror to the roadway ahead of us, "we can enhance our ability to discern those critical moments in which, if we act wisely, we can change the trajectory of the conversation" and even, more gloriously, the trajectory of our social worlds (Pearce 2007, p. 3).

Moving forward in this way requires breaking the pattern of normal interaction, getting out of the habitual rut of communication and acting *into* the conversation in a way that positively alters its course. The question in our minds, then, becomes "What are we making together?" (p.31) as well as "What are we becoming as we make this?" (p. 53). This focus helps both interpersonal and mass media conversationalists embrace a level of responsibility not only for their words but also for the worlds their words are creating. Giddens (2006) tells the story of an interview with a number of men from an Amish community. The author of the study was curious about the motivation for the Amish's rejection of certain technological devices, especially the telephone. In the interview transcripts, the Amish men in the community make some revelatory (and piercing) comments about the phone. What does it fashion in us and in our families, they ask, when we are constantly interrupted by this "interloper"? The peripheral becomes central. Minutiae take center stage. In similar fashion to Postman's earlier exhortations, these Amish were fully convinced that humans can become so distracted by technology that we become disconnected from what is most important.

The concept has far-reaching ramifications, and the message is too significant to be ignored, for, truly, the words that are spoken to us shape our social worlds. "(T)he world is far too complex and dangerous for us to adopt a laissez-faire approach to forms of communication. The issues confronting us—as individuals, as families, as nations, as a civilization—are too important to stuff them into inadequate forms of communication" (Pearce 2007, p. 161).

Before we begin with the social world, however, it is with our own internal inconsistencies that we must begin, for there is no conscientious possibility of removing the speck from another's eye without first plucking the plank from our own. Through education, re-socialization, and positive modeling, we can begin to refocus the communicative cultural lens, and, in just one generation, we can begin to see a radical transformation in culture.

There is a hope of change, of renewal, of caterpillar-turned-butterfly as people begin to recognize their own potential, their ability, and even their responsibility for healing. As Pearce (2007) says, we live in a world where we are pulled in three directions: backward, forward, and upward. This same triad of conflict is occurring constantly within our inner worlds as well as our social worlds. Throughout history, there has been one beneficial agent of prosocial change that has risen above all others. Its potential is great, but as other authors have noted, it is a sleeping giant.

Power of the Locals

Over the last 100 years, the government has thrown up its hands over and over and said, "Government can't do it. Give it to the church—they're the only ones who can make a difference." Does that surprise you? Consider these examples. Franklin D. Roosevelt sought funding for religious charities to decrease poverty and unemployment rates in the 1930s. In the 1960s, Lyndon Johnson sought to help churches create charitable nonprofit groups to help combat poverty and urban decay. In 1996, Clinton signed into law the Charitable Choice provision, with the intention of moving welfare responsibilities from the government's back to the church's shoulder. Finally, in 2005, President Bush signed the "Faith-Based Initiative" with the goal of "putting compassion in action," getting churches involved in the community. In many ways and for many reasons, the local church is the agent for positive change in our culture.

There have been numerous government initiatives, some certainly well-intentioned, for prosocial change, but none of them come close to the power of the local church. In the mid-1990s, the US government tried to create better student behavior through the school system, raising federal funding for "character education" in schools from just under 1 million in 1995 to $25 million in 2002. While 30 percent of young people did learn about being more "other-minded" within the school environment, the vast majority, nearly 70 percent, learned the behavior only through a religious institution. According to the Pew Life Project, the study concluded that "social service programs with a religious component are more effective than secular, government-run programs." Ultimately, the government found that "faith-based organizations" are the most effective agents for healing society's ills. The local church is the agent for positive change in our culture.

How do we apply what we know? Clinical psychologist Henry Cloud says that 95% of our behavior is automatic, habitual; only 5% is intentional. The path to change is to create an external structure that supports our internal goals. In the same way, we become transformed by renewing our minds, by rethinking our neural pathways until new habits form. What we hear becomes what we say. What we say becomes what we do. It's true in a spiritual sense, and it's true in the scientific and biological sense as well. What is compelling about this concept is the predictability of behavior from a scientific standpoint—because it's the concepts we are meditating on and talking over that impact our behavior. What we see, what we think about, becomes part of us, of who we are, over time. In order to change, we have to develop "rituals" that serve our mission.

What does that mean in the real world? It means that we develop an awareness of our world and our place in it. It doesn't necessarily mean we need more information, for we are certainly inundated with information in the information age. We aren't informationally-challenged; we are applicationally-challenged. We hear, but we fail to apply what we hear. Forging new habits means we begin to take seriously our role in community and that we take responsibility for how the words we digest through media affect us as well as how the words we spew out affect others. It means that we recognize that knowledge is power—if we do something with it. It means that we recognize our interdependence.

We are not islands unto ourselves, and our actions in the world do not affect us only. They affect others, who affect others, who affect others. It means realizing that all that glitters is not gold, and we must create a system of values that reinstates all that has been lost since the Values Clarification Movement swept across our society. It means recognizing that not everything that counts can be counted, that there is joy that comes in small packages, not just in expensive ones. It means we need to apply some antidotes to the pandemic of media influence. We need to make wise decisions about our intake and be conscious of the power of socialization as a result of both our neural and sociological propensity for influence. We need to crack the cocoon currently encasing us, mobilizing the massive, sleeping armies within our midst, pulling our heads up out of the sand, and taking a stand for those who cannot speak up for themselves, the impressionable children in our midst.

As a parent, I'm concerned about the world we are fashioning for future generations. I'm concerned about the oversexualization, the desensitization to human pain and suffering. I'm concerned about the number of children for whom emotionalism has run wild and who are taking antipsychotic medicines. I'm concerned about the anti-family values that the media is pouring out, the depth of brokenness from divorce, anger, adultery, perversion. I'm concerned about the doubling of obesity in children. I'm concerned about an increasingly intolerant, anti-faith culture, one that stifles free speech and free thought in the name of commerce.

What I am encouraged by, though, is the inherent potential that rests within each of us. Our great country has battled many massive monsters throughout its brief history, and we have proved ourselves to be resourceful, strong, and courageous. Here are a few recommendations for monitoring media intake.

Recommendations for Monitoring Media

- Visit media literacy sites with your children or other family members and learn how to become media literate. There are a number of excellent resources on media literacy available to the general public: The Center for Media Literacy is one of many (www.medialit.org). Invest some time and energy into your own research and find out what's available and what's comprehensive enough to meet the specific needs of your own family.

- If you're a parent, and you or your kids watch TV, do so together. Talk about it. Watch with one eye open, so to speak, knowing that the actions observed on TV can eventually influence the behavior of your child.

- Avoid letting children have separate TVs in their rooms. Keep the family together in a healthy pattern of mutual accountability.

- Mute the commercials.

- If you do watch television, limit viewing times to less than 2 hours a day so that you stay below the limits of couch potato status. Watch specific programming rather than simply vegging mindlessly in front of the fount of folly.

- Like junk food, consume junk media in moderation.

- Think for yourself. Cross reference. If you hear an opinion spouted out in mainstream media, get a second opinion. Contemplate and discuss the messages you are being fed before you digest them fully.

In addition to these tips, it's important to take proactive steps to helping your family become media literate and media savvy. First, create standards for family and self, and be aware of the power of media influence in altering those standards. Watch for signs of parasocial interaction and modeling behavior. If a show condones and regularly displays behavioral patterns that you do not wish to see emulated in your own life or the lives of your children, consider the cost and stop drinking from that fountain. Here are a few specific SMART goals for ongoing media consumption:

- Start somewhere. Set goals for balancing media intake.

- Make media-savvy decision: Choose programs wisely, not out of peer pressure

- Awaken: Stay alert for changes in worldview that are contrary to your values

- Reflect and assess: Check progress and continue to set goals

- Take time out: Trim down viewing time and build up connective time. Take a walk, ride your bike, play a game, get creative in the kitchen, or read a book! The possibilities are endless when you are living your life instead of watching others live theirs!

What's good about a recession? Togetherness, simplicity, and a refocusing of priorities are a few of the upsides. During a time of economic upheaval. we engender the creative American spirit and are forced to create ways to save. Perhaps the current recession will usher in other facets of social change. Perhaps our dependency ratio as a nation will be reduced, and we will begin planting and harvesting our own food, cutting down not only on our foreign dependency but also on the emissions and fuel costs (not to mention accidents caused by) from large trucks shipping goods we don't need all over the country. With less, we are forced to live on a budget. The billions of pounds of food that is thrown away in America each year is a testimony to our wastefulness, as is the 63% of us that are overweight or obese. It's a nation of excess, and as one popular songwriter put it, "The decision to excess wrecks us."

Given the importance ascribed to media, media personalities, and media content in the Western world, it is vital that we begin to think critically, to utilize media literacy skills, and to avoid being pulled into the undertow of the mass media pandemic sweeping our nation. In the words of the immortal Neil Postman, this book is, in essence, a plea to those who recall sailing upon "older and clearer waters," encouraging them to pass on a safe, healthy, compassionate nation to the next generation.

CHAPTER SIXTEEN

The Butterfly Effect: Butterflies and Epcot Rides

In 1972 weather expert Edward Lorenz posited a theory that the flapping of a butterfly's wings in one part of the world could set off a tornado in another part of the world. The concept is known metaphorically as The Butterfly Effect—how seemingly small events can have dramatic implications. One small shift in media modalities can create sweeping cultural changes over time. One small shift in human behavior holds the same inherent power. If media have played a power role in shaping culture in a deleterious fashion, then a small band of determined individuals, as Margaret Mead once put it, can change that trajectory for the better.

Two vital components of social behavior have been outlined in this book. First, we influence and shape others through both our beliefs and our behavior. Second, we are influenced and shaped by those with whom we spend our time. From childhood on, we are on a determined search for role models, set in motion by the sociological and biochemical drives deep within us. And, as we have seen, hundreds of studies around the world—at Harvard, USC, Stanford, and numerous European universities to name a few locations—demonstrate the powerful influence our virtual "friends" can have on our lives. We emulate the behavior of those we admire, whether in wisdom or in folly. As the adage goes, he who walks with the wise grows wise, but a companion of fools suffers harm; bad company corrupts good character. We mirror the behavior of others, and thus the butterfly effect is in effect in every one of our lives, for better or for worse.

The Restoration of Faith and Family

There is more to the media deluge than sassy teens sporting gangster apparel or the mocking of authority figures or even the rampant materialism plaguing the nation. Much of the pandemic of media-centrality points to larger issues of concern. As Goldsmith (1983) noted in the article "The Meaning of Celebrity," we have blurred the distinction between "fame and notoriety, between talent and its lack, between accomplishment and merely being well known, between heroes and villains." And when these "synthetic personalities," as Warren (1935) calls them, become our national heroes, "it is a sign a society is absenting itself from the ethical judgment needed for social health" (p. 176). Our current generation of Western youth has been largely isolated from family ties, connected instead to a virtual family, whether that's the computer, the TV, the latest celebrity, or a friend. The parent must be returned to the driver's seat. As Drs. Neufield and Mate (2006) point out, there is compelling scientific evidence regarding the vital role that parent-child attachment—and not peer attachment—plays in mental health.

And certainly, for those who identify with a faith-based lifestyle, there are other troubling cultural issues that must be considered in light of the cultural shift. One of the most profoundly problematic of these may be the lack of connection to the written word. The rapid decline of reading scores means that comprehension levels have reached an all-time low in modern Western civilization. If the current trend continues, how will the next generation understand, and be challenged by, the writings of the faith? How will they hear the "still, small voice of God" when they are constantly bombarded by a cacophony of voices blaring at them from all directions? As Warren (1935) noted in *Seeing through the*

Media, the mesmeric, undiscriminating "experience" of media consumption is "not conducive to the refinement of the critical faculties: logic and imagination, linguistic precision, historical awareness, and a capacity for long, intense absorption. These—and not the abilities to compute, apply or memorize—are the desiderata of any higher education, and it is critical thinking that can best realize them" (p. 16). If the critical thinking capabilities that permit us to "come and reason together," to think, to inspire, to invent, to create, and to lead positive change are absent from our collective cultural personalities, who will lead us into the next wave of industry or technology or morality or creativity or education?

These are serious questions to be contemplated, for as the anecdotal village story at the beginning of this book pointed out, the visionaries are the gatekeepers of the next generation. We are the guardians. We are the defenders of the faith. If we don't speak, who will? If we believe our children are a generation worth fighting for, if we truly believe in the principles of faith and truth, then we must be compelled to stand. We must be compelled to action. "But the problem is too great!" you might say. "It's overwhelming, impossible work." Are we strong enough to fight the current and swim upstream to begin redirecting the water source?

The answer to the question lies not in one of us alone, but in all of us together. As we saw in the last chapter, one of the greatest resources for prosocial change is the local church. If the citizens of this well-endowed nation begin spending less time "amusing ourselves to death," to borrow that Postman power line again, then we will be less likely to subsist under the veil of narcissism, materialism, isolationism. We will discover a new meaning for life. We will graduate from self-centeredness and become connected to the welfare of others. Instead of living in a television-induced stupor, a mass-media coma, we will awaken. The *nephia* of life will be breathed into us. This cultural shift will free up now entangled resources of time, energy, and finances to truly make a difference in the next generation. To do this, we need to arouse some sleeping giants, and we need to connect our creative resources to their intrinsic drive for the common good.

I read recently a heartbreaking letter from the much-respected organization Focus on the Family. Because donations to the organization had dropped to critical levels, the company had been forced to cut long-term staff members and operate on a bare bones budget. At the end of the beautiful letter, the then-president of the company made a selfless plea; yes, our company needs financial support, he said, but don't give to us if it means you must stop giving to the local church. Why would an organization of such depth of wisdom and such experience at the global level defer its request for financial support to the local church? Because Focus on the Family (as much as the organization deserves our support and recognition) knows the inherent power of the local church. When a small group of determined individuals band together around a common goal, they become a powerful force of social change.

Though there are thousands of available stories of compassion in action, I offer two examples of current local and global prosocial work being carried out by churches in the United States. In California, a young church decided to donate its sparse resources to an abandoned shantytown in Africa, where thousands of AIDs orphans eat daily from garbage dumps in an attempt to survive. This young church was ultimately able to build a working, sustainable community with a school and an orphanage, where villagers are learning viable trades and helping to stop the spread of the AIDS virus through personal and social responsibility.

The vision began in the heart of one woman and has now touched a village of millions. A church in Florida makes annual trips to Uganda and other poverty-stricken regions of the world, bringing to these destitute areas talented surgeons who perform free operations for the villagers. The doctors provide eye surgery, repair birth defects, and bring hope to the villages they reach. Instead of living for the pursuit of material pleasures, these men and women give of themselves to change someone else's world for the better. One small group with a common vision can make a significant impact on the world.

Gladwell's (2000) exhortations and insights in *The Tipping Point* provide a compelling conclusion to the ideas posited here.

Gladwell says it is extraordinarily difficult for humans to envision geometric progression (as in the case of an epidemic) because the end result and the cause seem disproportionate to one another. "To appreciate the power of epidemics," Gladwell says, "we have to abandon this expectation about proportionality. *We need to prepare ourselves for the possibility that sometimes big changes follow from small events*, and that sometimes these changes can happen very quickly" (p. 11, italics mine).

Gladwell gives an example of a professor at California State University in Sacramento, Ken Futernick, who was inspired by Tipping Point principles to leverage connective support in tackling a social need. The professor found that neither teachers nor principals were willing to take on assignments in violent neighborhoods ruled by gangs and crime—though help was clearly needed in these regions. No matter what incentives they were offered, from bigger salaries to smaller classes, the teachers wouldn't budge—until Professor Futernick discovered the impact of community. He selected top principles and gave them a year to assemble their own team of top teachers. Together, the teams felt capable and motivated to accomplish the goal that none was willing to tackle alone (p. 264). This is an excellent example of the power of community.

When a few determined individuals come together with focus and intention, they can shape society—for better or for worse. The persuasive position we find ourselves in today is largely a result of media centralization and the tragic timeline of social disconnect, the results of a culture embedded so deeply in media socialization that it has lost its moral anchor and its sense of purpose. Those of us who are looking around the bend at the potential ramifications of this current trajectory are the ones who must initiate the efforts of change. The flapping of one seemingly insignificant "butterfly wing" in a small farm town in southern Illinois can set off a thunderous waterfall of sweeping social change across the nation. Maybe *you* are that butterfly.

The Coming Change

Mass media does not have the same identical effect on every individual, every family, or every community. That is not to say that it does not have predictable effects on a significant portion of the population. Cigarette smoking does not cause lung cancer in every smoker. Drinking alcohol does not cause cirrhosis of the liver in every drinker. Nonetheless, these products must be labeled with the potential dangers in order to educate and thus protect the general public. Mass media should fall under the same guidelines. Education and media literacy programs should be offered at schools, community centers, religious centers, or anywhere that social change is discussed and deciphered. It is not enough to sit back and hope the next generation will "turn out okay." Cultures do not improve with inertia. It takes the sustained and collective efforts of courageous men and women to direct, or in this case, to alter, the course of history.

Whether it is within the timeframe of the current recession or the next recession, perhaps an economic downturn will lead to an interpersonal upturn. Yes, we may have to learn some new coping skills. We may have to clean our own houses and wash our own cars and labor in our own back yard gardens. If that is the case, we will learn to spend more time at home, to be more industrious, to share more time in true community. Perhaps we will discover anew that the human body was built for physical labor and the human mind wired for interpersonal interaction. Perhaps we will find that our collective socio-emotional growth has been stunted by a lack of face-to-face connectivity. Perhaps we will discover that the rest we've been seeking isn't a vacation in Hawaii; perhaps the true rest of the human spirit is found within the pragmatism of a new paradigm.

The World of the Future

An old ride at Epcot Center in Orlando, Florida once took children through a magical land of the future, where computers talked to moms in the kitchen, where Grandma could play a game with a computerized opponent, and where big sister could talk on the phone and actually see her friend on a screen as they spoke! When I boarded the ride as a child, it seemed amazing, futuristic, a scientific fantasy that lay completely outside of the realm of possibility. However, when we hop on those little cars and travel through "time" today, the ride is not so impressive, for that future is here. Those high-tech dreams have been realized. Computers talk, play games, and transport images every day. It's commonplace now—but once, it was an impossible dream in the mind of a creative imagination.

In similar fashion, will you imagine a world of the future with me? Imagine a world of caretakers who hold seriously the responsibility of stewardship for the planet they are leaving behind for the next generation. Imagine that instead of commuting to work for an hour each way every day, wasting valuable resources and time with family, these citizens work in their own village at a job they can reach by foot, a job that contributes to the common good of the village and of the planet, and a job that gives people a sense of purpose and meaning in life. Imagine that the families in each village, centered together around a collective, share in the care of, and the rewards from, a common vegetable garden and fruit grove, which enables them to cut down on the greenhouse emissions that were once spewed out from trucks traveling hundreds of miles across the country to deliver produce. The garden gives the children rich lessons in science and nature—the lessons of hard work, seed planting, patience, and harvesting. Imagine the metaphors of possibility circling in the children's minds when they learn what mighty oaks grow from tiny seeds-when those seeds are properly cared for, properly nurtured.

Imagine a world where parents don't ship their young children off to be raised by someone else for 8 or 10 hours a day, but where they share together in the growth process and the rich and joyful heritage that comes from being a parent. Imagine a world where people talk face to face, where interaction is warm and caring instead of harried and frantic, where games are played, where books are read, and where true critical-thinking skills develop—not in the artificial laboratory of a school classroom, but in a real, hands-on, natural laboratory. Imagine a world where belongingness is not represented by a clothing label or a shared innuendo from a TV show but from a sense of connection to what really matters, family and friends—real friends, not the intimate strangers on TV or the 400 names listed on a Facebook account. Genuine friends.

Imagine a world where crime is the exception rather than the rule, where the broken men and women of the past have been given hope and purpose. They have meaningful work and families that truly love them. They no longer seek attention through harmful, antisocial behaviors, for they have the healthy attention and boundaries they require. The love and value they have been shown as children helps them develop a sense of warmth, empathy, and respect for all creatures, including their fellow citizens. Imagine a world where citizens can think for themselves, without the interposition of media, where they can form opinions, discuss and debate ideas, fostering growth both as individuals and as a culture. Imagine a world where a foundation of respect allows people to agree to disagree and to listen to the viewpoints of others in a mature and open manner.

Climb aboard the ride and imagine the possibility.

I believe that this world is within our grasp, and I believe it is not only our right but our obligation to begin laying the foundation for this world, a better world, a stronger world, for the sake of the next generation. And unlike the villagers in our watery fairytale of corporate blindness, may the next generation to follow after us be able to look back on our decisions today with gratitude instead of frustration, knowing that we cared enough to pay the price, that we were willing to push forward and emerge from the cocoon of socialization for the sake of our freedom as well as theirs.

About the Authors

Lisa Dunne

For the last 15 years, Lisa Dunne has worked as an educator at the high school, community college, and university levels in the fields of English, humanities, public speaking, and psychology. She holds undergraduate degrees in Humanities and Secondary Education as well as two Master's degrees, an M.A. in Communication Studies from Regent University, and an M.A. in Organizational Systems from Fielding Graduate University. She is currently completing her Ph.D. in Human Development with a dissertation on relational distress and responsiveness theories. Lisa's writing has been recognized by the Columbia Scholastic Press Association, the Florida Community College Press Association, and the Academy of American Poets. Her educational accolades include Teacher of the Year, Who's Who among America's Teachers, and recognition from the City and County of San Francisco, California.

Lisa has been married to her British husband, Adrian, for 19 years. Adrian is the associate pastor of Mosaic Christian Church (www.mosaiccc.com), a thriving faith-based community in Rocklin, California with humanitarian outreaches stretching across the street and around the globe. In addition to speaking and writing, Lisa teaches Developmental Psychology and Interpersonal Communication at William Jessup University in Rocklin, California (www.jessup.edu). Adrian and Lisa have two intelligent and compassionate children, Ethan Reiley and Cymone Azariah, who serve alongside their parents in community-strengthening endeavors. Lisa speaks regularly on holistic parenting, socialization, organizational and interpersonal communication, home education, nutrition and behavior, and similar topics.

For more information or to book Lisa for a presentation, visit www.4GenPress.com.

Joel Johnson

Over the last decade, Joel Johnson has spoken before over two million young people in stadiums and arenas across North America as a host for Acquire the Fire.

Acquire the Fire is the largest-attended youth event in the world, with approximately a quarter of a million teens in attendance every year. As a youth, Joel surmounted the challenges brought about by poverty, a broken home, and abuse. His inspirational stories and teaching have helped thousands to overcome their own past difficulties.

Joel is also an avid adventurer. Some of his adventures include navigating down the Amazon River, living with a native tribe in the Darien Jungle of Panama, partaking in traditional Maori Hangi feasts and ceremonies in New Zealand, playing music throughout the war-torn city of Beirut, trekking to the top of Yosemite's Half Dome and Pike's Peak, walking the streets of Hanoi, riding an elephant through the jungle of Change Mia, and overseeing the remodeling of an orphanage playground in Change Rai, Thailand.

Joel received a B.S. in Political Science from the University of Texas at Tyler. Beyond keeping up with his busy speaking schedule, he is also currently enrolled in law school at Texas Wesleyan University. Joel resides with his wife, Casey, and newborn son, Lincoln, in Keller, Texas.

References

Alston, Frances. "Latch Key Children." New York Child Study Center Website. Giving Children Back Their Childhood page. http://www.aboutourkids.org/aboutour/articles/ latchkey.html.

AMA Guidelines Regarding Industry Interactions; Drug Makers Pay for Lunch as They Pitch, New York Times, July 28, 2006.

APA Names DSM-V Task Force Members - Leading Experts To Revise Handbook For Diagnosing Mental Disorders, USA. Main Category: Mental Health News.25 Jul 2007 - 1:00. http://www.medicalnewstoday.com/articles / 77663.php

Arvind and Rogers, *Entertainment-Education: A Communication Strategy for Social Change*

Bain, Helen Pate; Lintz, Nan and Word, Elizabeth. "A Study of Fifty Effective Teachers Whose Class Average Gain Scores Ranked in the Top 15 Percent of Each of Four School Types in Project STAR." 12 Feb. 2004. <http://www.heros-inc.org/eff-tchr.pdf>.

Baker, T. R. (2005, January). "Notifying Parents Following a College Student Suicide Attempt: A Review of Case Law and FERPA, and Recommendations for Practice." NASPA Journal Online, 4, 42. Retrieved May 5, 2006, from http://firstsearch.ocle.org.

Ball, Catherine. "Web Chi Square Calculator." Georgetown University. Retrieved Aug. 10, 2006. http://www.georgetown.edu/faculty /ballc/webtools/web_chi.html.

Barna, George. "Gracefully Passing the Baton." April 6, 2004. Perspectives Page. October 22, 2004. http://www.barna. org/FlexPage.aspx?Page=Perspective>.

Barnes, Robert. *Raising Confident Kids*. Zondervan: Grand Rapids, 1992.

Berta, Dina. "Workforce Said to Enter a New Age with Changing Values. Operators Prepare Yourselves: The Workforce has a New Attitude." Nation's Restaurant News. 06-11-2001.Page: 76 Copyright Lebhar-Friedman, Inc. Jun 11, 2001.

Berger, Kathleen. *The Developing Person: Through the Life Span*. Worth: New York, 2008.

"Beyond Vicary's Fantasies" Department of Social and Organizational Psychology, The Netherlands. http://www.tcw.utwente.nl/theorieenoverzicht/ Theory%20 clusters/Health%20Communication/ Elaboration_Likelihood_Model.doc/

Biby, Clara Mae. Personal Interview. 2 Feb. 2004.

Bittner, Christopher J. (1931). "G. H. Mead's Social Concept of the Self." Sociology and Social Research, 16: 6-22. http://www.brocku.ca/Mead Project/sup/Bittner_1931. html.

Blumer, Herbert. "What is Wrong with Social Theory." American Sociological Review 18 (1954): 3-10. http://www.brocku.ca/MeadProject/Blumer/Blumer_1954.html

Blumer, Herbert. "Sociological Analysis and the "Variable." American Sociological Review 21 (1956): 683-690. http://www.brocku.ca/MeadProject/Blumer/Blumer_ 1956.html.

Boorstin, Daniel. *The Image*. New York: Atheneum, 1987.

Boorstin, Daniel. *The Landmark History of the American People*. 1987 InquisiCorp: Littleton, CO

Booth, Fran A. "Back to the Basics: Generation X Needs to Connect to People, Not Just Computers." Nation's Restaurant News 03-22-1999 Page: 30. Copyright Lebhar-Friedman, Inc. Mar 22, 1999.

Bouman, Martine (1999). *Collaboration for Prosocial Change: The Turtle and the Peacock: The Entertainment-Education Strategy on Television*. Wageningen Agricultural University, The Netherlands.

Bouman, Martine. *The Turtle and the Peacock*. Gouda, The Netherlands: The Entertainment-Education Foundation, 1999.

Bowie, J. V., Ensminger, M. E., & Robertson, J. A. (2006, January). "Alcohol-Use Problems in Young Black Adults: Effects of Religiosity, Social Resources, and Mental Health." Journal of Studies on Alcohol, 67(1), 44-53. Retrieved April 5, 2006, from http://firstsearch.oclc.org.

Bradbury, Ray. *Fahrenheit 451*. 1953 Del Ray Books, New York.

Brookfield. *The Skillful Teacher*. San Francisco: Jossey Bass P, 1990.

Burger, Chester. "Jesus the Communicator." Public Relations Quarterly; Fall2000, Vol. 45 Issue 3, p29, 3p. < http://search.epnet.com.eres.regent.edu:2048/login.aspx?direct =true&AuthType=cookie,ip,url,uid&db=ufh&a >.

Burke, Peter (2005). *History and Social Theory*, 2nd edition. Cornell University Press. Ithica, NY.

Burr, Vivien. *The Person in Social Psychology*. Psychology Press, East Sussex, UK. 2002.

Burtell, Wendy. Personal Interview: Dallas, Texas. 22 January 2005.

Cacioppo, Petty, Feinstein, & Jarvis, (1996). Need for Cognition Scale. January 2nd, 2007. http://fp.dl.kent.edu/fcubed/modules /modules/learningstyles/ need%20for%20cognition.html

Cairncross, Frances. *The Company of the Future*. Harvard Business Press: Boston, 2002.

Cano, Jamie. "What Is Known about Effective Teaching?" The Agricultural Education Magazine 74 (2001): 6-8.

Carey, James. Communication as a Culture. University of Colorado Department of Communication homepage. http://www.colorado.edu/communication/meta-discourses/Theory/carey.htm.

Carnes, Tony. *Christianity Today*. "A Church for Internet Enrepreneurs."Carol Stream: Aug 6, 2001.Vol.45, Iss. 10; pg. 37, 1 pgs. Copyright Christianity Today, Inc. Aug 6, 2001 <http://gateway.proquest.com/openurl? url_ver=Z39.88-2004&res_dat=xri:pqd&rft_val_fmt= info:ofi/fmt:kev: mtx:journal&genre=article&rft_dat=xri: pqd:did=000000076020116&svc_dat=xri:pqil:fmt=text&req_dat =xri:pqil:pq_clntid=3927>.

Carpini, Michael X. Delli. "Youth, Civic Engagement, and the New Information Environment." Generation Communication. October-December 2000, Vol. 17, Issue 4."Characteristics of Effective Teachers." Center for Teaching and Learning, Stanford University. 13 Feb. 2004. <http://www.stanford.edu/dept/CTL/TA/char. html>.

Childhood Obesity Epidemic a Long-Term Challenge. http://health.msn.com/pregnancykids/kidshealth/articlepage.aspx?cp-documentid=100170840&GT1=10412

Children, *Adolescents, and the Media*. Victor C. Strasburger and Barbara J. Wison. Sage Publications, Thousand Oaks, CA, 2002.

Christian Century, *The*. *Chicago*: Apr 6, 2004. Vol. 121, Iss. 7; pg. 15, 1 pgs Copyright

Christian Century Foundation Apr 6, 2004. <http://gateway.proquest.com/openurl?url_ver=Z39.88-

Church of Fools Web site. Accessed 20 December, 2004. <http://churchoffools. com/index.html>.

Clay, Rebecca. "Molding Effective Teachers." Monitor on Psychology. 12 Feb. 2004. <http://www.apa.org/monitor/sep03/molding.html>.

Coley, Ann. "Gender-Linked Differences in the Style and Content of E-Mails to Friends <http://search.epnet.com/ login .aspx?direct=true&AuthType=cookie,ip,url,ui d&db=ufh&an=8624889>.

"Community Service Requirements in Schools." Issues and Controversies. December 25, 1998. Accessed November 5, 2004.
<http://eres.regent.edu:2285/ICOF/temp/68707temi0302700.asp>.

Cook, Scott. "The Cultural Significance of the American Front Porch." The Evolution of the American Front Porch.
<http://xroads.virginia.edu~ACLASS/am483_97/projects/cook/cultur.html>.

Cook, William (2005) . *Journal of Advertising Research*, Cambridge University Press UK, , It takes a village to raise an idea. Retrieved July 30, 2006.
http://web116.epnet.com/externalframe.asp

Contini, Lisa Marie. "Values Clarification Destroys Conscience."
http://www.catholicculture.org/docs/doc_view.cfm?recnum=3512

Cosgrove, Lisa and Sheldon Krimsey et al. "Financial Ties between DSM-IV Panel Members and the Pharmaceutical Industry."
http://www.tufts.edu/~skrimsky/ PDF/DSM%20COI.PDF

Covey, Stephen (2003). *Living the Habits: Personal Workbook*. Franklin Covey: Simon & Schuster, New York.

Cressey, Paul G. "The Social Role of Motion Pictures in an Interstitial Area." Journal of Educational Sociology 6 (1932): 238-243
http://www.brocku.ca/MeadProject/ Cressey/Cressey_1932.html

Cressey, Paul G. "The Motion Picture Experience as Modified by Social Background and Personality." Journal of Educational Sociology 7 (1934): 504-515.
http://www.brocku.ca/MeadProject/Cressey/Cressey_1933.html

Cressey, Paul G. "The Motion Picture Experience as Modified by Social Background and Personality." American Sociological Review 3 (1938): 244-230.
http://www.brocku.ca/MeadProject/Cressey/Cressey_1938a.html

Cressey, Paul G. "The Motion Picture as Informal Education." Motion Picture Study, New York University.

Cristie, Les. *When Church Kids Go Bad: How to Work with Rude, Obnoxious, and Apathetic Students.* Zondervan (2008)

D'Alonzo, Karen Therese, PhD. "Effects of an Intervention to Enhance Exercise Self-Efficacy among Black and Hispanic College-Age Women." Rutgers the State University of New Jersey - Newark. Aug 2002.

Donovan, Gill . "A Quarter of Web Surfers are Looking for Religion."National Catholic Reporter. Kansas City: Jan 11, 2002 Vol.38, Iss. 10; pg. 6, 1 pgs. Copyright National Catholic Reporter Publishing Company Jan 11, 2002. <http://gateway.proquest.com.

Dubinsky, James M. "Civic Engagement and Technical Communication." Technical Communication Quarterly. v. 13 no. 3 (Summer 2004) p. 245-349. <http://wilsontxt.hwwilson.com/pdffull/00433/L5TA3/2S5.pdf>.

Duvoli, John. "Volunteerism Down; Not-for-Profits Suffer." Hudson Valley Business Journal. Copyright County Business Journal Publications. Banking and Finance. August 12, 2002.

Duvoli, John. "Volunteerism: The Original Win-Win Situation." Hudson Valley Business Journal. Copyright County Business Journal Publications. Volume 14, Number 25. December 15 and 22.

Eiseman, Leatrice. *Pantone Guide to Communicating with Color.* North Light Books: Cincinnati, 2000.

Freudenheim, Milt. "Showdown Looms in Congress Over Drug Advertising on TV." New York Times. January 22nd, 2007. http://washingtontimes.com/national /20050425-122707-1314r.htm

"Faith-Based Initiatives." Issues and Controversies. March 16, 2001. Accessed November 6, 2004.

Franken, Darrell, Ph.D (2006)."Friendship and Self-Disclosure." The Life Skills Training Center, Holland, MI. http://lifeskillstraining.org/friendship.htm.

Garfield, Bob. "The Rise of the Net-Generation: Passive Media of Past are Passe for I-Minded Offspring of Baby Boomers." Advertising Age; 12/11/95, Vol. 66 Issue 50, p3, 2/5p, 5c <http://search.epnet.com.eres.regent.edu

General Social Survey. http://www.norc.org/projects/General+Social+Survey.htm

Gerbner, G., Gross, L., Morgan, M., Signorielli, N., and Jackson-Beeck, M. (1979). The Demonstration of Power: Violence Profile No. 10. Journal of Communication, 29, 177-196.

Gerbner, G., Gross, L., Morgan, M., & Signorielli, N. (1986)." Living with television: The dynamics of the cultivation process." In J. Bryant & D. Zillman (Eds), Perspectives on media effects (pp. 17-40). Hilldale, NJ: Lawrence Erlbaum Associates.

Giddens, Anthony et al. *Essentials of Sociology*. Norton: New York, 2006.

Glenn, Robert E. "What Teachers Need to Be." The Education Digest 67 (2001): 19-21.

Gladwell, Malcolm. *The Tipping Point: How Little Things Can Make a Big Difference*. Back Bay Books: New York, 2000.

Goldhaber, Gerald. "Email: Tool or Torment?" Communication World; Aug/Sep2001, Vol. 18 Issue 5, p25, 2p.http://search.epnet.com/login.aspx?direct=true&AuthType=cookie,ip,url,ui

Hathersmith, June. *From Akebu to Zapotec: A Book of Bibleless Peoples*. Wycliffe: Florida, 2002.

Heenan, John. New Zealand Foundation for Character Education. Cornerstone Values Site. http://cornerstonevalues.org/preview.pdf

Heinz, Ryan. "Governor Pushes for Mandatory Community Service for High School Students." Macomb Eagle. Eagle Publications. February 2004. <http://www.eaglepublications.com/article.jhtml?DB=dbase/dbase&DO=display&ID=1076343092_4466>.

Henderson, Kristina. "Starbucks Brewing Christianity." The Washington Times. January 23, 2003. Copyright © 2003 News World Communications, Inc.

Henry J. Kaiser Family Foundation. Issue Brief 2004. Entertainment Education and Health in the United States. http://www.kff.org/entmedia/upload/Entertainment-Education-and-Health-in-the-United-States-Issue-Brief.pdf.

Hill, Alexander. *Just Business: Christian Ethics for the Marketplace.* InterVarsity: Downers Grove, 1997.

Holcomb, Jesse. "Churches Shouldn't Ignore the Meetup Phenomenon." Sojourners Magazine. Washington: May 2004. Vol. 33, Iss. 5; pg. 9, 1 pgs. <http://gateway.proquest.com

Holcomb, Jesse. *Sojourners Magazine.* Washington: May 2004. Vol. 33, Iss. 5; pg. 9, 1 pgs. Copyright Sojourners May 2004. http://gateway.proquest.com

Holwerda, Thom. "The Elaboration Likelihood Model: Why People Won't Switch." http://www.osnews.com/story.php/15973/The-Elaboration-Likelihood-Model-Why-People-Wont-Switch/

Horrigan, John B. "Online Communities: Networks that Nurture Long-Distance Relationship and Local Ties." Pew Internet and American Life Project, 2001. <http://www.pewinternet.org/pdfs/PIP_Communities_Report.pdf>.

Kauffman, Richard A. "Keeping Silence: Christian Practices for Entering Silence." The Christian Century. Chicago: May 3, 2003.Vol.120, Iss. 9; pg. 40, 1 pgs. Copyright Christian Century Foundation May 3, 2003.

Keyes, Ralph. "Reversing the Decline of Community." International Leadership Forum. <http://www.wbsi.org/ilf/poltranscom.html>.

Kiecolt-Glaser, Janice K., & Newton, Tamara L. (2001). *Marriage and Health: His and Hers.* Psychological Bulletin, 127(4), 472-503

Kirk-Kuwaye, Michael R. Ph.D. "Academic Achievement Motivation in College Students: The Effect of Grade Information on Motivation." University of Hawaii. Jan 1995.

Kivisto, Peter(2005).. *Illuminating Social Life: Classical and contemporary theory revisited.* 3rd Edition Pine Forge Press. Thousand Oaks, CA.

Koch, James L. "The Decline of Community and the Growth of Hidden Work." Santa Clara University. 2004 http: <//www.scu.edu/bannancenter/publications/ explore/spring04/declineofcommunity.cfm>

Kollock, Peter. "Design Principles for Online Communities." PC Update. 15(5): 58-60. June 1998. University of California, Los Angeles. <http://www.sscnet.ucla.edu/soc/faculty /kollock/papers/design.htm>.

Kraus, Ruth, Ph.D., "The Teenage Brain: What were you thinking?" Retrieved August 8, 2006. http://life.familyeducation.com /teen/growth-and-development/36499.html.

Kull, Steven. "America's Image in the World." March 04, 2007. WorldPublicOpinion.org.http://www.worldpublicopinion.org/pipa/ articles/views_on_countriesregions_bt/326.php?nid=&id=&pnt=3 26&lb=btvoc

Lance deHaven-Smith & Jenne, K.C. II (2006, Ja/F). "Management by Inquiry: A Discursive Accountability System for Large Organizations." Public Administration Review, 66(1), 64-76. Retrieved April 5, 2006 from http://firstsearch.oclc.org. ezproxy.fielding. edu/WebZFTFETCH?sessionid=fsapp2-38009-elsoojut-qm7s0q:entitypagenum=33:0: rule=100:fetchtype=fulltext:dbname=WilsonSelectPlus_FT:recno+25:resultset=1:ftformat=HTML:format=BI:isbillable=TRUE:numrecs=1:isdirectarticle=FALSE:entityemailfullrecno=25:entitymailfullresutset=1:entityemailftfrom=WilsonSelectPlus_FT.

Langford, Jeremy. *God Moments: Why Faith Really Matters to a New Generation* Maryknoll, New York: Orbis, 2001.

Langlois, Donald E, and Zales, Charlotte Rappe. "Anatomy of a Top Teacher." The Education Digest 57 (1992): 31-34.

LaReau, Renee M. " "Net gains: How the Internet is Changing the Church." U.S. Catholic. Chicago: Oct 2001.Vol.66, Iss. 10; pg. 12, 6 pgs. <http://gateway.proquest.com/ openurl?url_ver=Z39.88-2004&res_dat=xri:pqd&rft_val_ fmt=info:ofi/fmt:kev:mtx:journal&genre=article&rft_dat=xri:pqd :did=000000082956722&svc_dat=xri:pqil:fmt=html&req_dat=x ri:pqil:pq_clntid=3927>.

Latterell, Catherine. *ReMix: Reading and Composing Culture*. Bedford St. Martins, Boston: 2006.

Leonard, Richard . "From Gutenberg to the Web, Church's Media Savvy Waxes and Wanes." National Catholic Reporter. Kansas City: Sep 19, 2003.Vol.39, Iss. 40; pg. 33<http://gateway.proquest. com/openurl?url_ver=Z39.88-2004&res_dat=xri:pqd& rft_val_fmt=info: ofi/fmt:kev:mtx:journal&genre= article&rft_dat=xri:pqd:did=000000421120011&svc_dat=xri:pqil :fmt=html&req_dat=xri:pqil:pq_clntid=3927>.

Loewen, James. "Something Has Gone Very Wrong." The Homepage of James W.

Loewen. Retrieved August 12, 2007. http://www.uvm.edu/~jloewen/ .

Loveless, David, Ph.D. Personal Interview: Roseville, California. October 2, 2004.

Malcolm, James and Paul Rodriguez, Mark Green, Mark Ree, "Leading Generation X: Do the Old Rules Apply?" Journal of Leadership & Organizational Studies. 04-01-2003. 67.

"Milestones in Faith-Based Initiatives." Issues and Controversies. March 16, 2001. 2004 Facts on File News Services <http://eres.regent.edu.2285/ECOF/Search/ ib600420.asp>.

Miller, K. (2005). *Communications theories: perspectives, processes, and contexts*. New York: McGraw-Hill.

Morgan, Gareth. *Images of Organization*. Berrett-Koehler: San Francisco, 1998.

Myrna, Smith J. "Editor's choice: Caring, Community, and Transcendence-Developing Spirit to Improve Learning." Community College Review 28 (2000): 57-75.

Neufeld, Gordon and Gabor Mate. *Hold on to Your Kids: Why Parents Need to Matter More than Peers*. Ballantine Books: New York, 2006.

Norris, Pippa. "The Bridging and Bonding Role of Online Communities." Harvard International Journal of Press/Politics.Vol. 7 Issue 3, p3, 11p. Summer2002 North West Regional Educational Library. "Parent Partners: Using Parents to Enhance Education." http://www.nwrel.org/request/march99/article5.html.

"Not just for visitors." *Christianity Today*. Carol Stream: pg. 17, 1 pgs Copyright Christianity Today, Inc. Feb 19, 2001. <http://gateway.proquest.com/openurl?url_ver=Z39.88-2004&res_dat=xri:pqd&rft_val _fmt=info:ofi/fmt:kev:mtx: journal&genre=article&rft_dat=xri:pqd:did=000000068829139& svc_dat=xri:pqil:fmt=text&req_dat=xri:pqil:pq_clntid=3927>.

Odell, Lee and Susan Katz (2006). *Writing in a Visual Age*. Bedford St. Martin's, Boston.

O'Donovan, Cheryl. "The X Styles: Communication Styles of Generation Xers." Communication World. 12-01-1997. COPYRIGHT 1997 International Association of Business Communicators.

Ong, Walter (1988). *Orality and Literacy: The Technologizing of the Word*. Routledge, London.

Ong, Walter J. (2002). *Orality and Literacy: The Technologizing of the Word*. Routledge, NY.

Paglia, Donald J. "Home Schooling: What the Church Could Learn From Families."

Pallarito, Karen. HealthDay. "It may take decades to reverse the health threats, experts say." http://www.washingtonpost.com/wp-dyn/content/article/2006/04/19/AR2006041902560_pf.html

Palmer, Parker. *The Courage to Teach*. San Francisco: Jossey-Bass P, 1998.

Parayre, Catherine Parayre, "The Conscience of the Past: An interview with historian Howard Zinn", Flagpole Magazine Online, 18 February 1998.

Patrikakou, Eva N (2006). "Family-School Partnerships Project." The University of Illinois at Chicago © 2006 President and Fellows of Harvard College. Published by Harvard Family Research Project.

Pharmaceuticals. Breast Cancer Suspects. Msn Health and Fitness homepage. http://health.msn.com/centers/breastcancer/slideshow.aspx?cp-documentid=100170347& imageindex=12

Pharmadaddy. "Too Much Information." August 12, 2007-08-13 http://pharmadaddy.wordpress.com/2007/08/12/too-much-information/

Postman, Neil (1985). *Amusing Ourselves to Death: Public Discourse in the Age of Show Business*. Penguin Books, London.

Postman, Neil (1982). *The Disappearance of Childhood*. Vintage Books, New York.

Postman, Neil (1992). *Technopoly: The Surrender of Culture to Technology*. Vintage Books, New York.

Preece, J. "Sociability and Usability in Online Communities: Determining and Measuring Success." Behavior and Information Technology. 20 (5): 347-356. 2001.

Price, Robert Arthur, III, PhD. "Civic Engagement in Texas." The University of Texas at Austin." Dec 1998.

Primer, Steve. A Primer for Social Persuasion. http://www.healthyinfluence.com/Primer/subliminal.htm

Primer, Steve. "Thinking: Grab the Head and the Heart will Follow"motivation and processing ability determine attitude change History and Orientation. http://www.healthyinfluence.com/ Primer/sectionsm.htm

Prosser, Michael and K.S. Sitaram. *Civic Discourse: Intercultural, International, and Global Media.* Stamford, Connecticut: Ablex, 1999.

Putnam, Robert. *Bowling Alone.* New York: Free Press, 2000.

Radford, Gary P. "Under the Threshold: Is There More Than Meets the Eye?" Fairleigh Dickinson University Magazine Winter/Spring 2007, pages 18-21 http://alpha.fdu.edu/ ~ gradford/subliminal.html

Reed, T.V (2006). http://www.wsu.edu/ ~ amerstu/tm /cultstud.html Theory and Method in American/Culture Studies: A Bibliographic Essay: http://en.wikipedia.org/wiki /Cultivation_theory:

Rena R. Wing and Robert W. Jeffrey (1999). *Journal of Consulting and Clinical Psychology* (1999, Vol. 67, No. 1, 132-138.) as quoted in Weight Watchers. http://www3.weightwatchers.com /wwocs/about/friends.asp.

Richwine, Lisa. "DSM Writers Had Industry Ties." Reuters Health Information, Medscape Today. http://www.medscape.com/viewarticle/530496

Rosenblum, Ava, PhD. "Connecting Online: An Ethnomethodologically Informed Study of Communication between Couples on the Internet." University of Oregon, 1998.

Rotolo, Thomas and John Wilson. "What Happened to the Long Civic Generation? Explaining Cohort Differences in Volunteerism." Social Forces.   03-01-2004.

Rutgers University, Cooperative Research and Extension Page. College Students and Credit Card Information. Retrieved August 19, 2006. http://www.rce.rutgers.edu/ru-fit/collegestudents.asp.

Sampson, Zinie Chen. "Medical Schools Rethinking Free Lunches from Drug Companies." Associated Press January 18th, 2007. http://www.commercialalert.org/ news/archive/2007/01/medical-schools-rethinking-free-lunches-from-drug-companies

Scanlon, Sean. "TV Ads Stress Children." The Press (Christchurch, New Zealand) http://www.commercialalert.org/news/ archive/2007/01/tv-ads-stress-children

Schaab, Richard D. "Corporate Volunteerism, Good Business." Westchester County Business Journal. November 3, 2003.

Schickel, Richard. *Intimate Strangers: The Culture of Celebrity in America*. Gideon Productions: New York, 1985.

Scheufele, Dietram Arend PhD. "Participation as Individual Choice: Comparing Motivational and Informational Variables and Their Relevance for Participatory Behavior." The University of Wisconsin-Madison. March 2000.

Schickel, Richard (2000). *Intimate Strangers: The Culture of Celebrity in America*. Gideon, Chicago.

Schilder, Kelly K.; PhD. "Thinking for Success: A Cognitive Restructuring Intervention for Female Adolescent Athletes." Iowa State University: 2002 Feb 2003.

Schor, Juliet. "The New Politics of Consumption: Why Americans Want So Much More Than You Need." Boston Review. http://bostonreview.net/BR24.3/schor.html

Sellers, Patricia. "Don't Call me SLACKER! Meet America's Top Talents under 30. They are Unorthodox, Rebellious, and a Challenge to Manage." Fortune . 12-12-1994. Sewall, Gilbert. "Textbook Publishing." Phi Delta Kappan. 2005. Retrieved August 12, 2007. http://www.pdkintl.org/kappan/k_v86/k0503sew.htm

"Should Public Housing Residents Be Required to Volunteer?" Issues and Controversies. November 6, 1998. Accessed November 5, 2004. < http://eres.regent.edu:2285 /ICOF/temp68682temib302260. asp >.

Sigman, Aric. "Television Can Harm Learning, Finds Study." The Guardian (UK). Commercial Alert Website: Protecting Communities from Commercialism http://www.commercialalert.org/news/archive/2007/01/television-can-harm-learning-finds-study

Silent Spring Institute, Updated Tuesday, July 17, 2007 http://www.silentspring.org/newweb/research/ssa2.html

Simon, Robin W. (2002). Revisiting the Relationship among Gender, Marital Status, and Mental Health. American Journal of Sociology, 107(4), 1065-1096 http://www.hope.edu/academic/psychology/335/webrep2/healthmarriage.htm.

Singhal, Arvind and Martine Bouman. *The Turtle and the Peacock*. Gouda, The Netherlands: The Entertainment-Education Foundation, 1999.

Singhal, Arvind and Maurine Cody, Everett Rogers, and Miguel Sabido, M. Entertainment-Education Worldwide: History, Research, and Practice. Maywah, NJ: Lawrence Erlbaum Associates, Inc.

Singhal, Arvind and Everett Rogers. *Entertainment-Education: A Communication Strategy for Social Change*. Mahwah, N. J.: Lawrence Erlbaum Associates, Inc., 1999.

Slaton, Rebecca Lee, PhD. "The Effect of Vividness, Perceived Efficacy, and Proximity on Empathy and Charitable Behavior: Hurting Till You Give and Giving Till It Hurts." University of California, Santa Cruz. Feb. 1995.

Smith, Gloria. "Philanthropy Can Be a Two-Way Street." Hudson Valley Business Journal. Copyright County Business Journal Publications. October 7, 2004.

Smith, Warren. "Community Commitment Leads to Prosperity." Hudson Valley Business Journal. Banking and Finance. Copyright County Business Journal Publications. October 7, 2004.

Social Psychology Network Website. The Social Psychology Network: http://www.socialpsychology.org

Speicher, Sara. "A Web of Concern: Modern Communication Technology in the Service of Peace-Making." The Ecumenical Review. Geneva: Apr 2001.Vol.53, Iss. 2; pg. 216, 11 pgs Copyright World Council of Churches Apr 2001. <http://gateway.proquest.com/openurl ?url_ver=Z39.88-2004&res_dat=xri:pqd&rft_val_fmt= info:ofi/fmt:kev:mtx:journal&genre=article&rft_dat=xri:pqd:did=000000075346261&svc_dat=xri:pqil:fmt=text&req_dat=xri:pqil:pq_clntid=3927>.

Spickard, Jim. *Thinking through Statistics: Exploring quantitative sociology*. Toroverde Press: Bulverde, TX 2005.

Stanford University Psychology Department homepage. http://www-psych.stanford.edu/graduate_areas.html

Stanley, Andy. *Creating Community*. Multnomah: Oregon, 2004.

Stanley Heshka, PhD, et al (2003). "Weight loss with self-help compared with a structured commercial program." The Journal of the American Medical Association Vol. 289 No. 14, April 9, 2003. 1792 to 1798. http://jama.ama-assn.org/cgi/content/abstract/289/14/1792?etoc.

Steenhuysen, Julie. "Why are kids overweight? Take a look around Surroundings to blame for obesity epidemic, researchers say." Reuters Sept 25, 2007. http://www.msnbc.msn.com/id/20967580/

Stice, James E. "Habits of Highly Effective Teachers." ASEE Prism 8 (1998): 28-31.

Stoltz, Eric. *America*. New York: Feb 19, 2001.Vol.184, Iss. 5; pg. 16, 4 pgs. Copyright America Press Feb 19, 2001. <http://gateway.proquest.com/openurl?url_ver=Z39.88-2004&res_dat=xri:pqd&rft_val_fmt=info:ofi/fmt:kev:mtx:journal&genre=article&rft_dat=xri:pqd>.

Strasburger, Victor C. and Barbara J. Wilson. *Children, Adolescents, and the Media*. Thousand Oaks, CA: Sage Publications, 2002.

Strupp, Joe. "Journalists, public hold divergent views on media." The Hollywood Reporter. May 25, 2005. http://www.hollywoodreporter.com/thr/media/article_ display.jsp?vnu_content_ id=1000931073

Suneel, Ratan. "The Workplace: Why Busters Hate Boomers." Fortune . 10-04-1993. Copyright 1993 Time Inc.

Sutherland, Max. "Advertising and the mind of the consumer." http://www.sutherlandsurvey.com/Column_pages/subliminal_advertising.html

"The Cyber church Is Coming: National Survey of Teenagers Shows Expectation of Substituting Internet for Corner Church." <http://webminister.com /growth01 /plan0011.htm>.

The General Social Survey homepage. http://www.norc.org/projects/ General+Social+Survey.htm. US Census. http://www.census.gov/population/socdemo/education/cps2006/tab 13.xls Table 13. Educational Attainment by the Population 25 years and older by state

US Department of Education. The Family Educational Rights and Privacy Act (FERPA) (20 U.S.C. § 1232g; 34 CFR Part 99).

Veenker, Jody. "Church of the Web." Christianity Today. Jun 14, 1999 Vol.43, Iss. 7; pg. 26, 2 pgs. Copyright Christianity Today, Inc.9 <http://gateway.proquest.com/openurl?url_ver=Z39.88-2004&res_dat=xri:pqd&rft_val_fmt=info:ofi/fmt:kev:mtx:journal &genre=article&rft_dat=xri:pqd:did=000000042347175&svc_dat =xri:pqil:fmt=html&req_dat=xri:pqil:pq_clntid=3927>.

"Volunteerism Summit Held: Clinton, Powell Urge Public Service." World News Digest. May 01, 1997. <http://eres.regent.edu: 2285/stories/index/1997067143.asp>.

Vygotsky, Lev (1986). *Thought and Language*. The Massachusetts Institute of Technology. MIT Press, MA.

Walsh, David, Ph.D., *Why Do They Act That Way? A survival guide to the adolescent brain for you and your teen*. Free press: New York, 2004.

Warren, Michael. *Seeing through the Media: A Religious View of Communication and Cultural Analysis*. Trinity Press: Pennsylvania, 1987.

Weight Watchers. 1999 Annual Meeting of the North American Association for the Study of Obesity (NAASO). "Self-help weight loss versus a structured commercial program after 26 weeks: A randomized controlled study" http://www3.weightwatchers.com/wwocs/about/selfhelp.asp.

Wherry, John, Ph.D. The Parent Institute, Selected Parent Involvement Research, The Parent Institute, Fairfaix, VA.

Williams, Rhys H. "Religion, Community, and Place: Locating the Transcendent." Religion and American Culture : R & Ac, 12(2), 249-263. 2002. Bloomington: Summer 2002. Vol. 12, Iss <http://proquest.umi.com/pqdweb? RQT=309&VInst= PROD&VName=PQD&VType=PQD&Fmt=2&did =000000144097121&clientId=3927>.

Wolburg, James and Joyce Pokrywczynski. "A Psychographic Analysis of Generation Y College Students." Journal of Advertising Research 09-01-2001.

Wood, Lamont. "When your significant other is a computer: Majority of Americans spend more time with PC than partner." Msn Tech and Gadgets page. Live

Science Website. Oct 5, 2007. http://www.msnbc.msn.com/ id/21154311 /wid/11915829?GT1=10450

Wubbels, Theo; Levy, Jack, and Brekelmans, Mieke. "Paying Attention to Relationships." Educational Leadership 54 (1997): 82-86.

Zunkel, Karen Ann Martinson PhD. "Relationships among Learning Community Participation, Student Self-Efficacy, Confidence, Outcome Expectations, and Commitment." Iowa State University. Feb 2003.

4GENPRESS